Investment
Theories and Analysis

Also by M.C. Baddeley

WHAT GLOBAL ECONOMIC CRISIS?
(*edited with Philip Arestis and John McCombie*)

Investment Theories and Analysis

M.C. Baddeley
Gonville and Caius College Cambridge

Foreword by G.C. Harcourt

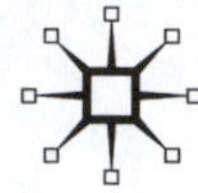

First published 2003 by
PALGRAVE MACMILLAN
Houndmills, Basingstoke, Hampshire RG21 6XS and
175 Fifth Avenue, New York, N.Y. 10010
Companies and representatives throughout the world

PALGRAVE MACMILLAN is the global academic imprint of the Palgrave Macmillan division of St. Martin's Press, LLC and of Palgrave Macmillan Ltd. Macmillan® is a registered trademark in the United States, United Kingdom and other countries. Palgrave is a registered trademark in the European Union and other countries.

ISBN 0–333–91569–0 hardback
ISBN 0–333–91570–4 paperback

This book is printed on paper suitable for recycling and made from fully managed and sustained forest sources.

A catalogue record for this book is available from the British Library.

Library of Congress Cataloging-in-Publication Data
Baddeley, Michelle, 1965–
Investment : theories & analysis / Michelle Baddeley.
p. cm.
Includes bibliographical references and index.
ISBN 0–333–91569–0 (cloth) — ISBN 0–333–91570–4 (pbk.)
1. Investments. I. Title: Investment : theories and analysis. II. Title.
HG4521 .B3428 2003
339.4′3—dc21 2002191249

10 9 8 7 6 5 4 3 2 1
12 11 10 09 08 07 06 05 04 03

Printed and bound in Great Britain by
Creative Print & Design (Wales), Ebbw Vale

For Damian

Contents

List of Boxes, Tables and Figures ix

List of Abbreviations xi

Foreword by G.C. Harcourt xii

Acknowledgements xiv

Part I Overview

1 Introduction 3
2 An overview of concepts and approaches 8

Part II Theoretical Issues

3 Intellectual ancestors: Irving Fisher and Maynard Keynes 23
4 Accelerator theory 47
5 Jorgenson's model of investment 57
6 The limitations of Jorgenson's model 66
7 Putty-clay models of investment 79
8 Adjustment costs and *q* theory 92
9 Uncertainty and investment 109
10 Post Keynesian analyses of investment 124

Part III Testing the Theories

11 Comparing Jorgenson's model and accelerator theory: evidence from the UK 139
12 Uncertainty in competing models of investment: evidence from the USA 149

Part IV Empirical Applications of Investment Principles

13 Computing investment in the New Economy: US evidence 163
14 Investment and development: a cross-sectional analysis 181

15 Residential investment: bubbles and crashes in the UK housing market, 1980–99 193

Part V Conclusion

16 Concluding remarks 211

Notes 217

Glossary 221

Statistical appendix: some basic econometric techniques 227

Bibliography 235

Index 249

List of Boxes, Tables and Figures

Boxes

2.1 Types of investment 9
2.2 Present value, internal rate of return and discount rates 11
3.1 Fisher's rate of return over costs and net present value 27
3.2 A brief biography of Irving Fisher 29
3.3 The marginal efficiency of capital 31
3.4 A brief biography of John Maynard Keynes 31
4.1 Simple accelerator theory 50
4.2 Flexible accelerator models 52
5.1 Jorgenson's model 60
5.2 The output and user cost elasticities in Jorgenson's model 62
6.1 Expectations and uncertainty in models of investment 71
8.1 Adjustment cost models 98
9.1 Applying real options principles in practice 116
14.1 Empirical convergence models 187

Tables

11.1 Results from the estimation of accelerator models 143
11.2 Results from the estimation of neo-classical models 144
11.3 Non-nested test results, p values 145
11.4 Results from the estimation of the hybrid model 146
12.1 Parameter estimates for q models without uncertainty 154
12.2 Parameter estimates for q models with uncertainty 155
12.3 Keynesian-Kaleckian models 156
12.4 Non-nested tests, p values 157
13.1 An estimation of computing investment in the USA 176
14.1 Absolute β convergence models 188
14.2 Absolute gap convergence models 188
14.3 Conditional β convergence models 189
14.4 Conditional gap covergence models – restricted versions 189
15.1 Owner occupation rates in the OECD, 1998 198

15.2 Policy changes affecting the housing market 199
15.3 Minskian bubble-crash models 202
15.4 Demand augmented bubble-crash models 203
15.5 Neo-classical models incorporating the user cost of housing investment 205
15.6 Non-nested test results, p values 206

Figures

2.1 Replacement investment 10
3.1 Keynes's investment demand schedule 33
7.1 Capital and labour as substitutes in putty models 82
7.2 Capital and labour as complements in clay models 83
8.1 Adjustment costs and investment 95
13.1 Growth in transistor count, logarithmic scale 165
13.2 Computing investment as a proportion of total investment 166
13.3 Average age of selected fixed assets, USA, 1978–2000 171
13.4 US venture capital disbursements to computer hardware, communications and the Internet 175
14.1 Growth in investment, 1988–98 185
14.2 Standard deviation of investment rates, 1988–98 186

List of Abbreviations

ADF	Augmented Dickey Fuller test
AMEX	American Stock Exchange
BEA	US Bureau of Economic Analysis
BLUE	Best Linear Unbiased Estimator
CAPM	Capital Asset Pricing Model
DC	Developed country
DF	Dickey Fuller test
FIRE	Financial, insurance and real estate sector
GDP	Gross domestic product
GLS	Generalized least squares
IT	Information technology
LDC	Less developed country
MIRAS	Mortgage interest relief at source
n/a	Not applicable
NASDAQ	US National Association of Securities Dealers
NDP	Net domestic product
NPV	Net present value
NYSE	New York Stock Exchange
OLS	Ordinary least squares
ONS	UK Office of National Statistics
R&D	Research and development
REH	Rational Expectations Hypothesis
UN	United Nations

Foreword

Michelle Baddeley's book, which started life as her PhD dissertation at Cambridge (I had the privilege of supervising her/it), exemplifies the best sort of relevant applied research. As the author rightly emphasizes, investment in physical assets, accumulation as our classical pioneers and Marx had it, is the concept most critical to our understanding of the processes at work over time in capitalist economies, ancient and modern. With this as the central focus, Dr Baddeley provides clear and comprehensive accounts of the principal rival theories of investment behaviour in the modern era. She starts with the theories of two modern giants, Irving Fisher and Maynard Keynes, from which virtually all subsequent developments derive – Dale Jorgenson's writings from the 1960s on, the various versions of accelerator (capital-stock-adjustment) theories, James Tobin's *q*, Avinash Dixit and Robert Pindyck's influential contribution, their real options theory, for example. (Dr Baddeley also gives Michal Kalecki rightful due for his independently derived and highly original theories of accumulation.) Not only does she provide a deep understanding of the issues and approaches involved, she is also a sympathetic and, where necessary, tough critic. With her astute and acute gaze no emperor is likely to get away with nakedness.

As is to be expected of an all-round economist, Dr Baddeley follows up her illuminating theoretical discussions with a number of thorough empirical studies. She uses econometric techniques as they should be used, to illuminate, to compare the respective merits of rival theories, while always keeping in mind the techniques' proper domain and limitations. There are cross-section and time-series studies, including a fascinating study of the UK residential market.

Dr Baddeley's conjecture has always been that Keynes and Kalecki were closer to a proper understanding of accumulation than were the neo-classicals, Fisher (great economist though he was), Jorgenson and even the late James Tobin, an eminent Keynesian economist (and superb human being) who, nevertheless, in his *q* theory drew on two, I have to say, incompatible approaches. From the evidence she so carefully presents, her conjecture is confirmed. I recommend *Investment: Theories and Analysis* as a model of what applied economic research should be, and I now ask readers to read on and judge for themselves. My conjecture is that they will not be disappointed.

Jesus College, Cambridge G.C. HARCOURT
April 2002

Acknowledgements

I would like to thank Geoff Harcourt for his help and advice as my PhD supervisor, for further advice and encouragement in more recent years, for commenting on drafts of this book, and for writing the Foreword. I would also like to thank Philip Arestis for encouraging me to write this book; my PhD examiners, Malcolm Sawyer and Kevin Lee, for their comments, many of which have been incorporated into the book; and the anonymous reviewers of this book for their comments and advice on a preliminary draft. My gratitude also goes to Rachel Wood for her careful yet enthusiastic proof-reading. Of course, all errors or omissions are my own. I would also like to thank my commissioning editor, Ursula Gavin, and copy-editor, Keith Povey, for their patient support. For general advice and encouragement I thank my friends and family, especially my parents.

MICHELLE BADDELEY

Part I

Overview

1 Introduction 3
2 An overview of concepts and approaches 8

1 Introduction

Why is investment important? 4
An outline of the book 5
Using this book 6
Understanding this book 6

This book is about aggregate physical, fixed asset investment expenditure. Physical fixed asset investment involves accumulating physical capital, including factories, machinery (for example, computers) and buildings (including houses). The aims of *Investment: Theories and Analysis* are first, to introduce some of the key theories of investment activity, explaining how the theories are related to each other; second, to test these theories empirically using recent data; and third, to apply theories of aggregate investment behaviour to some topical macroeconomic issues.

Why is investment important?

Investment activity is central to the promotion of economic well being because it is one of the most important economic activities that businesses, consumers and governments can undertake. Aggregate fixed investment is a substantial component of aggregate demand and a critical determinant of national income and GDP. Investment also has an important influence on employment and unemployment: if investment falters, capital stocks will dwindle and jobs may be lost. Investment today determines economic activity tomorrow because in the building-up of resources of capital that will be used to produce goods and services, future productive potential is determined. So investment will be an important determinant of future economic growth: if investment and growth in productive capacity are slow and sluggish, growth and employment will suffer and, as a consequence, labour productivity, wages and living standards will fall. As the most volatile component of aggregate demand, investment has an important impact on the business cycle. And investment doesn't only affect commercial businesses; some of the biggest economic decisions made by most ordinary people, i.e. the buying and selling of housing, is essentially an investment decision and, in aggregate, these housing decisions can have a critical impact on macroeconomic activity. Investment principles should be important to governments and government agencies too. The purchase of any sort of public infrastructure: the buildings, machinery and equipment purchased for hospitals, schools, railways, sanitation facilities, dams, etc. are all fixed investments.

Despite its importance, aggregate fixed investment is a topic often neglected in today's business and economics courses. This neglect may reflect a belief that other aspects of economic activity are more important; or it may reflect the fact that textbooks about aggregate fixed investment are few and far between. Also, investment concepts and ideas often seem difficult, esoteric and overly complicated, covering a wide range of theories that seem difficult to reconcile. And whilst most economists from a wide range of perspectives acknowledge the essential role of fixed asset investment, i.e. capital accumulation, they disagree about the determinants of investment. In fact, a coherent and plausible theory of investment has yet to be developed. This book aims to fill these gaps and analyzes the development of theories of aggregate investment activity in an attempt to clarify and crystallize the full spectrum of investment theories.

An outline of the book

In Chapter 2, to help those who do not know much about fixed investment, some basic concepts and issues are explained. Also in Chapter 2, in acknowledgement that, as with any other aspect of economics, there are substantial disagreements about the determinants of investment, the historical evolution of investment theories is traced in order to illustrate how differences between theories have emerged over time.

The theories

In Part II, the key theories of investment are explained in detail starting, in Chapter 3, with an outline of the ideas of Irving Fisher and Maynard Keynes. These two economists have had crucial influences on the evolution of investment theory right up until the recent development of real options theories of investment. In Chapter 4, accelerator models, in which output growth is the key determinant of fixed investment, are introduced. These models were initially associated with the Keynesian Revolution of the post-World War II era and were particularly influential up until the stagflationary episodes of the 1970s. In Chapters 5 and 6, Jorgenson's neo-classical model of investment is analyzed. Jorgenson responded to the accelerator approach by introducing relative price/cost factors into investment analysis, following in the tradition of Fisher. In Chapter 7, the ideas from accelerator theory and Jorgenson's approach are reconciled with an analysis of putty-clay models, which allow variability in the responsiveness of investment to relative factor prices. In Chapter 8, *q* models of investment are introduced. These models evolved out of a dissatisfaction with the treatment of expectations in the earlier approaches of the accelerator theorists and Jorgenson. The most influential version of *q* theory, the version associated with Brainard and Tobin, built upon some ideas from Keynes about the role of stock prices in signalling expected future returns from investments. In Chapter 9, real options theories of investment are analyzed. In these theories, the impact of quantifiable uncertainty (sometimes called 'Knightian risk') on rational investor behaviour is analyzed.

To conclude the theoretical section, an alternative group of investment theories, those associated with the Post Keynesian school, are outlined in Chapter 10. Post Keynesian theory is distinctly different because it emphasizes that unquantifiable uncertainty (sometimes called 'Knightian uncertainty') and non-rational behaviour invalidate the mathematical approaches to economic analysis usually associated with neo-classical or 'orthodox' mainstream economics. Whilst orthodox theorists and Post Keynesians would all agree that uncertainty is important, they disagree about how people respond to uncertainty. Differences about the nature of uncertainty are crucial to the analysis of fixed investment because fixed investment is all about planning for an uncertain future.

Testing the theories

In Part III, using data from the USA and UK the various theories are tested against each other using some simple statistical techniques. In Chapter 11, the debate between Jorgenson and the accelerator theorists is re-visited in an analysis of the importance of output versus relative factor prices in the determination of investment. In Chapter 12, some of the insights about the role of profit expectations and uncertainty are addressed in an empirical comparison of *q* theory with Keynesian-Kaleckian theories. In order to assess the relative explanatory power of these models, model comparison and non-nested testing techniques are applied in Chapters 11 and 12.

Empirical applications

In Part IV, investment principles are applied to a number of interesting current economic issues in an attempt not only to illuminate these topical issues but also to provide another, but more indirect, way of assessing some of the theoretical concepts introduced in the earlier chapters. The impacts of the IT revolution on computing investment in the USA are assessed in Chapter 13. In Chapter 14, the importance of investment activity to growth and development is addressed in an empirical assessment of the investment performance in a cross-section of countries. In Chapter 15, the role of financial constraints and speculation in exacerbating housing investment bubbles is analyzed, using data on UK residential investment from 1980 to 2000.

Using this book

This book is primarily designed for economics and business students studying core macroeconomic courses. It will be particularly useful to second- and third-year undergraduates studying aggregate investment as a component of their intermediate macroeconomics courses. It will also be helpful for students doing project work on aggregate investment as part of their statistics and econometrics courses. The book will be useful for MBA and other business/economics Master students who are studying macroeconomics and/or finance. Graduate students and researchers embarking on a research programme addressing aggregate investment will also find this book of relevance, as will anyone with a basic background in economics who is interested in current macroeconomic issues.

Understanding this book

Knowledge of mathematical economics is not necessary to follow the analyses presented in this book but for those who prefer a mathematical approach, simple mathematical explanations are separated into textboxes. To follow the mathematical textboxes, a basic understanding of differential calculus is required. A working knowledge of basic econometric techniques, i.e. multiple regression analysis, is helpful in following the statistical sections of Chapters 11–15 but, for those readers who are unfamiliar with econometric procedures, a brief explanation of the simple techniques used in this book is outlined in the Statistical Appendix: Some Basic Econometric Techniques. To help student readers, chapter summaries are included at the end of each chapter. Also, revision questions are provided, as a teaching aid, after each of the theoretical chapters. For those readers who need further explanation of some of the more unfamiliar technical terms used, a glossary of terms is included at the end of the book.

2 An overview of concepts and approaches

What is investment? 9
The evolution of theories of investment 10
Conclusion 18
Chapter summary 18
Revision questions 19

What is investment?

In the simplest economic models, there are just two factors of production: capital and labour. The stock of capital includes all fixed assets associated with productive capacity (for example, factories, machinery, plant and equipment, inventories) and/or future consumption for example, residential fixed assets. Some of the key types of investment are outlined in Box 2.1. The key defining characteristics of these fixed assets is that they represent postponed consumption: people invest in fixed assets because they expect these assets to deliver goods and services in the future. Investment is the flow into this stock of capital goods and is illustrated in Figure 2.1.

These flows of investment into the stock of capital are divided into the two categories of replacement investment and net investment. These two together make up gross investment, which is the total flow of investment goods into the capital stock.

Replacement investment

Replacement investment is necessary because the capital stock deteriorates naturally over time. The physical deterioration of the capital stock in use, reflecting wear and tear, is known as depreciation; without replacement

Box 2.1 Types of investment

- **Tangible, fixed asset investment** is investment in physical, fixed capital, such as plant and machinery.
- **Inventory investment** is investment in the 'working capital' of the firm, made up of goods produced but not yet sold.
- **Residential investment** is investment in housing (see Chapter 15).
- **Intangible investment** is the investment in non-physical assets that does not involve the accumulation of tangible physical assets but will nonetheless affect future productive capacity. Examples include goodwill, human capital investments such as staff training and some components of research and development (R&D) expenditure, for example, those associated with intellectual property. With recent technological changes associated with the IT revolution, intangible investments have become increasingly important (as is explained in Chapter 13).
- **Financial investment** is the purchase of financial, paper assets.

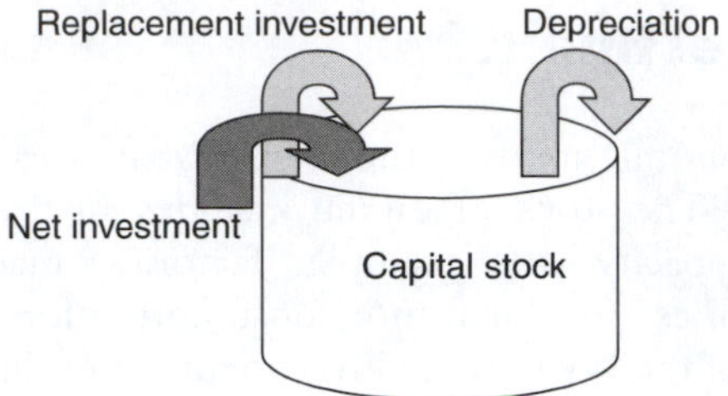

Figure 2.1 Replacement investment

investment, the capital stock would eventually disappear. Economic obsolescence will also affect the quality of the capital stock; it is the reduction in the economic value and useful life of capital which emerges as a consequence of technological and structural change. As illustrated in Figure 2.1, replacement investment is the investment that takes place to replenish the capital stock as it deteriorates.

Net investment

Net investment is the investment over and above what is needed for replacing worn-out plant and machinery. So flows of net investment augment the stock of capital and add to the overall productive capacity.

The evolution of theories of investment

The influences of Fisher and Keynes

In analyzing investment, the origin of modern theoretical ideas can be traced back to the debates between Fisher and Keynes. The theories of Fisher and Keynes provide the backbone of later analyses of fixed asset investment and some of the parallels and contrasts between these approaches are outlined in Chapter 3. In *The Theory of Interest* (1930), Fisher emphasized that investment is determined at the point where the rate of return on investment is equal to the prevailing interest rate. The modern concepts of present value and the internal rate of return are related to Fisher's ideas and are explained in Box 2.2. With its emphasis on relative price factors and benefits versus costs, Fisher's theory forms the basis of neo-classical models of fixed investment – for example Jorgenson's model, formulated in the 1960s.

Keynesian debates dominated theoretical developments in the immediate post-World War II period and the 'marginal efficiency of capital' was central to Keynes's analysis of investment. In its basic form Keynes's marginal efficiency of capital is very similar to Fisher's internal rate of return. However, in contrast to Fisher's approach, Keynes developed a theory of investment that allowed a central role for expectations and unquantifiable uncertainty. In Keynes's world of endemic uncertainty, monetary and financial factors have a decisive influence on fixed asset investment activity. Expectations are not necessarily quantifiable so investment projects cannot easily be assessed using Fisher's mathematical tools. Whilst Keynes argued that private entrepreneurship is important, he also argued that constraints on effective private decision-making mean that governments must play a role, for example in judging the desirability of investment projects and in moderating destabilizing forces, such as speculation.

Box 2.2 Present value, internal rate of return and discount rates

Present value (PV) and discount rates

When investors assess the value of investments in terms of the stream of revenues these investments deliver over time, they should calculate the 'opportunity cost' of investment, where the opportunity cost is the cost of committing funds, which could otherwise be earning interest, to an investment project. Revenue earned tomorrow does not have the same value as revenue earned today because money not spent on a project can be in a bank earning interest that will inflate its value tomorrow. For this reason it is important to look at the 'present value' or 'discounted' value of expected future revenues from investments, discounted by allowing that money banked today will be earning interest income over time.

Discounting involves using a 'discount rate' to establish the equivalence of future income with current income. In the simplest cases, the prevailing interest rate is used as a discount rate but this method does have limitations, as will be explained below. To illustrate present value with an example: a business is thinking of setting up a mobile phone factory expected to produce £1 million of revenue in 2012. In deciding about the present value of this potential revenue, the accountant decides to use a discount rate of 6 per cent. According to her calculations, the present value in 2002 of £1 million in 2012 is £558,395. This is because, if instead of building a factory, the business had banked £558,395 in 2002, this sum would be worth:

$1.06 \times$ £558,395 $=$ £591,899 in 2003;

$1.06 \times$ £591,899 $=$ £627,413 in 2004;

$1.06 \times$ £627,413 $=$ £665,057 in 2005, etc., etc.

and by 2012 would be worth £1 million: £558,395 $\times (1 + 0.06)^{10} =$ £1 million

So the present value of £1 million in 2012 is £558,395 in 2002, i.e. £1 million revenues from the investment project in 2012 is worth £558,395 in the bank today.

cont. overleaf

Box 2.2 continued

For investment projects, the present value of *streams* of revenues delivered from investments can be calculated. Mathematically, the present value (PV) of a stream of revenues over t years can be expressed as:

$$PV = \sum_{t=1}^{\infty} \frac{R_t}{(1+r)^t}$$

where R_t, is the revenue in each year and r is the discount rate.
If revenue is constant each year at $\overline{R}$, this gives:

$$PV = \left[\frac{\overline{R}(1+r)}{r}\right]$$

Internal rate of return/marginal efficiency of capital

Fisher's internal rate of return or rate of return over costs and Keynes's marginal efficiency of capital are mathematically equivalent. They are the discount rate that equalizes the present values of streams of future revenues from investments with the initial capital cost of installing those investments. The internal rate of return is the rate – ρ, which makes the present value of revenues in each year equal to the capital cost (C), i.e.:

$$C = \sum_{t=1}^{\infty} \frac{R_t}{(1+\rho)^t}$$

An investment will be worthwhile economically if the internal rate of return is greater than or equal to the prevailing interest rate, r, i.e. if $\rho \geq r$.

Accelerator theory: the role of output

The next step in the development of fixed asset investment theory was the refinement of Clark's (1917) basic accelerator model and different models of accelerator theory are outlined in Chapter 4. Accelerator models are simple models in which investment activity is the process of adjustment towards a desired capital stock. Investors will want to increase their stock of capital if they expect profits to increase. More complex versions of these accelerator theories developed in response to some of Keynes's observations about expectations: given uncertainty and limited information about future prospects of investment projects, there is no specific information about future profits. In addition, given technical rigidities, i.e. when the basic factors of production – labour and capital – cannot easily be swapped around as their relative factor prices change, the capital–labour and the capital–output ratios are likely to be fixed and unresponsive. Past output will be the best proxy for expected future profits given the absence of more detailed information and this means that investment and changes in the capital stock will be correlated with past output growth. In 'simple' accelerator models, the capital stock adjustment process is immediate and investment is a function of output growth in the previous period. In 'flexible' accelerator models, investment lags are introduced reflecting delays in decision-making, ordering, delivery, installation and adjustment.

Jorgenson's model and the user cost of capital

In the 1960s, returning to Fisher's approach, Jorgenson responded to what he saw as a lack of analytical rigour in Keynesian theories and the finer details of Jorgenson's model are outlined in Chapter 5. Jorgenson's model forms the basis of modern 'neo-classical' theories of investment because it assumes that firms are rational profit maximizers operating in a perfectly competitive world, able easily to calculate and balance the marginal benefits and marginal costs of investment decisions. For the neo-classical firm, the marginal benefits of investment can be represented as the addition to future expected output that will occur with increments to the capital stock. The marginal cost can be represented by the costs associated with buying or renting an additional unit of capital. These costs are captured within the 'rental' or 'user cost of capital' and include capital goods prices, depreciation rates and the real interest rate. A profit maximizing investor will adjust the capital stock until the marginal benefit of additional investment (in terms of the present value of future revenue) is equal to the user cost of capital. So investment increases as the user cost of capital decreases and decreases as output and revenue increase.

Jorgenson's original model embedded a number of restrictive assumptions, for example, that the capital stock will adjust to its optimal level instantaneously, that expectations do not change and that fixed asset investment activity is completely reversible. Some of the consequent criticisms and the subsequent refinements of these assumptions are outlined in Chapter 6. In addition, an empirical debate emerged about the merits of Jorgenson's model and accelerator models. This debate focused on the relative importance of output versus the user cost of capital, i.e. the importance of quantity adjustment versus relative price flexibility. Many studies emerged revolving around the estimation of what is known as the 'elasticity of factor substitution', which captures the responsiveness of the capital–labour ratio to changes in the user cost of capital. Accelerator theory assumes an elasticity of substitution of zero; that is that the proportions of capital and labour used in production do not change as the user cost of capital changes. On the other hand, Jorgenson's original model assumed an elasticity of substitution of one, i.e. that the capital–labour ratio will change in proportion with changes in the user cost of capital. In the middle ground are 'putty-clay' models, that allow the elasticity of substitution to vary over time between zero and one. In Chapter 7, putty-clay models are explained and the empirical debate about the importance of price flexibility and quantity adjustment is assessed.

Adjustment costs in *q* theories

In a more comprehensive response to the dynamic limitations of Jorgensonian models, a number of economists noted that expectations are crucial to an understanding of investment under uncertainty. They also argued that it is impossible to explain the timing of investment expenditure without allowing for the 'adjustment' and 'installation' costs associated with investment decisions, for example the costs of 'bolting-down' equipment, training new workers, etc. These factors were taken into account in the development of '*q*' theories of investment, incorporating rational expectations of future profits as the key determinant of aggregate investment activity. Early *q* theorists, such as Brainard and Tobin (1968) and Tobin (1969), formulated models of fixed asset investment in which Stock Market valuations of firms capture rational expectations of future profits from investments. This insight is developed, for example by Abel (1980), in describing adjustment cost models of investment in which investment activity is dictated by the 'shadow price' of investment (*q*), i.e. the total sum of net expected benefits over time expected from a given investment project. Within the adjustment cost *q* theories, *q* can be captured using share prices but adjustment cost models can also be captured via 'direct forecasting' and 'transformation' approaches. The development and analysis of adjustment cost theories of investment are outlined in Chapter 8.

Real options theories of investment under uncertainty

Another influential criticism of Jorgenson's theory focuses on his assumption that investment decisions are reversible. With 'asset specificity', i.e. when investment goods are designed for very particular types of production (for example, oil wells) firms cannot just re-sell their investment goods if they are unprofitable. This means that many real-world investment projects are likely to involve irrecoverable expenditures or 'sunk costs'; investors must therefore be cautious because they do not really know what will happen next. For this reason uncertainty has far-reaching consequences for investment activity. These ideas are developed by Dixit and Pindyck (1994), amongst many others, as real options models of investment. These models are based upon an analogy with 'call options', i.e. the options to buy assets in financial markets. Fixed asset investors will balance the benefits of exercising an option to invest today (for example, taking advantage of a new technological opportunity) against the benefits of delaying investments (for example, waiting for more information and/or better economic conditions). When there is a lot of uncertainty about the future, the value of waiting for more information and better conditions will increase, and so exercising the option to invest *today* will have a relatively lower value. Investors will prefer to wait and investment activity overall will decline. Models of investment under uncertainty, including real options models, are analyzed in Chapter 8.

Uncertainty, profits and finance in Post Keynesian theory

Increasing theoretical convergence can be seen in a wide range of the investment literature, with the modern adjustment cost and real options theorists introducing expectations and uncertainty, factors originally emphasized by Keynes but neglected by Jorgenson. So in the models discussed so far, there are certain parallels and degrees of theoretical convergence in the approaches.

However, key departures in methodological and philosophical approach can still be seen in the Post Keynesian literature. The Post Keynesians argue that Keynes's analysis was based on fundamentally different conceptions of human behaviour and uncertainty to the conceptions seen in mainstream analysis. In a Post Keynesian world, uncertainty is everywhere and it limits the ability of investors to form expectations rationally. The Post Keynesians argue that real options and adjustment costs models do not allow for this fundamental nature of uncertainty. Instead, the Post Keynesians focus on unquantifiable uncertainty (or 'Knightian uncertainty'), in contrast to the quantifiable risk (or 'Knightian risk') essential to mainstream analyses.

The Post Keynesians also argue that the determinants of reality are changeable or mutable: there is no objective model of the world waiting to be discovered: the world is irregular and unpredictable (or 'non-ergodic'). This means that, rather than focusing on the role of rational behaviour by dynamic optimizers, the Post Keynesians focus on non-rational, sub-rational and irrational forces, for example conventions, herd instincts and animal spirits. The inherently unquantifiable nature of uncertainty forces fixed asset investors to rely on non-rational motivations. It also means that investors are easily swayed by instability because they realize that the knowledge upon which they base their decisions is unstable and unreliable. In Chapter 10, some key Post Keynesian insights about the nature of investment activity are outlined, including the role of Knightian uncertainty, the nature of sub-rational and irrational expectations and the importance of monetary/financial factors (particularly profitability and the availability of finance).

Microeconomics versus macroeconomics: the aggregation problem

This book is about investment in the aggregate; it is about macroeconomic investment. In orthodox neo-classical theories, macroeconomics and microeconomics are not distinctly different disciplines. For example, in Jorgenson's model, q theories and real options theories, analyzing macroeconomic investment is analytically identical to analyzing microeconomic investment: both macroeconomic and microeconomic theories describe the profit maximizing behaviour of firms balancing their marginal benefits and marginal costs. This approach requires a 'representative agent hypothesis': i.e. by assuming that the macroeconomy is made-up of identical (or 'homogeneous') agents, the profit maximizing behaviour of one representative firm can be aggregated to describe macroeconomic investment in the aggregate. In this way, orthodox theories of aggregate investment are based upon rigorous microfoundations. The difference between the microeconomic behaviour of one individual profit maximizing firm and the macroeconomic behaviour of an infinite number of identical firms is just a matter of scale. This methodological approach is called 'methodological individualism' (MI).

In contrast, many Keynesians and Post Keynesians have rejected this atomistic view of the world in favour of 'methodological holism', allowing that the whole is not necessarily equal to the sum of its parts because of the interactions between agents. If the assumption of MI is abandoned, then an aggregation problem emerges: it is not possible just to add all the individual behaviours of microeconomic firms; macroeconomic theory requires a more complex approach. So Keynesian and Post Keynesian macroeconomic theories are not based upon rigorous microfoundations and tend instead to focus on large-scale forces such as herd behaviour, conventions, feedback effects, the state of confidence and aggregate uncertainty.

Real world investment appraisal techniques

The esoteric concepts discussed in the theoretical literature do have their parallels in the real world and form the basis of the investment appraisal techniques used by business managers. Government policy-makers also use these techniques when they appraise public investment projects, for example, in developing countries.

Net present value (NPV)

Net present value is a very common investment appraisal technique. The internal rate of return (explained in Box 2.2) and NPV are essentially just manipulations of each other. NPV focuses on the difference between the present value of expected future revenues (explained in Box 2.2) versus the current cost of investment projects:

$$NPV = \sum_{t=1}^{\infty} \frac{R_t}{(1+r)^t} - C$$

where r is the prevailing interest rate, *R* is the revenue generated in year *n*, and *C* is the capital of an investment project (e.g. the cost of buying a new machine).

NPV is equal to zero when the internal rate of return is equal to the prevailing interest rate. However, internal rate of return rankings of investment projects may differ from NPV rankings, depending on the interest rate and time span used in the calculations. The internal rate of return technique has the advantage that potential investment projects can be ranked even if information about the discount rate is unavailable. The NPV technique has the advantage that it is sensitive to the discount rate and in this sense captures a wider range of relevant information.

Estimating the discount rate for NPV calculations

For the investment appraisal techniques described above and in Box 2.2, future revenues are discounted using the prevailing interest rate as the discount rate. But how is this discount rate calculated in practice? In a very simple world, without inflation, the nominal interest rate *is* an appropriate discount rate. However, in an inflationary environment the real costs of borrowing are reduced by inflation and the real interest rate will be a more appropriate discount rate. In a world of uncertainty and risk, selecting an appropriate discount rate becomes even trickier because investors (and their financiers) may be committing money to an investment project that will turn out to be unprofitable in the future for reasons not anticipated in the present. In the real world, these risk factors are taken into account and so the discount rates used to appraise investment projects tend to be higher even than real interest rates.

Payback period

Another, simpler method of investment appraisal commonly used in the real world is the 'payback' method. The payback period is the length of time taken to recoup the costs of investments from the undiscounted streams of revenue generated as a result of investment projects. For example, if an investment project costs £1 million and it is expected to deliver revenues of £100,000 per year, the payback period is ten years. The surprising thing about the target payback periods used by real businesses is that businesses expect to recoup expenditures quickly, i.e. usually within five years. Expecting short payback periods and using high discount rates deliver the same result: both will mean that investors are focusing on the short-term rewards and this is consistent with investors believing that the long-term future is very uncertain.

What sorts of techniques are commonly used? Survey evidence from Baddeley (1996) suggested that larger firms are more likely than small firms to calculate NPV and rates of return. However, most firms used a range of techniques and overall the most commonly used technique used was the payback method; this technique was adopted by 81 per cent of the firms sampled. For the very small firms (i.e. less than ten employees) many firms just replaced their equipment when it stopped working.

Conclusion

This chapter will have raised a lot of questions – about the importance to investment activity of output growth, relative factor prices, risk and uncertainty. As mentioned already, the debates about these questions first emerged in the 1930s, when Fisher was writing *The Theory of Interest* (1930) and Keynes was writing *The General Theory of Employment, Interest and Money* (1936). The modern theories developed in the Chapters 4–10 can be placed into context with an analysis of Keynes and Fisher. In the following chapter, the two basic approaches are explained. Then, in Chapters 3–10, the various theories are outlined; in Chapters 11–12, the theories are tested empirically; and in Chapters 13–15, the ideas are applied to some topical macroeconomic issues. In Chapter 16, the various ideas are brought together with a concluding analysis of investment theories.

Chapter summary

1. Fixed asset investment involves purchasing physical, fixed capital, for example as plant and machinery. Gross investment is the total amount of investment expenditure and is equal to net investment plus replacement investment.
2. Inventory investment is the accumulation of working capital, i.e. goods produced but not yet sold.
3. Intangible investment is the accumulation of non-physical assets such as technical know-how.
4. The capital stock deteriorates over time, reflecting wear and tear in use. This deterioration is known as depreciation. The capital stock may also be affected by economic obsolescence; this occurs when existing capital stock becomes redundant as a result of technological or structural change.
5. Modern theories of investment have evolved from the ideas of Irving Fisher and Maynard Keynes. Modern investment appraisal techniques such as net present value (NPV) build upon concepts formulated by Fisher and Keynes; for example, the internal rate of return (called the marginal efficiency of capital by Keynes).

   Generally, modern theories differ in terms of their emphasis on price versus quantity factors. The accelerator theorists and the Post Keynesians emphasize the importance of quantity factors, such as output growth. The neo-classical theorists also emphasize the relative costs of investment projects.
6. Modern investment theorists now recognize the importance of expectations and uncertainty to investment decisions, although different theorists describe uncertainty in distinctive ways, with the neo-classical economists emphasizing quantifiable uncertainty (Knightian risk) and the Post Keynesians emphasizing unquantifiable uncertainty (Knightian uncertainty).

Revision questions

1. Explain why investment is often described as a flow variable and capital is often described as a stock variable.
2. Why is spending on housing regarded as a component of fixed investment?
3. What relevance do investment theories have for businesses in the real world?
4. In what ways has there been some theoretical convergence in the analysis of investment theories?
5. Why are expectations and uncertainty so important to fixed asset investors?

Part

II Theoretical Issues

3	Intellectual ancestors: Irving Fisher and Maynard Keynes	23
4	Accelerator theory	47
5	Jorgenson's model of investment	57
6	The limitations of Jorgenson's model	66
7	Putty–clay models of investment	79
8	Adjustment costs and *q* theory	92
9	Uncertainty and investment	109
10	Post Keynesian analyses of investment	124

Introduction

In this section, the evolution of the theories central to an understanding of fixed asset investment theory is outlined. These theories have their roots in the ideas of Irving Fisher (1867–1947) and John Maynard Keynes (1883–1946), arguably the most influential economists of the twentieth century. Some of Fisher's and Keynes's most influential ideas in the analysis of investment theory are presented in Chapter 3. Chapters 4–9 analyze mainstream investment theories generally in the order that they developed – starting with accelerator theory, moving to Jorgenson's neo-classical theory, then to *q* theory and then to real options theories. As will be seen, these theoretical developments involve a gradual recognition of some key insights, often foreshadowed by Keynes or Fisher years before the theories were fully developed. For example, Jorgenson and the *q* theorists developed Fisher's insights about time preferences and forward-looking economic behaviour; the *q* theorists attempted to incorporate more rigorous formulations of expectations into investment models, in recognition of Keynes's emphasis on the importance of expectations. Similarly, the real options theorists incorporated some of Keynes's and Fisher's insights about the importance of time and uncertainty. In addition, an alternative Post Keynesian theoretical literature developed at the same time as mainstream theories. This literature focuses closely on Keynes's ideas about economic behaviour but also examines the ideas of economists such as Kalecki. The Post Keynesians believe that uncertainty has a particularly profound impact on investment and macroeconomic activity in general. They also believe that human behaviour is not necessarily strictly rational in the sense postulated within the orthodox literature and that economic models based on assumptions of perfect competition and perfect markets are unlikely to be very illuminating, given the ubiquity of imperfect competition and market failure. For a Post Keynesian, this means that the abstract mathematical models of economic behaviour seen in the mainstream literature may have little practical relevance. Since the 1990s, more and more real-world evidence has been accumulating about the imperfect nature of markets and the ubiquity of uncertainty and so the Post Keynesian approach perhaps has more resonance now than it did 20 years ago. A selection of Post Keynesian investment theories are analyzed in Chapter 10.

3 Intellectual ancestors: Irving Fisher and Maynard Keynes

Fisher's ideas about investment and interest rates	24
Keynes's analysis of investment	30
Keynes on the subjective determinants of investment	36
Investment, speculation and the Stock Market	39
Keynes on investment policy	42
Conclusion	44
Chapter summary	45
Revision questions	46

For the range of theoretical approaches outlined in later chapters, it is important to emphasize that the divergent approaches are attempting to provide some answers to fundamental questions about the nature of economic behaviour. Are investors rational, maximizing machines easily described using mathematical models? Or does uncertainty and scarce information mean that psychological, subjective factors must predominate, making a mathematical approach redundant (or worse)? Knowledge of these debates is essential to a good understanding of how divergent modern investment theories have evolved.

The essential elements of Fisher's and Keynes's theories are presented in this chapter. In the mainstream orthodox neo-classical literature, models of profit maximization by rational investors are developed. These models build upon Fisher's mathematical approach to the analysis of economic behaviour and are essentially elaborations of Fisher's concept of the rate of return over cost. In the Keynesian and Post Keynesian literature, models of investment are built upon the insight that uncertainty limits the capacity of investors rationally to calculate the pros and cons of their investment projects. This means that investments will be affected by psychological factors, for example herd instincts and crowd psychology, rather than mathematical assessments. These ideas build upon Keynes's analysis of the limits to quantification under conditions of uncertainty. According to Keynes, using concepts such as the internal rate of return is difficult because information about the future is so limited.

The roots of the debate about the nature of investment activity can be traced back to the dialogue between Maynard Keynes and Irving Fisher in the 1930s. Both Fisher and Keynes assert that fixed asset investment will take place until the 'discount rate' used to balance the present value of an investment's expected future revenues with its cost is equal the prevailing interest rate. Fisher called this discount rate the internal rate of return or rate of return over costs; Keynes called it the marginal efficiency of capital. However, in practice, these theories are quite different and the key divergence lies in the contrasting descriptions of expectations formation and uncertainty. Fisher describes a world in which investors are responding to Knightian risk: risk is measurable and expectations are quantifiable. In contrast, Keynes's analysis is founded in a world of Knightian uncertainty: profound uncertainty about the future means that probabilities are rarely measurable and expectations are not necessarily quantifiable. This means that judgements of the prospective profitability of investment projects are affected by subjective, psychological factors.

Fisher's ideas about investment and interest rates

In *The Nature of Capital and Income* (1906) Fisher first outlined some of the principles that will affect macroeconomic activity and one of his key insights centres around the distinction between stocks and flows, a distinction that is important to an understanding of investment as the flow into the stock of capital. Fisher drew an analogy with water cascading down into pools at the bottom of a mountain. According to Fisher, understanding capital and wealth is like understanding streams and pools: when current income is saved, it flows into the pool of wealth, i.e. the stock of capital; if current income is spent, it flows out of the pool of wealth.

But Fisher does not focus on the stock of capital goods and instead concentrates on investment as circulating capital, consumed in the process of production. Output is determined, not by capital stocks, but by flows of investment. In this sense, Fisher's theory foreshadows adjustment cost versions of *q* theory (explained in Chapter 8) which are based around concepts of flows rather than stocks. This contrasts with stock adjustment based theories, such as accelerator theory and Jorgenson's neo-classical model (explained in Chapters 4 to 7). Fisher also foreshadows *q* theories in his focus on investment as an inter-temporal problem. Lags are important in his theory and he recognizes that investment in any one period cannot yield output until the following period.

Other links between Fisher's ideas and later theories can be seen in 'Fisher's Separation Theorem'. This theorem has two parts. First, firms' investment decisions are assumed to be independent of owners' preferences: Fisher believes firms' maximize profits and that is their only goal. Second, investment decisions are assumed to be independent of financing decisions. Again, these ideas re-surface in Jorgenson's neo-classical model and in adjustment cost versions of *q* theory, both of which adopt a profit-maximizing assumption and the Modigliani-Miller assumption of financing neutrality (explained in Chapter 6).

Similarly in Fisher's theory, labour is the only cost and capital has no role as an independent factor of production; it just reflects past savings. Savings are good for future prospects and current consumption limits future prospects. In this Fisher's approach contrasts radically with Keynes's focus on the 'paradox of thrift' in which savings are a leakage from the circular flow of income and will reduce multiplier effects, resulting in faltering aggregate expenditure and aggregate demand. But Fisher did not regard investment as a component of income. Only the consumption of the services of durable goods (for example, as depreciation) as well as consumption goods is counted as income; Fisher argues that to include in income both net investment and its later yields in terms of output and profits, will involve double-counting.

These ideas lead into Fisher's view that investment activity is propelled by inter-temporal allocation of preferences. In other words, investment is a response to the choice between consumption today and consumption tomorrow. In *The Rate of Interest* (1907) and *The Theory of Interest* (1930), Fisher outlines the principles that determine investment and interest rates in more detail. Fisher argues that the rate of interest is determined by the supply of savings and demand for savings; these he describes as the principles of 'impatience' and 'investment opportunity' and interest rates are determined when these forces are in balance. Fisher argues that 'impatience is impatience to spend, whilst opportunity is opportunity to invest' (1930, p. 177).

The impatience principle

The assertion that the supply of savings is constrained by the impatience principle was foreshadowed by John Rae in 1834. In assessing the value of future rewards, i.e. the present value of future income, a discount rate is selected that reflects economic agents' time preferences, i.e. the 'pure time preference rate'. Shortness and uncertainty of life explain agents' time preference. Interest is the reward for postponing consumption and income today will always be valued more highly than income tomorrow. Economic agents will not postpone consumption unless they will be rewarded by extra consumption in the future in compensation for the disutility of working and saving today. In this way, the inner impatience of consumers to shift future income towards the present is balanced against 'outer opportunities', that 'urge us to postpone present income' – and to shift income towards the future. If the consumption of present income is to be delayed, then value of future income must increase (Fisher, 1930).

The investment opportunity principle

The demand for savings is determined by the investment opportunity principle. Tobin (1998) observes that Fisher's investment opportunity principle does not seem to allow for capital as an independent factor of production; capital is just the accumulation of past savings. Investment decisions are made by comparing values of present income with the present values of future income. In comparing two optional streams of income, these judgements of the relative value of one over the other will be made by calculating the 'rate of return over cost'. As explained in Box 3.1, Fisher's rate of return over cost is 'that rate which, employed in computing the present worth of all the costs and present worth of all the returns, will make these two equal' (Keynes, 1936, p. 140). The investment opportunity principle involves a comparison of these internal rates of return. The advantages of holding money and holding goods will be equalized when the present value of expected future returns from an investment project are equal to the current cost of the investment project. Investors will only exploit investment opportunities if the rate of return over cost is in excess of the pure time preference rate.

In describing the intricacies of investors' decisions Fisher outlines four inter-related investment opportunity principles:

- Investors will select projects with the maximum net present value, given market rates of interest.
- Of competing investment projects, the one with the greatest advantages relative to its disadvantages will be selected.

Box 3.1 Fisher's rate of return over costs and net present value

Fisher's rate of return over costs (i.e. the internal rate of return) is the discount rate that equalizes the flow of future revenues R_t from investments and the capital cost C of installing those investments.

$$C = \sum_{t=1}^{\infty} \frac{R_t}{(1+\rho)^t}$$

It is the rate, ρ, that ensures that the difference between the present value of future revenues and the capital cost is equal to zero:

$$\sum_{t=1}^{\infty} \frac{R_t}{(1+\rho)^t} - C = 0$$

An investment will be worthwhile economically if the rate of return over costs is greater than or equal to the prevailing interest rate, r, i.e. if $\rho \geq r$. When $\rho = r$, the net present value of the proposed investment project with be zero because:

$$NPV = \sum_{t=1}^{\infty} \frac{R_t}{(1+r)^t} - C$$

- The project selected will yield a rate of return over cost greater than or equal to the interest rate.
- When investment options differ by 'continuous gradations', projects will be selected on the basis of *marginal* rates of return over cost.

In addition, Fisher introduced the idea that investment opportunities are 'options'. He separates 'eligible' and 'ineligible' options to invest and defines eligible opportunities as those investments that could be made to maximize present value, given the right rate of interest. These ideas foreshadow the real options theories outlined in Chapter 9.

Theory of the determination of interest rates

The balance of the two impulses of impatience and opportunity will move the investors towards equilibrium: 'if the pendulum shifts too far towards investment' then desires to invest will be moderated by a strengthening of impatience. The forces of opportunity and impatience are moderating each other. Assuming complete inter-temporal loan markets, the equality of savings and investment at every point determines the interest rate, the time path of production and the time path of consumption. This approach underpins the later development of the Arrow-Debreu's mathematical analysis of general equilibrium.

Fisher's legacy

Fisher's contributions extended beyond investment analysis to many other areas of economic theory and Tobin (1998) argues that Fisher's approach was 'very modern' and that the level of his reasoning was beyond that seen in other economic analysis of the time. Fisher indeed foreshadows a number of modern economic ideas. It is true that concepts of equilibrium, a marginalist approach and objective, mathematical analysis are emphasized within Fisher's writings and his concept of the rate of return over cost is a key building block of later neo-classical investment theory, such as the theory outlined by Jorgenson (discussed in Chapters 5–7). Fisher's ideas form the foundation of q and real options theories of investment too, as will be seen in Chapter 8. Fisher's concept of time preference (i.e. the timing of consumption expenditure) is also essential to other aspects of modern macroeconomic theory, for example, consumption and real business cycle theories.

According to Tobin (1998), Fisher was the most important American economist of the twentieth century. Fisher was the first to distinguish between real and nominal interest rates, although he was criticized by Keynes for not making clear the difference between inflation and inflationary expectations (Keynes, 1936, p. 142). Fisher also postulated the equation of exchange that underpins the quantity theory of money. He foreshadowed the life cycle theory of consumption smoothing. In statistics, he made contributions to the design of index numbers and, as a resolution to the contrasting drawbacks of the Laspeyres and Paasche price indicies, he formulated Fisher's Ideal Index (which is the geometric mean of the Laspeyres and Paasche formulae). He was very influential in econometrics as well and described distributed lag regression (particularly important to investment theory, as will be seen from Chapter 4 onwards).

In addition, Tobin (1998) points out that although Fisher is largely associated with neo-classical economics, he was in many senses an American Keynes. For example, Keynes drew on Fisher's ideas in his 1923 *Tract on Monetary Reform* (Skidelsky, 1992, p. 153). In the depressed environment of the early 1930s, Fisher's practical advice was to reflate the economy, for example, via public works spending (Tobin, 1998). Fisher's ideas about the trade cycle also have resonance within a Post Keynesian approach, for

Box 3.2 A brief biography of Irving Fisher

Irving Fisher was born on 27 February 1867 in New York. He was good at maths at school and studied maths at Yale College, graduating first in his class. He stayed on at Yale as a graduate student, researching economics and sociology, and was awarded his doctorate in 1892. His dissertation was entitled 'Mathematical Investigations in the Theory of Value and Prices'. He then became a tutor of mathematics at Yale. His mathematical background influenced his quantitative approach to economics. He was America's first mathematical economist, applying the quantitative method to a range of economic problems. He founded the Econometrics Society and he was President of the American Economic Association in 1918. Between 1923 and 1936 he headed his own Index Numbers Institute, an organization at the forefront of price index research.

Fisher came from a religious family (his father was a minister). This background gave him a sense of moral purpose; he was also a man of restrained habits. After an early episode with tuberculosis, he became a non-smoking, vegetarian teetotaller. He supported the Prohibition. He was a prolific writer on many subjects, including political commentary and eugenics. He also wrote poetry.

As an inventor/entrepreneur, Fisher was successful. He invented a card-index system, marketed by his Index Visible Company. He made a fortune when this company merged with Kardex Rand in 1925. Unfortunately, an avid speculator, Fisher lost this fortune in the Wall Street Crash of 1929. Even more unfortunately, adopting the maxim 'buy low', he continued to trade as share prices continued to fall. As a consequence he lost his wife's savings as well as his own and was forced to live in penury for the rest of his life. In spite of this, he was happily married to Margaret Hazard from 1893 until her death in 1940. They had one son and two daughters; one daughter died tragically after a nervous breakdown. Fisher died in New York on 29 April 1947 (Pressman, 1999).

example, the financial fragility theories of the Post Keynesians, such as Minsky (whose ideas are analyzed in Chapter 10). The neo-classical economists of the time argued that economies would be propelled back towards equilibrium, for example, via Pigou's real balance effect, in which deflation propels economies back towards equilibrium by increasing the supply of real balances and thereby generating falls in interest rates. In contrast, Fisher (1932) outlined a Schumpeterian debt-deflation theory of depression in which new innovations, financed with borrowings, fuel booms in economic activity. Fisher argued that real interest rates are pro-cyclical, reflecting money illusion. As inflation falls real interest rates fall but because investors suffer from money illusion, they do not recognize this fall in real interest rates and investment activity falters as a consequence. In the meantime, price falls mean that revenues fall as well, creating an unstable interaction between debt burdens and deflation (Tobin, 1998). In depressions, the fall in nominal interest rates leads to an increase in borrowing and investment because economic agents do not recognize that the real interest rate is sticky downwards in a deflationary environment. In this way, Fisher supported Keynes's emphasis on the economic consequences of deflation, arguing that deflation creates economic injustice for debtors, stockholders, enterprises, and similar groups and thus depresses trade (Skidelsky, 1992, p. 105).

Keynes's analysis of investment

The marginal efficiency of capital

In Chapter 11 of *The General Theory of Employment, Interest and Money* (1936), Keynes describes the marginal efficiency of capital (MEK) as the key determinant of investment. As described in Box 3.3, the MEK is a measure of the expected profitability of an investment; more specifically, it is the discount rate that makes the present value of an investment's future revenue (what Keynes calls its 'prospective yield' or an investment's 'demand price') just equal to its current supply price (or current replacement cost). So, in many ways, MEK is a concept similar to Fisher's internal rate of return. As the major determinant of investment, the MEK is a critical dynamic link in Keynes's analysis linking past, present and future. Today's capital stock represents the accumulation of investment goods in the past and thus reflects the past's influence on the present. Expectations of the future dictate the MEK and this reflects the future's influence on the present (1936, p. 145). So dynamic links and uncertainty about the future are central to Keynes's analysis.

According to Keynes, a mixture of subjective and objective influences will affect the MEK. Keynes's objective determinants of investment behaviour most importantly the relationship between MEK and interest rates, are similar to those outlined by Fisher and provide a basic description of investor behaviour. However, Keynes also argues that subjective influences profoundly affect the formation of expectations under uncertainty: the endemic nature of uncertainty means that precise mathematical tools cannot be used to judge the likely prospects of fixed asset investment decisions. Instead, subjective expectations and the state of confidence will play a key role. Given limited information and no basis for rational belief, psychological factors are important and investor behaviour will be affected by non-rational motivations, such as mass psychology, herd behaviour, animal spirits and conventions.[1]

Box 3.3 The marginal efficiency of capital

The **supply price** (p_k) of an investment or capital asset is the current replacement cost of capital assets.

The **prospective yield** (Q_t) is the expected future returns from the investment in a given year t.

The **demand price** of an investment is the present value of those expected future returns.

The **marginal efficiency of capital** (m) of an investment is the discount rate that will make the demand price exactly equal to the supply price.

Mathematically, the marginal efficiency of capital, m, will be determined when the discounted sum of revenues is equal to the supply price of the capital assets:

$$p_k = \sum \frac{Q_t}{(1+m)^t}$$

This is equivalent to Fisher's internal rate of return described in Box 3.2. Assuming that a fixed asset investment delivers the same revenue (Q) each year over an infinite time horizon and a one period lag before production commences, it can be shown that:

$$m = \frac{Q}{p_k}$$

This is the inverse of the payback period.

Box 3.4 A brief biography of John Maynard Keynes

Maynard Keynes was born on 5 June 1883, at 6 Harvey Road, Cambridge. His father was John Neville Keynes (1852–1949), a Cambridge academic and administrator. His mother, Florence Ada Keynes (1861–1958) was politically active; she was mayor of Cambridge 1932–3. So Keynes was brought up in an academic environment and this encouraged him to develop his intellectual skills. He had a younger brother (Geoffrey) and a younger sister (Margaret); he was closer to his sister than to his brother. Geoffrey Keynes became a surgeon after graduating with a First in Natural Sciences from Cambridge. As a hobby, Geoffrey wrote books and bibliographies. Margaret was interested in social work and wrote a pamphlet on *The Problem of Boy Labour*. She married A.V. Hill (physiologist, fellow and dean at Trinity College, Cambridge) in 1913.

cont. overleaf

Box 3.4 continued

Keynes went to Eton College and, in 1902, entered King's College as a maths undergraduate. At this time, he started to formulate his ideas on probability and expectations and these were influential in the development of his later theories of macroeconomic behaviour. Keynes was a sociable, charming and eloquent undergraduate and he was soon admitted into a select group of Cambridge intellectuals, the Apostles. In later years he was closely associated with the Bloomsbury group, including the writers Virginia Woolf and Lytton Strachey and the artist Duncan Grant. After graduating, he started work at the India Office but soon became bored; he then became a fellow (and later the Bursar) of King's College. He made a return to the Civil Service in 1915 when he joined the wartime Treasury but he became disaffected in 1919 writing the influential *Economic Consequence of the Peace*, criticizing the Versailles Treaty. Keynes was a gifted speculator and his knowledge of real-world financial behaviour informed his intellectual writings, for example, on financial instability. In his youth, he had a number of homosexual affairs and his Bloomsbury friends were disappointed when he married Lydia Lopokova, a ballerina, in 1925. In 1936, *The General Theory of Employment, Interest and Money* was published and, with its emphasis on demand management as the solution to depressions, it became one of the most influential economic works of the twentieth century. After World War II, Keynes became heavily involved with international policy design and was one of the principle architects of Bretton Woods. Keynes died on 21 April 1946 of a heart attack at his home in Tilton, Sussex.

There are some ironic parallels and contrasts between the lives of Fisher and Keynes. Both were talented mathematics undergraduates but there the similarities end. Although Keynes is popularly (though not entirely accurately) associated with a rejection of capitalism he was generally a very successful speculator. He is said to have made King's College one of the richest colleges in Cambridge at the time. In contrast, whilst Fisher was a successful entrepreneur and is often hailed as the father of modern neo-classical, free market economics, he was nonetheless an unlucky speculator. But Fisher did have more luck with his health – perhaps reflecting his vegetarian, teetotal, non-smoking lifestyle – he lived to 80. Keynes had a colourful but stressful lifestyle and was outlived by all his immediate family, including both his parents. In 1912, Keynes and Fisher met in London. They got on well and kept in contact until Keynes's death (Skidelsky, 1992, p. 168).

The investment demand schedule

The objective nature of the marginal efficiency of capital (MEK) is described fully in Chapter 11 of *The General Theory*. Here Keynes argues that the MEK for a given type of capital decreases with investment for two reasons – first, the prospective yield of a given type of capital good will decrease as increased supply in that market leads to falling prices and second, because the law of diminishing returns applies: 'pressure on the facilities for producing that type of

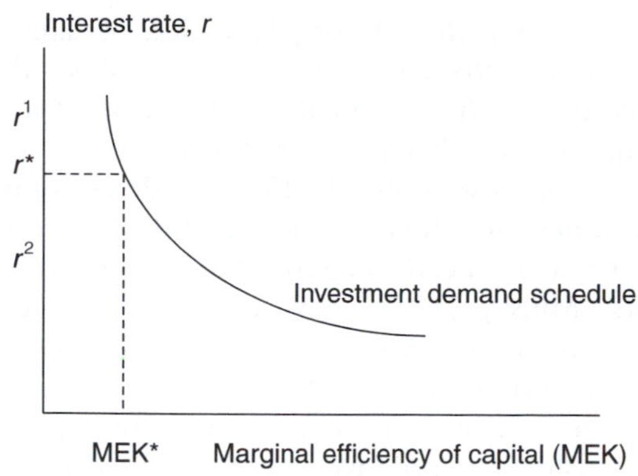

Figure 3.1 Keynes's investment demand schedule

capital will cause its supply price to increase' (Keynes, 1936, p. 136). The former factor has greater influence the longer the period considered and the latter has a greater influence in the short-term, before capital goods suppliers have had the opportunity to build up their own productive capacity. Keynes states that his investment demand schedule is in effect just the aggregate sum of the marginal efficiency of capital schedules for each type of capital good. As shown in Figure 3.1, investment will be determined at the point where the MEK in general is equal to the prevailing interest rate: that is where $\text{MEK}^* = r^*$. At this point the prospective yield from a marginal investment will exactly equal its supply price. So, at least in terms of its mathematical definition, Keynes's marginal efficiency of capital is the same as Fisher's internal rate of return.

Some Post Keynesians have criticized the objectivism implied by Keynes's construction of this investment demand schedule. They argue that it confuses subjective and objective elements, neglects dynamics, lags and conflates *ex ante* investment decisions and *ex post* investment expenditure. Also, Keynes's investment demand schedule is constructed employing a selective focus on *ex post* factors, thus ensuring a downward sloping curve. Finally, Keynes neglects the 'double-sided' relationship between investment and profitability in his construction of the downward sloping investment demand schedule (Asimakopulos, 1971, 1991; Kalecki, 1933, 1937a; Robinson, 1964a; Shackle, 1967; Targetti and Kinda-Hass, 1982). Lerner (1944), Pasinetti (1996) and Eisner (1996) point out that Keynes's concept of the marginal efficiency of capital is applied to investment flows and therefore should more accurately be termed the marginal efficiency of investment. Lerner shows that a full stock-flow equilibrium is reached not when Keynes's MEK equals the interest rate but when both the marginal efficiency of investment (Keynes's MEK) and the marginal efficiency of capital are equal to each other and to the rate of interest. Minsky also argues that Keynes may have confused the influence of stocks of capital assets and the rate of production of capital assets (Minsky 1975, p. 99). Pasinetti (1996) argues that Keynes confuses the MEK with the neo-classical concept of the marginal productivity of capital and thus, according to Pasinetti Keynes's approach is 'weak'.[2]

In resolving some of these problems, Keynes's description of the relationship between investment and interest rates can also be understood in terms of the demand price of capital, i.e. the present value of expected prospective yields from investments. Minsky (1975) advocates a greater emphasis on this demand price of capital rather than the investment demand schedule because the demand price captures influences of uncertainty, expectations and risk on investment activity more effectively. The demand price approach will capture the negative relationship between investment and interest rates. Interest rates will affect the calculations of present value of income streams from investment projects. As interest rates rise, the present value of income streams will fall so demand for investment goods will fall; conversely, investment will increase in response to a decrease in interest rates. New investment will be pushed towards the point at which the supply price of capital assets and prospective yield from investments bring the marginal efficiency of capital to equality with the rate of interest. Equating the MEK and the rate of interest is equivalent to equating the demand and supply price of capital (Keynes, 1936, p. 137).[3]

The role of interest rates

As explained above, Keynes did not argue with Fisher's assertion that interest rates play a crucial role in the determination of investment: Keynes shows that investment will take place until the marginal efficiency of capital is equal to the current interest rate: that is to the point 'where there is no longer any class of capital asset of which the marginal efficiency exceeds the current rate of interest' (1936, p. 136). The marginal efficiency of capital will also be affected by interest rate *expectations.* Keynes argues that if entrepreneurs expect a future decline in interest rates, then the desirability of current investments will decrease because these current investments will have to compete with future investments with lower rates of return given expectations of falls in future interest rates. However, Keynes concludes that expectations of interest rates are captured by the current complex of rates of interest and so should not have a significant independent influence.

Keynes defines 'full investment' as the level of investment associated with a 'full' capital stock, and the point of full investment is reached when the benefits from further investment are exhausted to nothing: i.e. when the MEK is equal to zero. However, the money rate of interest 'rules the roost', it is always positive and so 'knocks out' the production of capital goods (as well as other assets). Therefore, investment activity will stop whilst the MEK is still positive, even though the economy is below the point of 'full investment' and full employment.

Why is the interest rate always positive? Keynes adopts the liquidity preference theory of interest rate determination in arguing that the rate of interest is determined by the balance of money demand and money supply. Money has some unique attributes: it has no close substitutes; its supply, being controlled by government, is inelastic; and holding money involves negligible carrying costs. These attributes mean that there is a 'liquidity premium' – a premium on the holding of money. So the demand for money can never be fully 'choked-off' and the interest rate can never fall to zero. In addition, Keynes argues that there will always be a floor, beyond which interest rates cannot fall, on interest rates because of the transaction costs involved in getting borrowers and lenders together. For all these reasons, the interest rate will always be positive and so investment will always stop before the MEK falls to zero. Actual investment will almost always be below full investment.

Risk factors

Keynes argues that three types of risk will affect investment decisions: borrower's risk; lender's risk; and risks of changes in the monetary standard (inflationary risk). Borrower's risk is an entrepreneur's doubt about the probability of earning a given prospective yield. It is a real social cost but it can be reduced by increasing accuracy of foresight. By implication, borrower's risk is embedded in the discount rate used to calculate prospective yields. Lender's risk is a pure addition to interest costs but will involve some duplication of borrower's risk. This duplication of the different components of risk means that there are extra costs involved when borrowing and lending decisions are separated; in other words when an entrepreneur has to finance investment decisions via external borrowing rather than from retained profits. This is one of the reasons that interest rates (inclusive of risk premia) will be higher than objective factors indicate. Keynes argues that the estimates of lender and borrower risk become unusually and 'imprudently' low during booms. However, whilst lenders are affected by the state of confidence, they do require a wider margin between the base rate of interest and their lending rates because their decisions will not be affected by the spontaneous optimism that boosts the entrepreneur-borrowers.

Inflationary risk is the risk of an adverse change in monetary standard but Keynes argues that the independent influence of inflationary risk will not be great because expectations of inflation or deflation in the value of money loans will be absorbed within the price of capital assets (Keynes, 1936, p. 144). This dismissal of inflationary risk was probably more valid to the time in which Keynes was writing. In the stagflationary economic environment that characterized the 1970s and 1980s, inflationary risk probably had a significant independent influence.

Keynes on the subjective determinants of investment

The role of expectations

As mentioned above, expectations are central to Keynes's analysis. They provide a crucial link that reconciles the objective precision of investment calculations, as described in Chapter 11 of *The General Theory*, with the seeming subjectivism of investment decisions, as described in Chapter 12. Keynes divides expectations into two categories: long-term expectations and short-term expectations. Short-term expectations include expectations of the cost of output, wages and the price of output. Keynes argues that, in practice, short-term expectations are revised gradually and continuously in the light of realized results and this leads to an overlap in influence of past expectations and past realized results: past expectations will affect current decisions because these expectations are embodied in the current stock of capital equipment. However, current decisions will also be affected by current expectations, which in turn depend on current performance. This intermingling of past, present and future creates inertia and explains the convention of assuming stability in short-term expectations. So, whilst short-term expectations may take a while to work themselves out, they are not volatile and because of their stability, Keynes assumes that short-term expectations are not a crucial determinant of economic fluctuations.

In contrast, Keynes argues that long-term expectations can be very unstable. The long-term expectations of the profitability of investments are partly based on existing facts, including the existing capital stock and consumer demand. They are also based on forecasts of future events, for example, forecasts of future changes in the capital stock, in consumer tastes, in wages and in the strength of effective demand. These forecasts of future events are included in what Keynes calls the state of long-term expectation. In *The General Theory* the long-term expectations affecting investment and liquidity preference cannot be modelled accurately using existing data because individual decisions about investment and liquidity preference, decisions that have future consequences, are not necessarily quantifiable or even comparable. This insight has implications for the rationality of investors.[4] So, in forming their expectations, business decision-makers rely on a 'practical theory of the future' to overcome the limitations created by uncertainty. This theory incorporates a number of overlapping techniques including:

- **Projection** Investors assume that present conditions are the most reliable guide to the future and project them forward, even though past experience has shown that the present is often an inadequate guide to the future. This assumption is adopted because of lack of information about the nature of future changes. The technique will be used as long as there is no definite reason to expect change.

- **Convention** In forming expectations, investors accept the existing state of opinion at least until new information emerges because it is assumed to incorporate a more accurate assessment of future prospects. Thus conventional valuations are important determinants of investment decisions.
- **Herd behaviour** In response to new information, investors will often assume that other investors may have better information. So investors will rely on 'conventional judgements', the judgements of others. Investors will tend to follow the crowd.

These techniques all involve a judgement that the existing state of events will continue but this state of events is not determined by objective factors and so it is ephemeral and volatile; it changes rapidly as new information arrives. However, Keynes does emphasize that the state of long-term expectation associated with existing economic environment, although not strictly calculable, may sometimes be steady because of the influence of conventions, and these will be stable for as long as the belief in conventions is maintained (1936, pp. 162–3). The effects of long-term expectations will also be long lived because equipment will continue to be used in production until it is worn out or becomes obsolete. It follows that the past will continue to exert an influence on current production for a long time.

Animal spirits

Keynes argues that, given widespread uncertainty about the future prospects of investment projects, there will be no basis for forming a mathematical expectation of long-term profitability. Even if there were, it might often indicate that investments should not be undertaken. This results in a conflict between private and social objectives. For private entrepreneurs, it may suit them to be cautious in the face of uncertainty. But falling investment has negative social consequences in a Keynesian world and will generate falling output and rising unemployment. Keynes argues that the animal spirits of entrepreneurs partially resolve this dilemma. His precise definition of animal spirits is difficult to find but animal spirits are associated with 'spontaneous urges' to act now rather than wait for later. The existence of animal spirits as a subjective incentive to fixed asset investment can predominate over less encouraging objective signals and investment will be relatively robust as a consequence. In this sense, animal spirits are socially desirable. However, because animal spirits have no objective basis they are 'easily dimmed' by economic and political uncertainty and so the volume of new investment will be unnecessarily dependent on 'whim', 'sentiment' and the 'nerves', 'digestion' and 'hysteria' of business people. So whilst animal spirits may boost investment they will also contribute to its volatility and the fragility of the inducement to invest is compounded by the influence of animal spirits.

The emphasis in Chapter 12 of *The General Theory* on mass psychology, conventions and animal spirits seems to be very much at odds with the quantitative determinism implied by Keynes's Chapter 11 suggestion that the investment demand schedule is a neat, precise downward-sloping demand curve.[5] Shackle (1967) argues that Keynes's true message was lost in the 'curiously unsatisfying' Chapter 12 that contains only the 'scattered bones' of his real theory. Shackle observes:

> Chapter 11 shows us the arithmetic of the MEK and its relation with interest rates, as a matter for actuaries and slide-rules. Chapter 12 reveals the hollowness of all this. [In Chapter 12,] Keynes argues that the material for the slide-rules is absent or arbitrary. (Shackle, 1967, p. 130)

The overlap between the psychology of individual behaviour versus aggregate behaviour and the problems with precise quantification are some of the reasons that the investment demand schedule is seen as an inappropriate construction, in many senses unnecessary for, and contradictory to, the rest of Keynes's theory. But Chapters 11 and 12 of *The General Theory* can be reconciled by assuming that the investment demand schedule shifts abruptly and rapidly, reflecting the influence of volatile expectations and fickle animal spirits (Robinson, 1962; Shackle, 1967, p. 133). Even if there is an equilibrium level of employment associated with each state of long-term expectations, the economy is unlikely to reach this equilibrium before expectations change. In addition, the process of achieving new equilibria in response to changes in expectations will take time and in the period of transition there may be overshooting or undershooting of expectations (Keynes, 1936, p. 49). This suggests that Keynes believed, in stark contrast to neo-classical approaches, that concepts of equilibria are of no *practical* importance in understanding fixed asset investment.

The precariousness of expectations of the marginal efficiency of capital explains the focus by real world investors on short-term returns, as described in Chapter 2. This Keynesian assertion has been explored in various surveys, for example, the *CBI Industrial Trends Survey* and Baddeley (1996), and these indicate that investment decisions tend to have shorter pay-off periods and higher internal rates of return than would be expected from looking at the simple cost of borrowing as reflected in interest rates. Other factors mitigating the effects of the precariousness of expectations on the marginal efficiency of capital include the existence of contracts and risk-sharing, monopoly privileges and risks borne by public authorities undertaking activity for social purposes. So not all classes of investment are affected by volatility and complexity but, for Keynes, the volatility that does exist is enough to explain wide fluctuations in economic activity, particularly during times of extreme uncertainty.

Investment, speculation and the Stock Market

In the previous sections we have focused on Keynes's analysis of physical, fixed asset investment. But Keynes did also highlight some crucial links between financial investment and physical investment, and these links emerge via the Stock Market. According to Keynes, before Stock Markets evolved, physical investment depended on individual initiative and gambling instincts. The results of investment were often disappointing and because investment decisions were irrevocable in the short term, entrepreneurs were wary about committing their money to new investment projects. However, as financial markets have evolved, investment activity has been encouraged. This is because the rights to ownership of fixed assets can easily be traded in the Stock Market: individuals can revise their commitments to placements on a very short-term basis. So organized asset markets allow investments, while fixed for the community as a whole, to become liquid for individuals. Keynes argues that this liquidity often facilitates investment activity by calming the nerves of investors: investors will be more willing to commit their funds because they can trade their ownership very quickly in response to news and/or if they become pessimistic about an investment's prospects.

According to Keynes, Stock Markets have another important purpose. Uncertainty and limited information limit investment decisions. Uncertainty prevents the assignment of precise numerical values to expectations particularly for new forms of production in new markets. In such cases, there may be very little information about the prospective success of new projects. Anyone thinking of investing may have very little information about costs, demand etc. and so has difficulty quantifying the probability of making a profit. Existing competitors in the same market would have no incentive to circulate information. Given no objective basis upon which to estimate the likely profits of investment projects, Keynes argues that potential investors will look to the Stock Market valuations when considering new investment projects. If an entrepreneur is considering a new investment to be undertaken purely for profit, his/her decisions will be governed by the average expectations of the future performance of similar firms as revealed in share prices as much as by the genuine expectations of entrepreneurs. 'There is no sense in building up a new enterprise at a cost greater than that at which an existing one can be purchased' (Keynes, 1936, p. 151). So high share prices will have the same effect as low interest rates: a high quotation will boost the market valuation of a firm and therefore the firm's estimates of its future prospective yields. This insight forms the basis of the predominant modern approach to modern fixed asset investment analysis: q theories of investment, discussed in Chapter 8.[6]

Also, in using share prices as signals of future profitability, a dilemma does emerge because share prices themselves are based upon very limited information. Investors realize that they are not well informed and so will look to others in forming their judgements of future movements in share prices. They will apply the practical theory of the future, outlined above, to their financial investments. They will rely on the convention of assuming that the existing share price will prevail, unless they have definite reasons for expecting a change. This convention is not based on rational judgements because there is limited information about future share prices. In reality, investors know that the share price is likely to change but nonetheless believe that the existing market valuation is uniquely correct compared with existing knowledge and will change only in proportion to changes in that knowledge. In addition, investors form a judgement that the likelihood of changes in the market valuation in the short-term is small because the only risk is of a change in news in the short-term. Financial investments are therefore regarded as safe for short periods of time.

However, the fact that the convention is arbitrary and has no objective basis means that it will be precarious and weak. This precariousness reflects a number of inter-related factors affecting the links between the behaviour of entrepreneurs (the fixed asset investors) and speculators (the financial investors trying to make money out of changes in share prices).

For example:

- Owners of financial assets have little real knowledge of the value of shares so ephemeral factors will have disproportionate impacts on share prices.
- Mass psychology is volatile because there are no 'strong roots of conviction to hold it steady' creating herding behaviour. Thus financial markets will be subject to waves of optimism and pessimism.
- Expert speculators will devote their skill to outwitting the market and predicting changes in the mass psychology propelling the market. They will devote their expertise to forecasting average opinion of average opinion of future share prices rather than genuine expectations of prospective yield. In describing this behaviour, Keynes uses his oft-quoted analogy of the beauty contest in which a newspaper asks its readers to judge, not their opinion of the most beautiful woman, but the other readers' opinion of the most beautiful woman, i.e. the average opinion of the average opinion. This all means that genuine beliefs have little influence as everyone is focusing on outwitting the rest of the market. In this sort of market, speculative activity will overwhelm genuine entrepreneurship. Entrepreneurship is also constrained by the fact that forecasting genuine changes in the prospective yield of investments over the long-term is risky, costly, difficult, unconventional, and requires greater resources than predicting ephemeral changes in financial markets.

In particularly uncertain times, when the state of confidence in markets is very fragile, people will tend to rely on conventional behaviour of other financial investors. They will fall back on the judgement of the rest of the world because the rest of the world is perhaps better informed. Thus herd behaviour and crowd psychology will determine the movement of share prices. Furthermore, because people realize that their estimates of the values of shares are based on precarious foundations, the conventions propelling financial markets will be unstable and volatile. Speculative bubbles emerge as professional speculators chase average opinion of average opinion.

Keynes argues that this 'fetish' with liquidity seen in Stock Markets is a major destructive element in the capitalist system. The influence of the conventionally based market valuations on new physical investment will mean that fluctuations in aggregate private investment will be unplanned, uncontrolled and subject to the vagaries of the market. So whilst the existence of asset markets provides much-needed liquidity, the market valuation of assets will have no tendency to coincide with the fundamental value of a share: i.e. the discounted stream of expected future dividends. 'Certain classes of investment are governed by the average expectation of those who deal on the Stock Exchange as revealed in the price of shares rather than by the genuine expectations of the professional entrepreneur' (Keynes, 1936, p. 151). If speculative activity dominates asset markets, there will be substantial negative effects for real activity and output. During a bubble phase, entrepreneurial behaviour is driven by subjective factors such as animal spirits and spontaneous optimism. This subjectively-driven level of activity cannot endure because the estimates of the marginal efficiency of capital that determine investment decisions are based on precarious and over-optimistic expectations. This over-optimism precipitates a crisis as disillusion sets in at the end of a boom: investors realize that their subjectively based profit expectations are not justified and errors of pessimism replace errors of optimism and the marginal efficiency of capital collapses.

The predominance of speculative forces in modern capitalist economies compromises the development of economic potential:

> Speculators may do no harm as bubbles on a whirlpool of speculation. But the position is serious when enterprise becomes the bubble on a whirlpool of speculation. When the capital development of a country becomes a by-product of the activities of a casino, the job is likely to be ill-done. (Keynes, 1936, p. 159)

Speculation has increased as the organization of investment markets has improved. But the development of organized investment markets has not been a triumph for laissez-faire capitalism because the 'best brains' have focused their attention towards outwitting the market and anticipating changes in the market valuation of shares rather than directing new investment into the opportunities with the most potential. Therefore, organized Stock Markets, rather than increasing the volume of funds directed at new investment, have instead contributed to its increasing volatility.[7]

Keynes on investment policy

Keynes argues that securing a sufficient volume of investment is a central problem for economic policy-makers. Keynes goes on to argue that full investment (as defined above) 'has never occurred, not even momentarily' (p. 324). Keynes argues that full investment can never be reached in a free market even if agents possess perfect foresight, because interest rates are always too high and the subjective forces of optimism and animal spirits that determine the boom phase of the cycle are not strong enough to secure sufficient investment from a society's point of view. So whilst Keynes emphasizes the need to harness individual initiative and argues that individualism can foster the variety essential to the effective operation of the capitalist system, he is also pessimistic about the ability of free markets completely to correct problems of insufficient investment, excessive interest rates and consequent sub-optimal levels of output and employment. In his view, government intervention is essential:

> In conditions of laissez-faire the avoidance of wide fluctuations in employment may . . . prove impossible without a far-reaching change in the psychology of investment markets such as there is no reason to expect. I conclude that the duty of ordering investment cannot safely be left in private hands. (Keynes, 1936, p. 320)

Whilst making the purchase of fixed asset investments indissoluble would force investors to focus on the long-term, Keynes argues that this policy would be ineffective because uncertainty about future prospective yields would discourage a large number of people from investing. On the other hand, the liquidity allowed by organized investment markets creates its own dilemmas, contributing to fragility and volatility. Keynes suggests a compromise and argues that access to Stock Markets should just be limited via policy measures such as taxation (Keynes, 1936, pp. 159–60).

Interest rate management

Whilst an increased quantity of money should, in theory, lead to a decrease in interest rates and thus to an increase in investment, Keynes was sceptical about the likely success of monetary policy. The effectiveness of monetary policy is determined by the credibility of policies and may have little to do with the magnitude of an increase in the quantity of money because expectations and psychology are crucial. If an increase in the money supply is perceived to be an experimental policy, expectations of policy reversals will dilute the effectiveness of the policy. Similarly, in the situation of extreme pessimism, liquidity traps may develop. Liquidity traps emerge when an infinite elasticity of demand for money means that increases in money supply have no effect on the interest rate. Without interest rate falls, entrepreneurs will not be encouraged to invest more and the economy will not move along its investment demand schedule. In addition,

Keynes argues that a policy of decreasing interest rates may have limited effectiveness if interest rates cannot fall fast enough to keep pace with a falling MEK: 'the market estimation of the marginal efficiency of capital may suffer such enormously wide fluctuations that it cannot be sufficiently offset by corresponding fluctuations in the rate of interest' (Keynes, 1936, pp. 319–20). In contrast, if investors believe that the interest rate has an objective basis, monetary policy will be effective even if the resulting interest rate just reflects conventions. The influence of these and other monetary factors is assessed in detail by the Post Keynesians (see Chapter 10). Psychological factors are crucial (Keynes, 1936, pp. 201–3).

Investment and expenditure policies

Keynes is more optimistic about policies directed at the MEK rather than the rate of interest and argues that the state should act to internalize the social benefits and costs of investment projects by calculating the MEK, adopting a long-term view. He argues that the government should have control both of the allocation of resources to investment and over the MEK. However, the ownership of the means of production would remain in private hands allowing government intervention whilst harnessing the benefits of private initiative.

Famously, Keynes also recommends government expenditure policies as a means of boosting the level of investment, arguing that even government expenditure can be beneficial given the reluctance of policy-makers to pursue more constructive forms of investment. Public investment can be undertaken to increase the capital stock to a desirable level as well as to propel multiplier effects and Keynes argues that any sort of public investment will have positive effects in postponing contractions in economic activity. According to Keynes, while it is best that public investment is devoted towards productive ends, even wasteful expenditure can be beneficial: 'even the diversion of the desire to hold wealth towards assets, which will in fact yield no economic fruits whatever, will increase economic well-being' (Keynes, 1936, pp. 219–20).

However, Keynes does allow that investment in public works can sometimes create 'adverse reactions' on private investment. Interest rates may rise due to increased transactions demand for money to finance investment 'so retarding investment in other directions, unless the monetary authority takes steps to the contrary'. In addition, the MEK of private investments may increase with the increased cost of capital goods generated by increased public investment. Furthermore, fluctuations in the state of confidence and the 'confused psychology' created by changes to government policy may decrease the MEK unless offsetting measures are also implemented. Finally, the effects of government expenditure policies may be dissipated in an open economy as 'some part of the multiplier of the increased investment will accrue to the benefit of employment in foreign countries' (Keynes, 1936, pp. 119–20).

However, Keynes argues that overall, wealth-making tendencies, enterprise and skill should be harnessed for predicting prospective yields of investments rather than for speculative activity (Keynes, 1936, pp. 220–1). If the State intervenes to ensure full investment, then a 'properly run', modern community with manageable population growth should be able to bring down the MEK until capital is no longer scarce whilst still allowing sufficient rewards for risk-taking and entrepreneurship. Employment would increase and the consequent redistribution of income would boost consumption, generating positive effects for output and employment, propelled via the multiplier. Government policies to encourage the abundance of capital would overcome many of the 'objectionable features of capitalism'.

Conclusion

According to Fisher, investment is dictated by objective, quantifiable influences as captured by the rate of return over costs. According to Keynes, the inducement to invest is affected by a multiplicity of subjective and objective factors. The crucial role played by the subjective influences of the state of confidence, long-term expectations and animal spirits means that investor behaviour cannot effectively be modelled using the largely mathematical approach employed by Fisher. So the essential differences between Keynes's approach and Fisher's approach lie in the different understandings of the nature of rational investor behaviour and expectations formation. Fisher's model is firmly based within objective mathematical analysis. In Keynes's world, complexity means that simple mathematical descriptions of individual behaviour are inappropriate. Also, in Chapter 12 of *The General Theory* at least, Keynes suggests that it is not possible simply to aggregate from individual behaviour to macroeconomic behaviour using the methods described by more mainstream theorists because human behaviour is overlapping and interdependent. At every stage of Keynes's analysis, empirical observation, experience, generalization and intuition, rather than logical necessity and precision, are preferred to mathematical tools:

> The object of our analysis is . . . to provide ourselves with an organised and orderly method of thinking out particular problems. In ordinary discourse, where we are not blindly manipulating but know all the time what we are doing and what the words mean, we can keep 'at the back of our heads' the necessary reserves and qualifications and the adjustments which we shall have to make later on . . . Too large a proportion of recent 'mathematical' economics are merely concoctions, as imprecise as the initial assumptions they rest on, which allow the author to lose sight of the complexities and interdependencies of the real world in a maze of pretentious and unhelpful symbols. (Keynes, 1936, pp. 297–8)

So the contrasts between a Fisherian and Keynesian approach are founded not so much in terms of the basic determinants of investment. Keynes's marginal efficiency of capital is a concept similar to Fisher's rate of return over costs. Neither would argue about the importance of interest rates. The fundamental differences come in methodological approach and these methodological differences have been projected forward in the modern theories of investment outlined in the subsequent chapters. The neo-classical economists emphasize the objective quantitative approach of rational profit maximizing investors and the Post Keynesians emphasize the limits on quantification and the importance of psychology, subjective factors and non-rational behaviour in a world of uncertainty.

Chapter summary

1. Fisher's key contribution was in discussing the role of net present value and the internal rate of return over costs in the determination of investment decisions. Fisher also illuminated the relationships between internal rates of return and the interest rate in his ideas about impatience versus opportunity.
2. Keynes presents a basic theory of investment that is similar to Fisher's: Keynes's marginal efficiency of capital is, analytically at least, much the same as Fisher's internal rate of return.
3. However, a more thorough analysis of Keynes reveals that although he began his analysis of investment with an objective description of the marginal efficiency of capital, he also argued that subjective influences, such as conventional behaviour and crowd psychology, will have profound effects on judgements of the profitability of investments as captured by the marginal efficiency of capital. This is because uncertainty limits the ability of investors to calculate the marginal efficiency of capital objectively.
4. Given limited basis for rational calculation, Keynes also argues that animal spirits, i.e. forces of spontaneous optimism, will also encourage a larger, more socially desirable volume of investment than would result if investors relied only upon their rational calculations.
5. Keynes argued that there will be crucial links between investment, uncertainty and finance because investment activity will be determined by the state of the Stock Market and financial factors. These ideas link into discussions of the 'finance motive' and are developed by the Post Keynesians.
6. In addition, Keynes spent some time analyzing the relationship between Stock Market valuations of firms and investment decisions.
7. Many of the key ideas that surface in modern investment theory have their roots in the ideas of Fisher and Keynes. Fisher's ideas resonate in Jorgenson's neo-classical model of investment (see Chapters 5–7), in adjustment cost versions of q theory (see Chapter 8) and his approach is also broadly consistent with real options theories (see Chapter 9). Keynes's ideas have been influential not only in the construction of accelerator theories (Chapter 4) and Post Keynesian theories of investment under uncertainty (Chapter 10) but also in the evolution of q theories of investment, outlined in Chapter 8.

Revision questions

1. How do the principles of impatience and opportunity affect investment decisions?
2. What is the rate of return over cost?
3. What are the similarities between Keynes's and Fisher's approach?
4. In what ways does Keynes distinguish his theory from Fisher's theory?
5. Why has Keynes's analysis of investment been so influential?
6. What are some of the problems with Keynes's analysis?
7. Which of Keynes's ideas about investment have had an influence on modern understandings of investment?

4 Accelerator theory

Introduction	48
Simple accelerator theory	49
Flexible accelerator models	51
The empirical evidence for accelerator theory	53
Conclusion	55
Chapter summary	56
Revision questions	56

Simple and flexible accelerator theories are explained in this chapter. Accelerator theories describe fixed asset investment as the process of adjustment to a desired capital stock. Firms will want a larger capital stock if they expect demand for their products to rise. As investment is the flow into the capital stock, it will respond to changes in this expected demand for output. So accelerator models are built upon the insight that investment will be determined by output growth. Early 'simple' accelerator models were built upon the assumption that firms can adjust their capital stocks instantaneously and that expectations are static and lags are absent. Of course these assumptions are unrealistic and later formulations of flexible accelerator theory incorporated lag structures to capture delays in investment decision-making. The emphasis in accelerator theory on movements in quantity rather than price variables means that accelerator models are generally associated with a fixed-price, Keynesian approach.

Introduction

Keynes's writings had a crucial influence on the development of macroeconomic theory and policy after World War II. The dominant models of investment that evolved during this time were based around 'accelerator' theory and so accelerator theory is generally associated with a Keynesian approach. However, one of the first people to postulate an accelerator mechanism was J. Maurice Clark who observed:

> the demand for enlarging the means of production [net investment] . . . varies, not with the volume of demand for the finished product, but rather with the acceleration of that demand, allowance being made for the fact that the equipment cannot be adjusted as rapidly as demand changes. (Clark, 1917, p. 234)

In other words, Clark argues that businesses invest in response to *growing* demand for output and not to the *level* of demand.

Harrod (1936, 1939) elaborated upon these ideas with his development of the 'acceleration principle', essential to his multiplier-accelerator theory of growth and the trade cycle. Harrod argued that firms make investment decisions by looking at the capital–output ratio, which is determined by factors such as technological conditions, the state of confidence and interest rates. Firms make a decision about proposed increases in their output and use the capital–output ratio to estimate the value of capital goods needed to produce that increment to output. So net investment (the value of the increment to the capital stock) will be determined by proposed changes in output. These ideas form the basis of the simple accelerator theories described below.

The links between Keynes's approach and the predominant accelerator theories are not immediately clear as Keynes's analysis does not concentrate solely on processes of adjustment in quantities such as output. In fact, as explained in the preceding chapter, Keynes's argument is slightly more complex: he argued that factors such as expected future income from investments and capital goods prices are important determinants of investment activity because these factors are key components of the marginal efficiency of capital. Matthews (1959) clarifies the link. He explains that entrepreneurs (i.e. fixed asset investors) aim to make investment decisions in response to profit expectations. However, they are constrained by uncertainty preventing them from forming clear, quantifiable expectations of expected future profitability. So entrepreneurs will use readily observable quantity variables, i.e. output growth, as proxies for changes in expected future profitability.

Simple accelerator theory

As noted in Chapter 2, net investment is the flow into the stock of capital; it augments the capital stock. Simple accelerator theory describes the process of capital stock adjustment as follows: businesses accumulate capital, i.e. undertake net investment, when they want a larger capital stock and they will want a larger capital stock if they expect increases in demand for output. The mathematics of simple accelerator models are explained in Box 3.1. This shows that the desired capital stock is a function of the expected level of demand for output. Investors aim to accumulate enough capital in a given period to be able to produce this expected output. Since expectations of future output are not observable, current output is used as a proxy for output expectations and the desired capital stock becomes a function of current demand for output. It follows that net investment, being the change in the capital stock, is determined by *changes* in output. This insight can be extended by making simple assumptions about the capital stock in previous periods: for example, some simple accelerator models allow that net investment will be moderated if the capital stock was under-utilized in the previous period.

Accelerator theories are set in a Keynesian world of sticky prices. In this sort of world, there will be no substitution of one factor for the other and *relative* factor prices (i.e. of capital relative to labour) will not affect investment decisions. This is because, in an economy operating below full employment capacity, all factors of production are plentiful relative to demand. This excess supply of factors relative to insufficient *effective* demand will mean that factor prices do not change as aggregate demand increases. The economy will be operating on a horizontal aggregate supply curve and investment will not be choked-off by rising capital goods prices. Capital and output will rise in equal proportions. It follows that the capital–output ratio, the amount of capital needed to produce each unit of output, will be fixed. In addition, in accelerator theory, the capital stock is assumed to change slowly over time and the technological parameters (i.e. the capital–labour ratios) embodied within the existing capital stock are assumed to be constant, at least in the short-run. In other words, capital and labour will be complementary factors: increases in one factor cannot be used unless there are equivalent increases in the other. So capital–labour ratios will be constant. (These points are explained in more detail in Chapter 7.)

Box 4.1 Simple accelerator theory

Assuming full capacity utilization

In accelerator theory, the desired capital stock (K^*) is a function of future expected output (Y^e):

$$K_t^* = vY_t^e$$

where v is the capital–output ratio.

Assuming that Y_t can be used as a proxy for Y_t^e in the current period, $K_t^* = vY_t$ and $K_{t-1}^* = vY_{t-1}$:

$$\rightarrow \quad I_{nt} = K_t^* - K_{t-1}^* = v(Y_t - Y_{t-1}) = v\Delta Y_t$$
$$\text{and} \quad I_{gt} = v\Delta Y_t + \delta K_{t-1}$$

where I_{nt} = net investment (net of depreciation), I_{gt} = gross investment including depreciation and δ is the depreciation rate.

The model above incorporates the assumption that the capital stock was at its desired point in the previous period and that the capital stock is always fully utilized. However, the theory can be reformulated allowing capacity under-utilization and/or deviations from K* in the previous period.

Allowing capacity under-utilization

If the existing K is underutilized then that acts as a disincentive to further investment. From above, net investment, I_{nt}, is equal to:

$$I_{nt} = (K_t^* - K_{t-1}^*) - \gamma K_{t-1} = v\Delta Y_t - \gamma K_{t-1}$$
$$I_{gt} = v\Delta Y_t + \delta K_{t-1} - \gamma K_{t-1}$$

where γ = extent of capacity under-utilization.

Allowing $K_{t-1} \neq K_{t-1}^*$

$$I_{nt} = K_t^* - K_{t-1} = vY_t - K_{t-1}$$
$$I_{gt} = vY_t + (\delta - 1)K_{t-1}$$

There are a number of theoretical and empirical difficulties with these simple accelerator models. First, net investment is assumed to adjust the capital stock to its desired level within *one period of time* and this does not seem to be a particularly justifiable assumption. Matthews (1959) points out that the level of investment cannot be expressed as a function of the rate of change in output because the capital stock in the previous period was not necessarily at its optimal level. The capital stock is unlikely to adjust to its desired level in one period because investment lags will mean that current investment expenditure may reflect decisions taken many time periods earlier. It seems more likely that net investment will be a process of 'partial adjustment' to the desired capital stock. Second, empirically, the simple accelerator specification was rejected in tests by Chenery (1952), Harrod (1936), Koyck (1954), Kuznets (1935) and Tinbergen (1938). For example, Chenery (1952) found that the estimates of the capital–labour ratio derived from his models were considerably lower than the average capital–labour ratio. This poor empirical evidence for simple accelerator models was attributed to the omission of lag structures.

Flexible accelerator models

In response to some of these empirical shortcomings with simple accelerator models, Goodwin and Chenery formulated 'flexible accelerator' models. Goodwin (1948) outlined a rudimentary flexible accelerator model that showed entrepreneurs adjusting their desired capital stock over a number of time periods. Harrod (1939), whilst emphasizing that other factors were more crucial, did observe that producers' decisions to increase capital relate not only to the increase in total output in one period but also to prospective increases in subsequent periods and so the importance of time lags in investment decisions should be recognized; lags will lead to oscillations and instability in investment activity, and these will spread throughout the system via multiplier effects. Chenery (1952) developed Goodwin's insight by introducing 'reaction lags' into the simple accelerator model. These reaction lags reflect the interval between changes in demand and the response in terms of new investment activity and so will capture the delays between investment decisions and investment expenditures. So in flexible accelerator models, adjustment to the desired capital stock is assumed to take place over many periods. Expected future output is included as a weighted function of past output, allowing partial, delayed adjustment within the investment decision-making process. In this way, the effects of past output growth are spread over time, reflecting decision, financing, ordering, delivery, installation and adjustment lags.

This recognition that capital stock adjustment is not an instantaneous process is crucial to an understanding of the process of investment. Lags will appear in investment for a variety of reasons: there will be gestational delays between identifying investment opportunities, planning projects, making the investment decisions, ordering, delivering, and paying for investment expenditures as well as for commencement of new investment projects. Lags will be longer for large-scale capital goods made to order and shorter for investment in vehicles and for short-term investment projects. Institutional and legal constraints on investment activity will also create lags in the investment process. This delayed adjustment will mean that actual investment expenditure in any given period will reflect investment decisions made in the past.

The process of forming the *expectations* that affect investment decisions will also create relationships between current and lagged variables, for example, if current expectations are based upon past events. For example, investment decisions may be affected by expectational lags: firms may look at a series of lags on past output in forming expectations of future profitability or they may use adaptive expectations, correcting previous mistaken expectations by some constant amount. In either case, investment will respond sluggishly to current conditions.

Flexible accelerator models allow for all these sources of lags by describing investment in any given period as a function not only of current output growth but also of past output growth, as outlined in Box 4.2.

Box 4.2 Flexible accelerator models

The flexible accelerator model

Geometrically declining weights on past output growth are incorporated by including a coefficient of adjustment, μ, on the output growth terms, where $0 < \mu < 1$.

As μ is positive but less than 1, its effects are multiplied down over time and the parameters on output changes will become smaller as the lag lengthens. This can be summarized with the following notation:

$$I_{nt} = v(1-\mu)\sum_{n=0}^{\infty}\mu^n Y_{t-n} - K_{t-1}$$

$$v(1-\mu) < v, \text{ given } 0 < \mu < 1$$

The Koyck transformation

This transformation can be used to simplify flexible accelerator models as follows, beginning with a definition of K_t

$$K_t = v(1-\mu)\sum_{n=0}^{\infty}\mu^n Y_{t-n} \qquad (0 < \mu < 1) \tag{1}$$

$$= v(1-\mu)Y_t + v(1-\mu)\mu Y_{t-1} + v(1-\mu)\mu^2 Y_{t-2} + \cdots + v(1-\mu)\mu^{\infty} Y_{t-\infty}$$

Lagging K_t by one period and multiplying it by μ:

$$\mu K_{t-1} = v(1-\mu)\sum_{i=0}^{\infty}\mu^{n+1} Y_{t-(n+1)} \tag{2}$$

$$= v(1-\mu)\mu Y_{t-1} + v(1-\mu)\mu^2 Y_{t-2} + \cdots + v(1-\mu)\mu^{\infty} Y_{t-\infty} + v(1-\mu)\mu^{\infty+1} Y_{t-\infty-1}$$

Box 4.2 continued

Subtract (2) from (1) and note that all terms but the first cancel out and the last term approaches zero as $n \to \infty$ (because $0 < \mu < 1$). So:

$$K_t - \mu K_{t-1} = v(1-\mu)Y_t$$

Subtracting $(1-\mu)K_{t-1}$ from both sides:

and $\quad \therefore\ K_t - K_{t-1} = I_{nt} = v(1-\mu)Y_t - (1-\mu)K_{t-1}$

So the econometric estimation of these models can be simplified to a regression of net investment on current output and lagged capital stock.

The empirical evidence for accelerator theory

A large number of accelerator models have been estimated since Clark first introduced the approach in 1917. Once the problems with simple accelerator models had been resolved, subsequent empirical evidence verified that current and lagged output growth was an important determinant of fixed asset investment activity (Chenery, 1952; Diamond, 1962 amongst many others). Survey evidence supported the assertion that not only output but also other quantity variables such as demand, sales and capacity utilization were more important than price factors (such as the cost of funds and interest rates) in propelling investment activity (Hall and Hitch, 1939; Morris, 1974; Neild, 1964; Rockley, 1973). These survey findings were also confirmed in econometric analyses that favoured flexible accelerator theories of investment over interest rate models (Eisner, 1965; Kuh, 1971; Modigliani and Weingartner, 1958).

More specifically, in addressing some of the empirical shortcomings of simple accelerator models outlined above, Chenery found that the flexible accelerator coefficients in his model were less than the upwardly biased average capital–output ratio estimated for simple accelerator models. However, a key practical problem for flexible accelerator models (and other models incorporating many lagged variables) lies in empirically specifying the lag structure. There may be little clear *a priori* guidance about how many lags on output growth to include. Specifically, two key questions emerge:

1. Over what sort of time periods should the lag structure be distributed? Economic theory and/or other empirical evidence rarely gives a clear answer.
2. In practice, estimating long lag structures using standard statistical techniques can be statistically 'expensive' – involving the loss of many degrees of freedom, thereby limiting the accuracy of the parameter estimates for output growth.

In answering these questions, it is difficult to get reliable quantitative information about lag structures although survey data does reveal some information about lag length. For example, Nobay (1970) conducted a survey revealing that, for engineering investment in the UK, the average lag length was about five quarters, comprising a four-quarter lag between order and delivery and a one-quarter planning lag. For US industrial investment in the 1950s, Mayer (1960) found a seven-quarter lag between investment planning and completion.

Lag lengths have also been quantified using econometric approaches. A 'top-down' econometric modelling strategy involves the statistical estimation of large models with many lags on the relevant variables. The statistically insignificant lagged terms are removed from the model gradually.[1] A large literature evolved assessing the relative explanatory power of a wide range of distributed (and more complicated) lag structures estimated using this top-down approach. Following an econometric approach, Bean (1981) detected a bi-modal lag structure with a minor peak at a lag of three quarters and a major peak at seven quarters. He argued that this bi-modal response reflects the long lags between investment project decisions and installation of investment goods made to order, and short lags as investment orders are changed in response to recent events. Evans (1967) also found a double peak on a distributed lag specification reflecting impacts from the investment decision period at five quarters, with an additional lag on output at one quarter reflecting last-minute modifications to investment plans in response to changes in capacity utilization. In contrast, Anderson (1964) found only a single-peaked lag structure, with lags of five quarters on capacity utilization and interest rates.[2]

Koyck (1954) devised another way to address some of the problems associated with capturing the lagged effects of output on investment. Allowing that the effects of output growth would be distributed over successive time periods, he captured the process of adjustment using a 'Koyck transformation': assuming geometrically declining weights on output, distributed lags on past output can be captured with a lagged capital stock term. This Koyck transformation is explained in Box 3.3. However, there are problems with this approach: the weights on lagged output may not be declining geometrically and, there is no theoretical reason to assume that they will. Also, the econometric evidence presented above suggests that they are not. In addition, models based around a Koyck transformation are vulnerable to econometric problems, such as serially correlated errors and inconsistent estimation.

Following on from some of the debates discussed in this chapter, a large empirical literature has developed comparing accelerator theories with Jorgenson's approach, the latter allowing that investment responds to changes in the relative cost of capital and labour as well as to output growth. Jorgenson's model is explained in Chapter 5. As will be seen in Chapter 7, most analyses have confirmed that the elasticity of factor substitution seems to be closer to zero than to one and so accelerator theory is often credited with having superior explanatory power relative to Jorgenson's theory. However, there are a number of empirical problems with the estimation of accelerator theory and despite its apparently superior explanatory power, accelerator theory is not necessarily convincing as a *complete* explanation for investment behaviour. This is because, in accelerator theories, expectations are essentially static, the direction of causality is not established and lags are often introduced in an *ad hoc* way. However, accelerator theory *does* show us that demand and output growth may signal changes in future profitability and play a key role in propelling investment decisions. So accelerator models were an important step in developing an economic understanding of the determinants of fixed asset investment.

Conclusion

In this chapter, we have examined the relationship between fixed asset investment and output growth in simple and flexible accelerator models. We have also examined some of the problems with the accelerator approach. Overall, whilst the flexible accelerator model performs well empirically, the lag structures underlying these models were still criticized as being *ad hoc*, without theoretical underpinning (Griliches, 1967; Nerlove, 1972). The empirical support for accelerator theory can also be criticized as being tautological: given that capital is a key input into the production process, it is not surprising that there should be a correlation between capital accumulation (i.e. net investment) and output; multiplier theory tells us that investment dictates output as much as output dictates investment. As Tinbergen (1938) points out, 'there is some doubt about the causal direction of the relationship'. Although these problems can, to an extent, be addressed via statistical testing and alternative estimation techniques, neo-classical theorists argue that the accelerator theorists have left too much out.

Neo-classical economists would not deny that investment is correlated with output growth but they would argue that an equally crucial determinant of investment is the relative cost of capital goods. And rational expectations theorists would argue that the adaptive/extrapolative expectations hypotheses embedded within accelerator models are not consistent with fully rational behaviour; they do not properly capture the forward-looking nature of investment decision-making. (Rational expectations models are presented in Chapters 8 and 9.) From the other end of the spectrum, modern Post Keynesians would criticize accelerator theory because of the limited role allowed in these approaches for psychological forces, subjective expectations, uncertainty and financial/monetary factors. (Post Keynesian theories are analyzed in Chapter 10.) So overall accelerator theory seems to form an incomplete explanation for investment activity.

Chapter summary

1. Accelerator theories describe investment as the process of capital stock adjustment. Desired capital stock is determined by expected demand for products of a firm so net investment, as the change in capital stock, is described as a function of output growth in simple accelerator theory.
2. Simple accelerator specifications focus on output growth in one period as a determinant of investment decisions. However, this ignores the importance of lags in investment decision-making and expectations formation.
3. These shortcomings are addressed in flexible accelerator models. Flexible accelerator models incorporate lag structures describing investment as a distributed lag function of output growth over many time periods. The distributed lag function will capture many sources of lags: for example, lags reflecting delays in decision-making, planning, ordering, delivery and installation of new investment projects. In addition, lags can be used to capture the formation of expectations. However, one problem with the distributed lag structures seen in flexible accelerator models is that they do not allow the different sources of lags to be separated.
4. The econometric evidence on accelerator theory is generally good but there are a number of theoretical and empirical problems with these models.
5. Accelerator theory is generally associated with a Keynesian approach because of its emphasis on quantity rather than price variables. The neo-classical economists argue that this focus is misplaced. In neo-classical models of capital stock adjustment, such as Jorgenson's model, the relative cost of capital goods as well as output growth is taken into account as an important determinant of investment. These neo-classical models are discussed in Chapters 5–7.

Revision questions

1. Why are accelerator theories usually associated with a Keynesian approach?
2. How are profits captured within accelerator theories?
3. What are the key limitations of accelerator theory?
4. How are expectations incorporated into accelerator models?
5. Why is the finding that there is a positive relationship between investment and output growth not necessarily a confirmation of accelerator theory?

5 Jorgenson's model of investment

Introduction	58
Optimal capital stock adjustment in Jorgenson's model	59
Jorgenson's simplifying assumptions	61
Appendix: Jorgenson's model in continuous time	63
Chapter summary	64
Revision questions	65

As outlined in the previous chapter, accelerator theory paved the way for the development of models in which quantity factors determine investment decisions. In this chapter, Jorgenson's (1963) neo-classical model of investment, which as well as allowing a role for quantity factors also introduces the relative cost of capital. As will be seen, the basic building blocks of Jorgenson's model are similar to the building blocks of accelerator theory. Both theories describe a process of capital stock adjustment to a desired or optimal level. However, a crucial difference between the two models emerges in the role that each credits to relative factor costs. In accelerator theory, the capital stock does not adjust in response to changes in factor costs because production processes are like 'clay', with fixed capital–output ratios. In these models, capital and labour are complementary factors, used in fixed proportions with a fixed capital–labour ratio. In contrast, in Jorgenson's theory, the capital stock does adjust to changes in relative factor costs and investment will be affected by these changes in costs. The relative cost of capital is captured in Jorgenson's model by the *user cost of capital.* Optimizing investors will balance this user cost of capital with the marginal productivity of capital when they decide about their optimal capital stock.

Jorgenson's theory incorporates a wide range of simplifying assumptions that compromise the realism of his theory. However, Jorgenson's model is path-breaking in the sense that a wide range of modern orthodox investment theories have developed in response to Jorgenson ideas, by relaxing one or a number of Jorgenson's simplifying assumptions.

Introduction

Jorgenson's neo-classical model of investment forms the basis of modern neo-classical approaches to investment theory and some of Fisher's ideas resonate in Jorgenson's analysis. But Jorgenson refines Fisher's analysis in two ways. First, he applies Fisher's principles of balancing present values of future returns over current costs to the profit maximizing behaviour of firms using a marginalist approach, by showing when the marginal productivity and marginal cost of capital are in balance. Second, he refines Fisher's concept of current cost by including depreciation and expected capital value changes, as well as the interest rate, into his concept of the cost of capital. In this way, Jorgenson (1963, 1964, 1967, 1971) describes the optimal accumulation of capital by firms maximizing the net worth of their production and investment activities over time.

Jorgenson assumes that investment by perfectly competitive firms takes place costlessly and instantaneously to adjust the discrepancy between the optimal capital stock in the current period and the optimal capital stock in the previous period. Jorgenson assumes that the capital stock is like 'putty': inputs of capital and labour are perfectly substitutable both in the *ex ante* planning stage and in the *ex post* expenditure stage. Investment expenditures are completely reversible. In early models, Jorgenson also assumes static expectations in arguing that predictions of future optimal capital stocks are irrelevant to current capital stock adjustment because gaps between actual and previous desired capital stock are closed instantaneously. In other words, according to Jorgenson, the firm always adjusts to its optimal capital stock immediately; and forming expectations of the future is unnecessary if an investor can respond to changes immediately and costlessly. This neglect of expectations is one of the weakest links in Jorgenson's theory. Investment is all about planning for the future and so forecasting the future is central to investment activity and Jorgenson did recognize this in later formulations of his theory, as will be seen in Chapter 6.

Optimal capital stock adjustment in Jorgenson's model

As outlined in Chapter 3, Fisher (1930) emphasizes the rate of return over cost as the basic determinant of investment behaviour and, although he does not develop the point in detail, one of his four 'investment principles' suggests that projects can be judged against each other on the basis of *marginal* returns over costs. Jorgenson takes this marginalist approach further. He assumes that all capital is homogeneous and shows that the optimal capital stock will be determined at the point where the value of a firm's productive activities is maximized: i.e. at the point where the expected marginal benefits and costs from an additional unit of capital are equalized. This point will be reached when the marginal productivity of capital, MP_k, is equal to the marginal cost of capital.

The user cost of capital[1]

Jorgenson calls the marginal cost involved in using capital the 'user cost of capital' and it has three components:

- The opportunity cost of investing in real rather than financial assets: i.e. the relative cost of financing real investment. In a world of certainty and perfect capital markets, the user cost of capital will be exogenously determined and will equal the real interest rate. Given perfect markets, it will also equal to the opportunity cost of present consumption forgone: the discount rate.
- The rate of depreciation for the existing capital stock.
- Capital gains/losses emerging from changes in the value of capital goods.

One of the key differences between Fisher's approach and Jorgenson's approach is that Jorgenson incorporates both *expectations* of changes in the value of capital goods and depreciation in his formulation of the user cost of capital. As shown in Box 5.1, the relationship between user cost and MP_k can be used to derive the optimal capital stock (K^*):

$$K^* = \alpha \Upsilon / C$$

where Y = output and C = the user cost of capital.

Box 5.1 Jorgenson's model

Defining the optimal capital stock

In the simpler formulations of his theories*, for example, Jorgenson (1964), Jorgenson shows that the marginal product of capital can be derived from a Cobb-Douglas production function of the form:

$$Y = AK^{\alpha}L^{\beta}$$

where *Y*, *K* and *L* are output, capital and labour respectively, *A* is a constant, α is the elasticity of output with respect to capital and β is the elasticity of output with respect to labour. Jorgenson then shows that the marginal product of capital (MP_K) is equal to the first partial derivative of *Y* with respect to *K*:

$$MP_k = \partial Y / \partial K = \alpha K^{\alpha-1} L^{\beta} = \alpha Y / K$$

The optimal capital stock (K^*) is determined at the point where the marginal benefits and marginal costs of investment projects are balanced: i.e. when the MP_k is equal to the relative cost of capital, i.e. the user cost of capital, *C*, i.e.:

$$\alpha \frac{Y}{K^*} = C$$

Re-arranging to give an expression for the optimal capital stock, gives:

$$K^* = \alpha \frac{Y}{C}$$

Where the user cost of capital (*C*) is defined as:

$$C = \frac{p_K(r + \partial) - \dot{p}_K}{p_O}$$

where p_K = price of investment goods
p_O = price of output
r = real interest rate
∂ = depreciation rate

* Jorgenson's original 1963 model is outlined in the Chapter Appendix.

Adopting this simple formulation of K^* and assuming that the capital stock is at its optimal point in the preceding period, net investment (I_n) in each period of time will take place instantaneously to adjust the current capital stock to its new optimal level:

$$\begin{aligned} I_{nt} &= \alpha(Y/C)_t - \alpha(Y/C)_{t-1} \\ &= \alpha\Delta(Y/C) \end{aligned}$$

Investment is a function of disequilibrium in the capital stock and so will be dependent on changes in the ratio of output to the user cost of capital rather than its level. Net investment is therefore a function of changes. However, as noted above, this specification assumes that the capital stock was at its optimal level in the previous period. If this assumption is relaxed, then lagged capital cannot be expressed as a function of output and user cost and must be included separately. In which case, the following model applies:

$$I_n = \alpha Y/C - K_{t-1}$$

In other words, if the capital stock is not at its optimal level in the previous period then net investment will be a function of the current period's optimal capital stock and the possibly sub-optimal capital stock in the previous period. The fact that the determinants of the current optimal capital stock and the previous capital stock cannot be combined will mean that output and the user cost of capital enter as levels rather than changes. For net investment equations, the failure to include a lagged capital stock term in a regression that assumes that the capital stock was not at its optimal level in the previous period will lead to inconsistent estimates of the parameters because a crucial explanatory variable will have been omitted.

It can be shown that, in this putty-putty world of Jorgenson's simple model, adjustments to the desired capital stock are completely elastic in response to changes in the user cost of capital, as well as to output (i.e. the elasticities are equal to +1 for output and −1 for user cost – see Box 5.2). These elasticities define the mathematical difference between Jorgenson's model and accelerator theory. Adopting a representative agent hypothesis, that the microeconomic behaviour of one representative investor can be used to describe all investors, Jorgenson's description of the microeconomic behaviour of a single firm is used to describe aggregate investment behaviour at the industry-wide and macroeconomic levels, for example, see Jorgenson and Stephenson (1967).

Jorgenson's simplifying assumptions

The real-world applicability of Jorgenson's approach is constrained by the range of assumptions incorporated into his model. Jorgenson assumes that there

Box 5.2 The output and user cost elasticities in Jorgenson's model

It can be shown that, in this putty-putty world of Jorgenson's simple model, the elasticity of desired capital stock in response to changes in output is the same (but of opposite sign) as the elasticity of desired capital stock in response to changes in the user cost of capital, i.e. is unitary.

Developing the analysis presented in Chapter 4, the elasticity of the capital stock with respect to output is equal to:

$$\frac{dK^*}{dY}\cdot\frac{Y}{K^*}=\frac{\alpha}{C}\cdot\frac{Y}{K^*}=1$$

given $K^* = \alpha Y/C$

Similarly, the elasticity of the capital stock with respect to the relative user cost of capital is equal to:

$$\frac{dK^*}{dC}\cdot\frac{C}{K^*}=-\frac{\alpha Y}{C^2}\cdot\frac{C}{K^*}=-1$$

are no delivery lags and no adjustment costs. He assumes that investment decisions are independent of financing decisions and that capital depreciates at a geometric rate. For Jorgenson, investment is completely and costlessly reversible. There are no 'vintage' effects: the capital stock is made up of homogeneous capital goods and capital goods accumulated in one year are the same as capital goods accumulated in other years. This means that the production technology (as reflected in capital–labour ratios) is not constrained by past investment decisions as it is in accelerator theory. In Jorgenson's world, adjustment to the optimal capital stock is instantaneous and complete.

A key analytical problem emerges because the assumption of instantaneous adjustment implies that the rate of investment per unit time is infinite and this means that the *rate* of investment will be undefined (Haavelmo, 1960). If there is a shortage of capital relative to its optimal level, optimal capital stock adjustment theories of investment, such as Jorgenson's, do not describe how investors time their responses to capital shortages (Junankar, 1972). But once the assumption of instantaneous adjustment is abandoned, an exogenous mechanism must be imposed to describe the rate at which the capital stock adjusts to its new desired level. Therefore, just as for accelerator theories, the speed of response to discrepancies between the actual and optimal capital stock is imposed *ad hoc* onto Jorgenson's model; dynamics are introduced *ex post* rather than from behavioural hypotheses incorporated into the determination of demand for capital. The Jorgensonian firm does not need to look deeply into the future and 'the multi-period optimization problem becomes essentially static' (Chirinko, 1993, p. 1878).

Whilst many of Jorgenson's building blocks can be criticized as unrealistic descriptions of real world investment behaviour, Jorgenson's model did form a starting point for the development of families of investment models based upon the basic premise of the profit-maximizing investor responding to relative factor costs. Jorgenson's model both parallels and contradicts the accelerator approach of the Keynesians. Some of the issues associated with the relationship between Keynesian and neo-classical theory are outlined in Chapter 7. Developments of orthodox approaches to the analysis of optimizing investors, that take explicit account of adjustment costs and expectations, are outlined in Chapter 8. The assumption of costlessly reversible investment is relaxed in real options models, for example, the models of Dixit and Pindyck (1994) and Abel and Eberly (1996, 1999) amongst many others and these models are analyzed in Chapter 9. However, it should be noted that all these models assume that investor behaviour is rational, maximizing and quantifiable. The Post Keynesians adopt a fundamentally different methodological approach in their analysis of investor behaviour, and some of these models are presented in Chapter 10.

Appendix: Jorgenson's model in continuous time

Adapting Jorgenson's model to a world with no taxes (for simplicity), firms maximize the present value of their investment and production activities where this present value is the integral of discounted net receipts from the firm's production activities over an infinite time horizon. Assuming that the time rate of discount (in this simple case Fisher's real interest rate, r) is constant, the net present value (NPV) is as follows:

$$NPV = \int e^{-rt} R(t) \mathrm{d}t$$

$$R(t) = p_o Q - wL - p_k I$$

where R is revenue, Q is the flow of output, w is the wage rate, p_k is the price of capital goods, I_s investment and p_o is the price of output. So the total value of production and investment activities includes flows of income from production (i.e. cash flow minus expenditure on variable inputs, including labour and investment goods). Income flows will also be augmented by net investment and by increments to the value of the existing capital stock.

The NPV will be maximized subject to two constraints: first, levels of output and labour/capital inputs are constrained by the production function (which Jorgenson assumes to be strictly convex and twice differentiable with positive marginal productivities of capital and labour); second, the rate of change in the capital stock must be equal to gross investment less replacement. These two constraints can be expressed as:

$$\Upsilon = F(Q, L, K) = AK^{\alpha}L^{\beta} \quad \text{and} \quad \Delta K = I - \delta K$$

So the following Lagrangian, Λ, can be formulated to represent the optimizing conditions, as follows:

$$\Lambda = \int e^{-rt}\{R(t) + \lambda_0(t)[\Upsilon - AK^{\alpha}L^{\beta}] + \lambda_1(t)[\Delta K - I + \delta K]\} \cdot dt$$

Solving the Lagrangian gives the following necessary condition for capital input is:

$$\lambda_0(t)\frac{\partial Q}{\partial K} = e^{-rt}p_k[\delta + r - \frac{\dot{p}_k}{p_k}]$$

This gives:

$$MP_k = \frac{\partial \Upsilon}{\partial K} = \frac{p_k}{p_o}(\delta + r - \frac{\dot{p}_k}{p_k}) = \frac{c}{p_o} = C$$

This gives the user cost of capital, C, equal to the ratio of the price of capital services and the price of output.

Chapter summary

1. Jorgenson's neo-classical model describes investment as a process of capital stock adjustment. Building upon ideas from Fisher, Jorgenson argues that rational, profit-maximizing investors will calculate the present value of rewards from investment decisions and will balance the marginal benefits and marginal costs of investment plans.
2. The marginal benefit of investments will be the marginal productivity of capital, as derived from a Cobb–Douglas production function.
3. The marginal costs will be captured by Jorgenson's 'user cost of capital'. This describes the costs involved in using capital, including interest costs, depreciation and capital gains/losses from changes in capital goods prices.
4. Jorgenson builds a model of aggregate macroeconomic investment from microeconomic foundations by describing the behaviour of a representative profit-maximizing firm.
5. Jorgenson's model incorporates a number of simplifying assumptions, for example static expectations, instantaneous capital stock adjustment, no adjustment costs and completely reversible investment decisions.

Chapter summary continued

6. One of the major analytical shortcomings of Jorgenson's theory arises from the assumption that capital stock adjustment happens instantaneously. If capital stock adjustment takes time then the rate of investment over time is undefined in Jorgenson's model. In addition, issues related to expectations formation/uncertainty are ignored in Jorgenson's early model. Jorgenson assumes static expectations because investors do not have to worry about forming expectations of the future if they can reverse their investment decisions and/or adjust their capital stock instantaneously. Some of the problems that emerge from these assumptions are addressed by later orthodox analyses, as outlined in Chapters 8 and 9.

Revision questions

1. How is Jorgenson's model similar to Fisher's theory? How is it different? How is it similar/different to accelerator theory?
2. Derive the elasticity of factor substitution from Jorgenson's model.
3. Discuss the restrictive assumptions incorporated into Jorgenson's model. How do you think that unrealistic restrictive assumptions can be defended?
4. How are the assumptions of static expectations, instantaneous capital stock adjustment and irreversible investment connected?

6 The limitations of Jorgenson's model

Revision of the microfoundations of aggregate investment models	67
Lag structure	68
Expectations and uncertainty	70
Adjustment costs	72
Financing of investment and the Modigliani–Miller assumption	73
The Cambridge Capital controversies and the neo-classical parables	73
Conclusion	76
Chapter summary	77
Revision questions	78

As was seen in Chapter 5, Jorgenson describes investment as a process of optimal capital stock adjustment in which the current costs and future benefits of investment activity are balanced. However, Jorgenson's model did not escape criticism; it is based upon a number of restrictive assumptions. Some of the key criticisms of Jorgenson's theory are discussed in this chapter, including:

- the problems associated with aggregating a macroeconomic model of investment from the microfoundations of perfect competition;
- the failure formally to specify the expectations formation process;
- the related neglect of issues to do with rationality and uncertainty;
- the absence of an explicit dynamic structure reflected in the *ad hoc* nature of lag specifications;
- the absence of adjustment costs;
- the neglect of financing issues; and
- problems with measuring and defining capital goods in a world in which the capital stock is heterogeneous and made up of capital machinery of many different vintages.

Revision of the microfoundations of aggregate investment models

As explained in Chapter 5, Jorgenson's theory is based upon rigorous microfoundations describing a world of profit maximizing, perfectly competitive firms balancing the benefits and costs of investment expenditures. From the 1960s onwards, microeconomic theories of the firm were being substantially modified to fit more closely with observed behaviour by real world decision-makers. This led to developments such as Baumol's theory of sales maximization, Marris's model of maximization of balanced growth, Williamson's model of utility maximization by business managers, and Cyert and March's behavioural theory of the firm (addressing the implications for optimizing behaviour of bounded rationality and the use of average cost pricing principles, Cyert and March, 1963). As a consequence, the assumptions of perfect competition and profit maximization were widely criticized. Survey results collected by Baddeley (1996), Hall and Hitch (1939), Morris (1974), and Neild (1964) suggest that businesses are not necessarily profit maximizers and that managers do not use marginalist rules in their decision-making. Furthermore, it seems unlikely that assumptions of atomistic behaviour and perfectly competitive firms will hold in a reality in which oligopoly is the predominant market structure. Uncertainty about the future will mean that businesses will pursue goals associated with security and stability rather than profit maximization.

On the other hand, Friedman (1953) defends marginalist theory by arguing that it is not the realism of assumptions that is important but the predictive power of theories. Earley (1956) provides survey evidence indicating that marginal costs and marginal revenues *are* used by businesses in their decision-making. Machlup (1946) argues that the survey evidence against neo-classical marginalist assumptions is unreliable and inconclusive: business decision-makers have incentives, such as presenting a good public image, to distort their responses to surveys and so surveys are not a good method for assessing economic behaviour. Furthermore, lack of information is not a real constraint on marginalist behaviour because businesses can make subjective assessments of costs and revenues and still apply these beliefs in a way consistent with marginalist principles.

In terms of empirical validity, Jorgensonian statistical models of investment have rarely out-performed accelerator models and these are not dependent upon assumptions of perfect competition and profit maximization. This suggests either that investors are not using marginalist principles in their investment decision-making or that the complexity of real-world decision-making by heterogeneous firms means that any marginalist behaviour is difficult to detect. The failure of aggregate empirical models of investment to detect investment behaviour based on marginalist principles can also be attributed to problems of aggregating data across large numbers of firms (Chirinko, 1993, p. 1899).

Lag structure

As noted in Chapter 4, Jorgenson's original model was widely criticized for its neglect of lag structures. In response, in later Jorgensonian models, lag structures were super-imposed onto models of optimal capital stock adjustment. The inclusion of lags within these models is achieved by describing investment expenditure as a function of lags of past gaps between the optimal and actual capital stock, distributed over past time periods.

In other words, investment is a distributed lag function of the difference between the optimal capital stock (as described above, $K^*_{t-j} = \alpha(\Upsilon_{t-j}/C_{t-j})$ and the actual capital stock in the previous period:

$$I_n = \sum_{j=0}^{J} \{\beta_j[\alpha(\Upsilon_{t-j}/C_{t-j}) - K_{t-j-1})]\}$$

As explained in Chapter 5, for empirical tractability the capital stock in the previous period is often assumed to be at the optimal capital stock (Jorgenson assumes that the capital stock adjusts instantaneously to its optimal level). Therefore, Jorgenson's investment model can be simplified to:

$$I_n = \sum_{j=0}^{J} \{\alpha\beta_j\Delta(\Upsilon_{t-j}/C_{t-j})\}$$

In practice (as explained in Chapter 4 in the context of accelerator theory), lag structures are incorporated into such models either by assuming a deterministic distributed lag structure, such as a Koyck transformation, or by econometric estimation of the lag structure using a 'top-down' approach of excluding statistically insignificant lagged terms. A disadvantage for Koyck lag structures is that the deterministic weights imposed on different lags of the explanatory variables may be inappropriate. In addition, in the presence of autocorrelated errors, the autoregressive form of Koyck distributed models will create inconsistent Ordinary Least Squares (OLS) estimators. Many of the standard statistical tests for specification error will be invalidated in the presence of the lagged dependent variables seen in some Koyck specifications. Furthermore, the inclusion of Koyck lag structures can be criticized on the grounds that distributed lag structures have only weak theoretical justification as they are not derived as an implication of a particular behavioural hypothesis (Griliches, 1967).

Whilst *ad hoc* lag structures allow the selection of past explanatory variables for inclusion in investment models without the constraints on the relative weights given to different lag lengths that is seen in Koyck models, Nerlove (1972) was also critical of the 'ad-hockery' implicit in the top-down econometric approach and emphasizes the need for a theoretical underpinning of the lag structures incorporated into empirical models of investment. Anderson (1981, p. 88) argues that unless the dynamic structure of investment is known *a priori*, complicated lag structures may be incorporated into investment equations because they fit the data rather than for more substantive reasons. This will be a particular problem for analyses adopting specification search methods: if a large number of lags are included in the unrestricted model, the process of 'testing-down' to an acceptable model may be creating misleading results. A similar problem emerges with models in which lag structures and orders of differencing are 'determined empirically', without attending to signs of model misspecification.

Both approaches to lag specification are also prone to the criticism that they omit explicit dynamic structure (Chirinko, 1993) and little was done to give lag structures an explicit theoretical basis until the advent of the rational expectations approaches to investment in the 1980s. (These models are discussed in Chapter 8.) In response, Jorgenson (1971), whilst acknowledging the importance of the explicit integration of dynamics into the representation of investment and capital accumulation, argued that some models incorporating distributed lag structures (namely, Jorgenson and Siebert [1968] and Jorgenson and Stephenson [1967]) are justifiable because they confirm Mayer's (1960) survey evidence relating to lag length (Jorgenson, 1971, pp. 1137–8).

Econometrically, even with lags included, Jorgensonian models yielded large, unwieldy models characterized by micronumerosity and multicollinearity (Abel, 1980, p. 61). A further problem emerges because lag structures in these models usually reflect a convolution of gestational, adjustment, expectational, informational and technological delays (Bean, 1981). Thus the parameters estimated in *ad hoc* and distributed lags models will be an amalgam of different parameters and it is impossible to separate the different sources of lags. This complexity is exacerbated by the fact that different determinants of lags will operate within different time frames. 'Vintage effects', reflecting the accumulation of different capital goods at different times, will dilute the responsiveness of investment decisions to changes in relative factor prices, leading to additional lags on the user cost of capital.

Finally, theoretical problems emerge in terms of specifying the lag structure because it creates a dynamic contradiction: K* is derived assuming that the delivery of investment goods is immediate yet the investment equation is derived assuming a distributed lag function reflecting adjustment costs and delivery lags. Once this problem is taken into account, the investment path described by Jorgenson may not be optimal (Anderson, 1981; Gould, 1968; Nerlove, 1972). This difficulty can only be escaped by incorporating static expectations assumptions: i.e. by assuming that the benefits and costs of acquiring capital are the same at any given point in time and are therefore independent of any delivery or adjustment lags. The assumption of static expectations is itself subject to numerous criticisms as explored below.

Expectations and uncertainty

As discussed in Chapter 5, Jorgenson assumes in his simple model that expectations of output and the user cost of capital are static. Changes in expectations are unimportant in a world of instantaneous capital stock adjustment and completely reversible investment. If the capital stock can adjust instantaneously within a given period, then there is no need for investors to worry about future changes in the present because they can deal with changes immediately when they materialize. However, with irreversible, sluggish investment, current investment decisions will depend crucially upon expectations of future optimal capital stocks. Investment is by nature forward-looking behaviour and an understanding of uncertainty and the processes dictating expectations formation is essential to a meaningful theory of investment decision-making. However, identifying the roles played by expectations and uncertainty in aggregate investment models is an extremely complex exercise: first, because it is difficult, if not impossible, to quantify expectations and uncertainty and second, because investment is the outcome of the interaction of so many influences operating over a number of periods. To illuminate some of these issues, the key approaches to expectations are outlined in Box 6.1.

In recognition that the static expectations assumption was simplistic, Jorgenson's approach was refined to allow that decision-makers base their expectations of optimal capital stocks on future expectations of the determinants of the optimal capital stocks, output (Y) and the user cost of capital (C) and these expectations were assumed to be a function of the current and past values of Y and C: adaptive and extrapolative approaches to expectations specification were incorporated into neo-classical models via the use of the

Box 6.1 Expectations and uncertainty in models of investment

Different approaches to investment incorporate different definitions of uncertainty and this will affect the way that expectations are described. In mainstream models of investment, people are assumed to be able to quantify their expectations; they operate in of world of what is known as **Knightian risk**, or quantifiable risk. Knightian risk is implicitly assumed in the models described in Chapters 5–9.

The descriptions of these quantifiable expectations in the mainstream literature has gradually evolved from static expectations to rational expectations:

Static expectations are unchanging, or unimportant if economic agents can adjust instantaneously to changes in the economic environment. Jorgenson originally assumed static expectations.

Extrapolative/Regressive expectations are formed by looking at past events and extrapolating them forward. Flexible accelerator theories are often based upon an assumption of extrapolative expectations, and these are modelled using distributed lags.

Adaptive expectations hypothesis (AEH) describes the revision of expectations according to past mistakes. In other words, expectations will be formulated by looking at expectations in the previous period and adjusting these by some factor of the mistake from the previous period. For example in forming expectations of output, y:

$$y^e_{t+1} = y^e_t + \lambda(y^a_t - y^e_t)$$

where y^e_t is the expectation of output in period t and y^a_t is actual, realized output in period t and $0 < \lambda < 1$ is the adjustment factor.

Rational expectations hypothesis (REH) Some theorists, for example, Muth (1961), argue that the simple models of expectations outlined above suggest that economic agents make systematic mistakes. For example, if people use the AEH, they will be consistently over-estimating or under-estimating variables that are falling or rising. In contrast, according to the REH, economic agents are forward looking, make complete use of all available information; their expectations will change immediately as new information arrives and agents do not make systematic mistakes. The REH is incorporated into the *q* theories and real options theories outlined in Chapters 8 and 9.

In contrast, the Post Keynesians describe a world of **Knightian uncertainty**, or unquantifiable uncertainty. They develop some of the ideas outlined by Keynes in his *A Treatise on Probability* (1921) and *The General Theory of Employment, Interest and Money* (1936) about the problems with quantifying probabilities. The Post Keynesians believe that uncertainty is so profound and overwhelming that quantifying probabilities and expectations is very difficult. This is particularly true for the expectations that govern investment decisions because many investment projects are expected to deliver revenues over long time horizons. Some of these ideas are discussed in Chapter 10. The mainstream literature has also gradually recognized the importance of uncertainty as a macroeconomic force, as will be explained in Chapter 9, but there is still considerable theoretical dispute about the extent to which uncertainty limits rational behaviour.

distributed lag structures, just as described in the preceding section. There are a number of problems with this approach:

- As for accelerator theory, the adaptive and extrapolative expectations assumptions are adopted in an *ad hoc* way with little theoretical basis and no clear explanation of the role played by lags in the formation of expectations.
- A given lag structure cannot separate the independent influence of expectations because it will also reflect the influence of other sources of lags.
- Specifying the optimal capital stock and the lag structure in separate stages results in an inconsistent treatment of expectational and other sources of lags. To be consistent expectations should be incorporated into the representative firm's original optimization problem from the start.
- It is difficult to get reliable information about expectations formation (Anderson, 1981). Without a theoretical basis to support adaptive and extrapolative expectational assumptions, researchers have considerable discretion in selecting lag specifications.
- Adaptive expectations are formed on the basis of current and past values of the explanatory variables. Proponents of the Rational Expectations Hypothesis (REH) argue that this denies the essentially forward-looking nature of expectations formation by rational agents and implies (erroneously) that rational agents make systematic mistakes.
- The adaptive expectations hypothesis does not reflect any underlying behavioural hypothesis (Griliches, 1967) and expectations are only captured implicitly in these models (Chirinko, 1993; Eisner, 1996).

Chirinko (1993) argues that, in order to resolve these problems and properly to assess the independent influence of expectational variables, expectations must be incorporated explicitly into the firm's optimization problem as described in Chapter 8.

Adjustment costs

Another theoretical difficulty with Jorgenson's simple model lies in the assumption that adjustment to a new desired capital stock can take place instantaneously. If this is the case, the rate of investment will be undefined (Haavelmo, 1960; Junankar, 1972; Lerner 1944). When lag structures are super-imposed, the rate of investment can take almost any value depending upon the lag structure super-imposed onto the model. Also, whilst Jorgenson assumes constant returns to scale, Nickell (1978) argues that the optimal capital stock is not well defined in Jorgenson's simple model unless the production technology exhibits diminishing returns to scale although the assumption of diminishing returns to scale can be relaxed if the firm is assumed to face a downward-sloping demand curve (Nickell, 1978). As will be seen in Chapter 8, the problem of an undefined rate of investment is resolved within q theories of investment by assuming that the integration of new equipment into the firm's production process imposes adjustment and installation costs upon the firm.

Financing of investment and the Modigliani–Miller assumption

Jorgenson's model is founded upon the Modigliani–Miller assumption. Modigliani and Miller (1958) asserted that the cost of capital and the value of a firm is independent of the firm's internal financial structures and financing decisions. Firms finance investment decisions using external funds (including borrowings and share issues) and internal funds (including retained profits). Modigliani and Miller argued that, assuming a world of perfect capital markets, the costs and returns on these different forms of investment financing will be equalized. So the nature of the funding will not affect investment decisions because financing costs are exogenously determined and common to all firms in a given risk category (Modigliani and Miller, 1958).[1] However, this assumption is problematic: given uncertainty and firm-specific risk, the Modigliani–Miller theory will not hold: each firm is unique and in its own risk class so the cost of different forms of funds may depend on an individual firm's past investment history. If risks of bankruptcy are perceived to be high by lenders, this may add to the cost of borrowing versus retained profits. Similarly, share issues may be more risky for the firm, adding to the costs of raising equity relative to retained profits. Information asymmetries will increase the relative cost of external funds (Meyers and Majluf, 1984). Capital market imperfections will mean that other financial factors, such as the sourcing and availability of funds, are also important.[2] Certain types of funds are more limited than others: for example, small firms will be particularly reliant on internal funds and will be unable and/or reluctant to borrow or issue equity. There may be discontinuities in the cost of capital for a given firm, for example at the point where internal funds are exhausted. Empirical evidence suggests that internal fund are the principle source of funding for most real-world firms (Gomes, 2001). For all these reasons, the Modigliani–Miller assumption of financing neutrality does not hold in the real world; investment, the cost of capital and the financing of investments are in fact interdependent.

The Cambridge Capital controversies and the neo-classical parables

Jorgenson's model is based around a neo-classical formulation of the production function and this embeds many assumptions: for example, that technical progress is disembodied (i.e. not incorporated within plant and machinery), that the capital stock is comprised of homogeneous capital goods and that investments are reversible. A number of 'neo-classical parables' form the basis of this axiomatic, assumption-based approach and these parables were criticized by the 'Cambridge (UK) school', generating the 'Cambridge Capital Controversies' of the 1960s and 1970s (Harcourt, 1976). Joan Robinson instigated the debates when she argued that the assumptions of neo-classical theory are unrealistic and out-dated (Robinson, 1953/4; 1960a). The controversies that developed centred on the related problems of measuring and defining capital; aggregating the capital stock; assuming factor substitutability; and capital re-switching/reversal.

Measuring and defining the capital stock

Keynes (1936) raised this issue when he observed that there is no unit of measurement that allows 'a quantitative comparison between the new items of equipment produced during the period and the old items that have perished by wastage' (Keynes, 1936, p. 38). The 'index number problem' was expounded by economists from the Cambridge school, who argued that fundamental problems with the definition and measurement of capital compromise neo-classical theory. The Cambridge economists argued that it is unclear whether capital should be measured in physical terms or value terms. To measure the value of capital, an index independent of relative prices and the distribution of wealth/income is needed. But measuring capital in terms of the wage rate and the interest rate, as attempted in neo-classical theory, is problematic (Harcourt, 1966; 1972; 1976). Definitional problems compound measurement problems (Harcourt, 1976) – for example, Robinson (1975) argues that the 'meaning' of capital will change as institutional frameworks and social relationships change.

Aggregation problems

These problems are compounded by the fact that the capital stock is made up of many different machines of different vintages, each incorporating different technologies as reflected in the capital–labour ratios. Even if the value of capital goods is measurable in theory, in reality the aggregate capital stock is made up of many heterogeneous capital goods acquired at different times and so describing an aggregate capital stock is problematic. Robinson (1960b, 1973a, 1973b) argues that it is not possible to aggregate heterogeneous capital goods to give a macroeconomic theory based on microeconomic principles. Sen (1970) argues that heterogeneous capital goods accumulated at different times cannot be aggregated because the rates of gain on capital assets will change over time; value weighted aggregation is only possible when prices are unchanging (Sen, 1970; Wan, 1971). In Post Keynesian literature the importance of vintages and the heterogeneous nature of the capital stock has always been emphasized: see, for example, Harcourt (1966, 1969, 1972, 1976); Harcourt and Kenyon (1976) and Salter (1966).

Limits to factor substitutability

Jorgenson's investment theory is based upon a neo-classical aggregate production function in which capital and labour can respond completely to changes in relative factor prices. But key questions emerge in assessing whether or not production processes respond smoothly and continuously to changes in the user cost of capital. The Cambridge economists argued that existing technologies, embodying different capital–labour ratios, will limit the ability of firms to substitute capital for labour and vice versa. In this way, 'vintage effects', i.e. effects that emerge from the existence of machines of different vintages, will influence the relationship between past investment and current investment, constraining the responsiveness of investment to factor prices changes. Samuelson (1962) responded to some of these criticisms by formulating a 'surrogate production function', in which the assumption of factor substitutability is replaced with an assumption that there is an infinite number of techniques, each incorporating different capital–labour ratios. In this way, he shows that substitutability of techniques can replace factor substitutability. Solow (1970) proposed a more convincing solution than Samuelson's based around the insight that technologies are more flexible in the investment planning stage, and his 'putty-clay' model is explained in the following chapter.

Capital re-switching and capital reversal

Following from above, other critiques of neo-classical theory focused on the assumption of a smooth, continuous response of capital to changes in relative factor prices. Kregel argues that a 'well-behaved' relationship between capital scarcity and interest rates will not hold if the assumptions of neo-classical theory are relaxed. In this case even surrogate and putty-clay production functions will be discontinuous (Kregel, 1972, pp. 84–5). Production functions may not be smooth, continuous or 'well-behaved' because of 'capital re-switching' and 'capital reversals'. Capital re-switching occurs when a given technique, embedding a particular capital–labour ratio, is used at two or more separated rates of profit (Harcourt, 1976). To explain: in its simplest form, neo-classical theory postulates a negative relationship between capital accumulation (investment) and interest rates. Capital re-switching occurs when, for two techniques with the same capital–labour ratio, one technique is preferred at very high or very low interest rates but another is preferred at moderate interest rates. This will create 'capital reversal': i.e. for some parts of the production function, capital will accumulate even as interest rates rise.

Why does this happen? To illustrate with a simple example, firms may interpret extreme interest rates as a signal that economic conditions are changing. And they may respond to this uncertainty by delaying or abandoning investment decisions. In the meantime, they will favour labour-intensive techniques and so the relationship between capital–labour ratios and interest rates will be non-linear: when interest rates are very low, firms will use more labour but as interest rates rise and firms start to feel happier about the future, they will be prepared to accumulate more capital – capital reversal takes place.

Sen (1970) argues that liquidity traps (i.e. when interest rates do not respond to expansionary monetary policy because of an infinite elasticity of money demand) will also affect the relationship between capital and interest rates. When there is a liquidity trap, the floor on the rate of interest will limit the adjustment of the capital–labour ratio. Capital–labour ratios will not be perfectly flexible in response to changes in the interest rate (or, by extension, the user cost of capital).

The Cambridge Capital Controversies generated much discussion but are now largely ignored by mainstream theorists. So the questions raised remain unanswered and orthodox neo-classical economists retain homogeneous capital stocks and well-behaved production functions within their theories. The orthodox view is that, until the critics can come up with a better, replacement theory, the abstractions of neo-classical theory are justifiable. Solow argued that 'the whole episode now seems to have been a waste of time, a playing-out of ideological games in the language of analytical economics' (Solow, 1988, p. xiii). In contrast, the Post Keynesians have incorporated many of these insights into their theories and in the process, eschewed the abstract, axiomatic approach of orthodox economics. Some of these Post Keynesian theories of investment are outlined in Chapter 10.

Conclusion

One of the key limitations for neo-classical models of investment lies in the fact that they are built up from microfoundations: aggregate behaviour is just a scaled-up version of the behaviour of a representative profit-maximizing, perfectly competitive firm. Essentially, the neo-classical approach assumes that the difference between macroeconomics and microeconomics is just a matter of scale. This dependence on the representative agent hypothesis is misleading because the whole is not necessarily equal to the sum of its parts; there are essential differences between macroeconomics and microeconomics particularly if macroeconomic behaviour is affected by interdependencies, herd behaviour and feedback effects. So, overall, the theoretical interpretation of the neo-classical investment model has been blurred by the recognition that a complex amalgam of forces affects investment decisions. This may explain the large volume of contradictory empirical evidence relating to the relationship between the user cost of capital, output and investment. This chapter has focused on some of the theoretical issues but the range of econometric evidence on Jorgenson's putty model and alternative models is summarized in the following chapter.

Chapter summary

1. In this chapter, some of the problems with Jorgenson's neo-classical model are outlined. These problems are associated with some of the restrictive assumptions imposed upon his basic model.
2. Jorgenson aggregates microeconomic relationships, i.e. the profit maximizing behaviour of individual firms, to give an aggregate investment model. However, interdependencies between firms and feedback effects in the macroeconomy will limit the practical applicability of this aggregative approach.
3. Jorgenson assumes no adjustment costs, instantaneous capital stock adjustment and reversible investment decisions. This creates a theoretical problem because the rate of investment over time is undefined in a world of instantaneous capital stock adjustment.
4. In his initial model, Jorgenson assumes static expectations because his assumptions of instantaneous capital stock adjustment and reversible investment mean that firms do not need to form expectations of the future. However, as investment is inherently forward-looking behaviour it is important that expectations and uncertainty are modelled explicitly. So Jorgenson superimposes lag structures on top of his model in an *ad hoc* way, to capture extrapolative or adaptive expectations. The interpretation of these lag structures is difficult because there are numerous sources of lags in investment decision-making and expenditure, including the lags important to expectations formation.
5. Jorgenson's model incorporates an assumption of financing neutrality: that sources and availability of finance are not important determinants of investment decisions.
6. Jorgenson's model disregards some of the problems that surround the measurement and definition of capital goods. In reality, the capital stock is heterogeneous and made up of capital machinery of many different vintages, so an approach that assumes all capital goods are homogeneous will lead to misleading conclusions.
7. Some of the problems discussed in this chapter were resolved via refinements to Jorgenson's basic model although fundamental theoretical problems still remain. This led to the development of other orthodox approaches to investment, including *q* theories (discussed in Chapter 8) and options costs theories (discussed in Chapter 9). These theories extend and refine the basic postulate that investment can be described as a process of profit maximization by rational investors. In contrast, Post Keynesians adopt a fundamentally different approach to analyzing investment under uncertainty (as explained in Chapter 10).

Revision questions

1. Why is the rate of investment undefined in Jorgenson's model and can this problem be resolved? If so, how?
2. What are some of the problems with the lag structures seen in Jorgenson's neo-classical model?
3. How does Jorgenson explain the relationship between microeconomic and aggregate macroeconomic investment activity?
4. How are expectations specified in refinements to Jorgenson's approach and what are some problems that arise as a consequence?
5. Why is the neo-classical assumption that all capital goods are homogeneous a problematic assumption?

7 Putty-clay models of investment

The production process 80
The empirical testing of putty-clay models 84
Conclusion 89
Chapter summary 90
Revision questions 91

As discussed in previous chapters, a key point of divergence between Jorgenson's neo-classical model and accelerator models of investment lies in the assumptions about the nature of the production process and the capital stock. Investment models can be separated into the three categories of putty-putty, putty-clay and clay-clay models according to the assumptions made about the responsiveness of investment to changes in relative factor prices. The difference between these three types of model is captured by the parameter describing factor substitutability, i.e. the elasticity of factor substitution (σ), which captures the responsiveness of capital inputs to relative factor costs. In putty-putty models, such as Jorgenson's model, the elasticity of factor substitution is assumed to be equal to one, meaning that a given rise in the relative cost of capital will lead to a proportionate fall in the demand for capital. In clay-clay models, such as accelerator models, the elasticity of factor substitution is equal to zero; demand for capital does not respond at all to changes in the cost of capital. In putty-clay models the elasticity of factor substitution *ex ante* and in the short-run is equal to zero. *Ex post* and in the long-run the elasticity of factor substitution is equal to one. This is capturing the fact that production processes are more likely to be flexible in planning stages and over longer time periods because time is needed to allow the capital stock to adjust to changes in factor costs. During the 1960s and 1970s a lot of econometric work was conducted to assess the relative predictive power of accelerator theory versus Jorgenson's model and its variants. The empirical evidence discussed in this chapter confirms the finding from accelerator theory – that investment keeps pace with output growth. However, the evidence on the magnitude of the elasticity of factor substitution is very mixed with different researchers estimating a wide range of possibilities from close to zero to close to one. This suggests that the econometric modelling of Jorgensonian models has not provided any substantial empirical evidence about the validity of simple neo-classical models.

The production process

The differences between the putty and clay approaches can be explained by describing the isoquants in these models. An isoquant describes the various combinations of capital and labour that will produce a given, fixed level of output. In a world of only two factors of production, labour and capital, the neo-classical economists, such as Jorgenson, assume that capital and labour are perfect substitutes and the isoquants that describe production are smooth, convex functions. In other words the production process is very flexible and responsive, like jelly or putty. In contrast, in accelerator models the isoquants are 'L-shaped' in form, reflecting fixed factor proportions. Once investments are in place, subsequent investments will be constrained to fit in with old technologies. The production process will be more like clay than putty: i.e. capital–labour ratios will be fixed and unresponsive to changes in the cost of capital.

Putty-putty models: Jorgenson's model

Jorgenson's original model is a putty-putty neo-classical model of investment in which the isoquants are the smooth, continuous convex functions depicted in Figure 7.1. Along each isoquant, output is fixed. But if a firm can move to a higher isoquant, then this means that it will be producing more output. In the diagram, the iso-cost line depicts the combinations of labour and capital that can be afforded from a given, fixed budget. The relative cost of capital and labour is captured by the slope of the iso-cost line. In Figure 7.1, as capital becomes more expensive (or in Jorgenson's terminology, as the user cost of capital increases), the iso-cost line pivots anti-clockwise and flattens reflecting the fact that fewer units of capital but more units of labour can be bought from a given budget; capital has become relatively more expensive. On the other hand, if the iso-cost line pivots clockwise and steepens this means that capital has become relatively cheaper in comparison with labour. If the cost of capital decreases (the iso-cost line pivots clockwise from iso-cost line 1 to 2), then two effects will determine the change in the optimal capital stock. The 'output effect' will ensure that, as capital becomes cheaper, output will increase reflecting the overall decrease in the costs of production. There will be an overall increase in the demand for both capital and labour and the producer will shift to a higher isoquant. This effect is reinforced by the 'substitution effect'. As capital becomes relatively cheaper than labour, producers will switch to production processes that are more capital intensive, also leading to an increase in demand for capital goods and a concomitant increase in investment.

On the other hand, if labour becomes cheaper, i.e. if the wage rate falls, the increase in the relative cost of capital goods will cause substitution away from capital goods leading to a fall in demand for capital and therefore a fall in investment. But this effect will be counter-balanced by the output effect: the decrease in overall production costs allowed by the lowered wage rate will lead to a positive output effect and so the demand for capital will increase. In neo-classical economics, the substitution effect is assumed to predominate: the changes in demand for capital following from the substitution effect will exceed the changes in demand for capital arising from the output effect. With the substitution effect predominating, the capital–labour ratio will fall as labour becomes relatively cheaper.

Overall in putty-putty models, changes in relative factor prices lead to equal and proportionate changes in factor inputs: i.e. there is a unitary elasticity of factor substitution. This perfect substitutability of factors both *ex ante* and *ex post* does not allow for partial, delayed adjustment of the capital stock in response to changes in the cost of capital on investment in subsequent periods. Even when lags are superimposed on top of the model, as described in Chapter 6, the responsiveness of investment decisions to output changes and to relative factor price changes is assumed to be equal. So lags on relative factor prices will be equal to the lags on output because the optimal capital

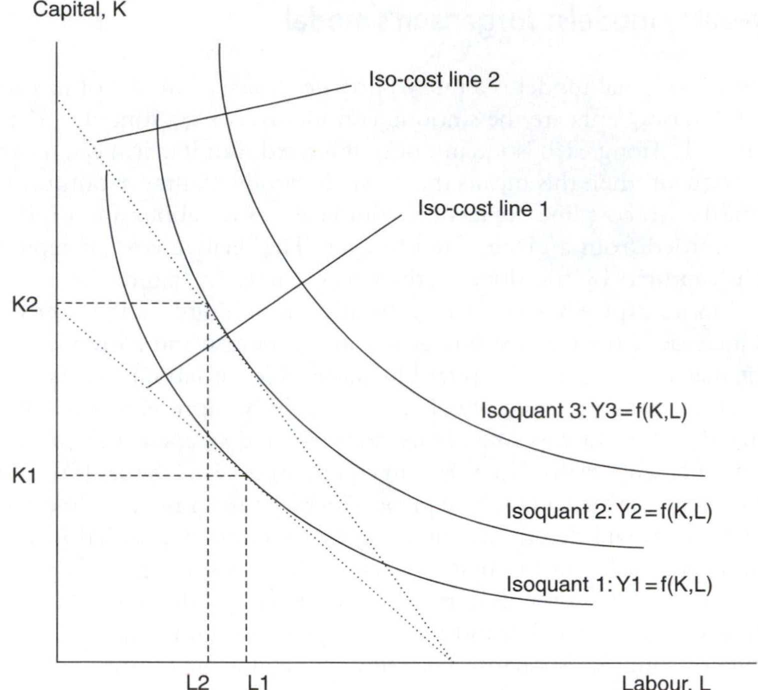

Figure 7.1 Capital and labour as substitutes in putty models

stock will respond equally and simultaneously to scale effects and relative factor price effects.[1]

Clay-clay models: accelerator theory

Mathematically at least, the accelerator model can be derived from the neo-classical model by assuming clay-clay technology: i.e. that the elasticity of substitution of capital for labour in response to factor price changes is equal to zero and, in this case, the isoquants will be L-shaped, as depicted in Figure 7.2. This reflects the fact that, in accelerator models, capital and labour are complements. In other words, they must be used together, in fixed proportions (though not necessarily in one-to-one proportions). A simple example of a production process in which labour and capital are used in fixed proportions might be a clothes factory. Each worker can use only one sewing machine and each sewing machine can employ only one worker. Therefore, the use of the different factors will not respond to relative factor prices: as one factor becomes relatively cheaper, the use of *both* factors will increase. To follow the analogy: if sewing machines become relatively cheaper and the firm

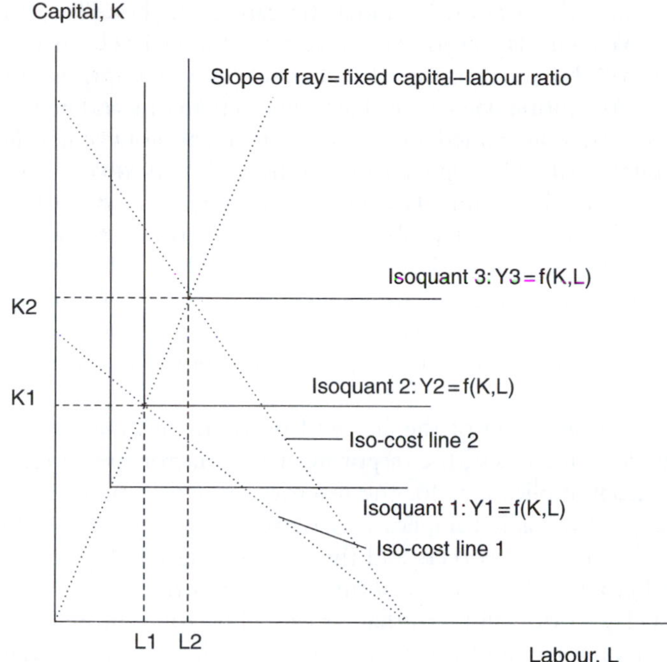

Figure 7.2 Capital and labour as complements in clay models

buys more machines, the firm will only be able to employ as many new workers as new machines and vice versa because each worker requires one machine. In other words, there will be no substitution effect: the output effect from changes in relative factor costs will dominate. Overall, capital and labour will not be substituted for one another either *ex ante* or *ex post* and the optimal capital stock will be determined solely by expected future output, not by relative factor costs. The elasticity of factor substitution is equal to zero. Technology will be fixed and immutable, associated with constant capital–labour and capital–output ratios.

Putty-clay models

As explained in Chapter 6, in response to the assertion that capital and labour are not easily substituted for each other, Samuelson (1962) bridged the gap between putty and clay approaches by showing that a surrogate production can be constructed assuming the existence of different techniques embodying different capital–labour ratios, even if given techniques have a fixed capital–labour ratio. In Samuelson's approach the substitutability of factors can be replaced by the substitutability of techniques. Solow (1970) also developed a response to the problem of limited factor substitutability in the formulation of his vintages model. In Solow's model the capital stock is like putty or jelly *ex ante* but 'baked in clay' *ex post*. So, once capital stock has been accumulated, investment will be unresponsive to changes in factor prices: the *ex post* elasticity of substitution will be considerably less than one and new investment decisions will be constrained by the existing technology embodied in the current capital stock. The capital–labour ratio will be flexible in the long-run but not in the short-run. However, different vintages of machinery incorporate different capital–labour ratios and these allow firms extra flexibility: as relative factor prices change, firms will be able swap production to the appropriate vintage of machinery. This is possible because Solow assumes no depreciation and therefore an infinite number of past vintages, representing an infinite number of capital–labour ratios, is available for use by the firm.

While the construction of the clay and putty models may seem similar in terms of basic foundations, the responsiveness of factor use to relative factor costs has crucial implications for the macroeconomy. In neo-classical theory, relatively expensive capital implies that there will be an increase in employment opportunities for workers and these increasing employment opportunities exist because of factor substitution. In contrast, relatively expensive capital in a clay world will mean that, as capital becomes more expensive, the employment opportunities for workers will actually decrease because capital and labour are complements. Unemployment will rise. The key point of divergence here lies in the differing assumptions about full employment versus involuntary unemployment. In Keynesian models of unemployment, declines in investment will lead to a dwindling capital stock and faltering aggregate demand. These in turn will create increased involuntary unemployment, as seen in capacity scrapping models of unemployment. This links in with a second key difference between Keynesian clay accelerator models and neo-classical putty models: neo-classical analysis assumes full employment of factors of production including capital stock: i.e. capacity is always fully utilized. In contrast, as was seen in the analysis of accelerator theories, accelerator models often incorporate a term to capture the extent of capacity utilization. Investment will be affected by the extent of capacity utilization because the capital stock is not always fully employed in a world of deficient aggregate demand.

The empirical testing of putty-clay models

The literature on the empirical estimation of putty-clay models is vast. But to simplify: three broad approaches have been used to test the relative impact of output and factor prices: estimation of the elasticity of substitution; estimation of the different lag lengths on changes in the user cost of capital and output; and model selection techniques, such as non-nested tests, to assess the comparative performance of putty-putty, putty-clay and clay-clay models.

Estimation of the elasticity of substitution and lag lengths

Given an unknown elasticity of substitution less than one and effects of changes in the user cost of capital changing over time, investment equations can no longer be expressed in terms of the Y/C ratio. Even if output and user costs lags are the same, the neo-classical investment model specification described above is not linear in the parameters therefore the elasticity of substitution cannot be estimated independently using the popular ordinary least squares (OLS) procedures. Therefore, in much of the empirical testing of putty-clay models the following linear approximation of Jorgenson's model is estimated (a net investment version of model in Chirinko, 1993, p.1880):

$$I_{\mathrm{nt}} = \sum_{j=0}^{J} \alpha\beta_{Y_j}\Delta Y_{t-j} - \sigma\sum_{j=0}^{J}(\alpha\beta_{Cj}\Delta C_{t-j}) + u_t$$

The lags in this model will reflect not only all the factors outlined in Chapter 6, such as adjustment costs, expectational parameters and gestational lags but also the technological lags implied by sluggish adjustment to changes in the user cost of capital. All these influences are captured in the parameters β_C and β_Y.

As explained above, a non-zero elasticity of substitution of capital with respect to user cost is the crucial element in neo-classical investment theory and differentiates it from accelerator approaches. Whilst there is consensus that the *output* elasticity is approximately equal to one, there has been considerable disagreement about the magnitude of the elasticity of substitution with respect to the user cost of capital. Hall and Jorgenson (1967) and Jorgenson and Stephenson (1967) estimate a neo-classical investment model which incorporates a composite output-user cost term: investment is estimated as a distributed lag function of changes in desired capital, assuming that desired capital is proportional to the ratio of the value of output to the user cost of capital. The use of this composite term restricts the elasticity of substitution to −1 (the negative sign indicates that demand for capital decreases as the user cost of capital increases) and is justified by Hall and Jorgenson who argue that statistical tests suggested that an absolute value of unity was appropriate.

Coen (1969) argued that this approach is not a good test of neo-classical theory and overstates the responsiveness of the capital stock to changes in the user cost of capital. Furthermore, he argues that Hall and Jorgenson's own results were inconsistent with an elasticity of substitution of one. Coen tested models with composite output-user cost terms incorporating elasticities of substitution (σ) less than one in absolute terms. He found the best fit to the data in a model with an elasticity of substitution of −0.2, indicating that the responsiveness of investment to changes in the user cost of capital is quite muted. Coen's results confirmed those of Eisner and Nadiri (1968) who, in an unconstrained estimation of the elasticity of substitution, found an elasticity of −0.2. Their estimate of the elasticity on output was +0.7. Bischoff (1969), again using unconstrained estimation and using his own data on the user cost of capital, found a significant elasticity of substitution approaching −1. Eisner (1970) confirmed this result finding an elasticity of −0.88 using Bischoff's data but of only −0.28 using Jorgenson's measure. The results from the estimation of the elasticity of substitution seem to be very sensitive to the measure of user cost used (Hay and Morris, 1991, pp. 452–4). Feldstein and Flemming (1971) found that the elasticities on output and the components of the user cost of capital varied greatly and that the elasticity of substitution was much closer to zero than to one. Similarly, Bean (1981) found that both the user cost of capital and output terms in his neo-classical model are significant, with output elasticity of +0.91 and an elasticity of substitution of −0.05. Bean also runs a regression with the user cost of capital term decomposed into its constituent parts. He finds that the crucial determinants of investment expenditure are the prices of capital goods relative to output prices and the marginal retention ratio on corporate profits, with elasticities of +0.39 and +0.34 respectively (though the positive elasticity on the relative price of capital goods is an anomalous result). These terms are not highly significant in themselves. Furthermore, hypothesis tests revealed that the restrictions implicit in amalgamating the different constituents of the user cost of capital did not significantly increase the variance of the errors in the model, suggesting that investment is determined by the user cost of capital overall rather than the separate influences of its constituent parts.

As mentioned above, the testing of putty-clay models has also focused on establishing the relative length of the lags on determinants of investment, by estimating linear approximations of Jorgenson's model. If investment responds slowly to relative factor prices, then the effects of changes in the user cost of capital will be spread out over time and the lags on the user cost of capital will be longer than those on output. In empirical putty-clay models, such as Bischoff (1969) and Feldstein and Flemming (1971), longer lags are introduced for the user cost terms compared with the output terms in order to capture the relative delays in capital stock adjustment in response to factor cost changes. Eisner and Nadiri (1968) also found that the responsiveness of investment to changes in relative prices was slower than responsiveness to output, with longer lags on the user cost of capital relative to output.

Model selection/non-nested tests

A number of studies of investment determination compare the relative performance of different types of models rather than focusing on the results from one model. Early analyses compared industry-wide models on the basis of the significance of the coefficients and the size of R^2. Testing time-series data on a sample of 15 individual firms, Jorgenson and Siebert (1968) compared their neo-classical models against other models according to the magnitude of the residual variance of each model. They also examined the fitted coefficients and assessed goodness of fit. They found that the putty-putty neo-classical specification performed better than a flexible accelerator model. Using time-series data on 15 sub-industries, Jorgenson and Stephenson (1967) confirmed these results.

Jorgenson and Siebert's and Jorgenson and Stephenson's results were based on very small samples of firms and therefore further analyses were conducted to test the generality of their results. Elliott (1973) replicates Jorgenson and Siebert's approach using time-series and cross-sectional data from 184 US firms. He finds that the estimated R^2 from various models of investment are comparable to Jorgenson and Siebert's. However, his precise empirical findings vary considerably from Jorgenson and Siebert's findings. For his time-series data, Elliott finds that the residual variances of putty-putty models are not markedly lower than those in the alternative models. In the cross-sectional regressions, the performance of the neo-classical model was inferior to that of the other specifications. Elliott concluded:

> The major conclusion of the [Jorgenson-Siebert] studies that the neoclassical model of investment is more effective than other alternatives simply does not stand up to the enlarged test [incorporated in Elliott's study], and must now be interpreted as having no general implication beyond their sample. (Elliott, 1973, p. 206)

The problem with the econometric approaches outlined above is that the interpretation of results was necessarily somewhat subjective. More rigorous model selection tests, non-nested testing techniques, were developed in the 1970s and 1980s. The rationale underlying these tests rests on the insight that good empirical models should be able to explain not only the data-generating process but also the empirical results from alternative models (Davidson and MacKinnon, 1981). Anderson (1981) regressed nominal investment on nominal output and liquidity flow and found that both variables were significant. He argues that this result is not inconsistent with a putty-clay specification for investment. He tests his putty-clay specification against clay-clay and putty-putty specifications and finds that the increased residual variances, resulting from excluding either the output or the user cost terms in his putty-clay model, were significant. He argues that his results support his putty-clay specification and suggest that capital stock adjustment is more responsive to output signals than to the supply of funds or the relative cost of capital.

Bean (1981) tested competing investment models against each other using Pesaran-Deaton non-linear non-nested test procedures. He found that his putty-clay models out-performed clay-clay and putty-putty specifications. Putty-putty and clay-clay models are soundly rejected although clay-clay models performed better than putty-putty models, confirming earlier findings that output effects are stronger than price effects. Bean's putty-clay model also out-performs other alternative models (for example, Eisner and Nadiri, 1968;

Hines and Catephores, 1979). In Baddeley (1996) neo-classical models were tested against Keynesian and accelerator alternatives for UK manufacturing investment between 1975 and 1992, using a range of non-nested testing techniques. These tests revealed that various measures of the user cost of capital contribute no significant independent explanatory power when super-imposed upon accelerator specifications. However, the accelerator model contributed significant independent explanatory power when tested against other models.

Problems with the estimation of putty-clay models

So throughout the 1960s and 1970s, a large number and range of putty and clay investment models specifications were estimated.[2] The range of contradictory results is almost as large as the number of models estimated so these econometric exercises have provided little conclusive evidence about investment activity. Some of the problems may reflect econometric rather than theoretical issues. For example, Hay and Morris (1991) discuss a number of factors that might lead to the delayed response to the user cost of capital and explain the evidence on differential lag lengths. The assumption of a constant elasticity of substitution across all types of capital good may not be justified (Abel, 1990). Harcourt (1966) argues that assuming a constant elasticity of substitution across machines of different vintages will lead to biases in the estimates of the elasticity of substitution. Hay and Morris also comment that user-cost will vary for different types of equipment because depreciation rates vary: for example, structures are not depreciated as rapidly as equipment. Also, the accounting conventions that dictate measured depreciation rates may not reflect the *actual* rate of deterioration of equipment and the associated replacement costs. It may also be difficult to establish when actual investment decisions were made and thus which lag on the user cost is important. As noted above, the results from the estimation of putty-clay models depend greatly upon the precise measure of the user cost of capital used. Furthermore, different measures of the user cost of capital are highly dependent on interest rates and tax rates (Anderson, 1981).

In addition, given the existence of heterogeneous firms in reality, assuming that one aggregate measure of the user cost of capital describes all firms may be an inappropriate test of neo-classical theory. There may be interactions between investment and its various determinants. If the user cost of capital and output are related then multicollinearity may limit the power of inference procedures. For example, if profit expectations are determined by demand expectations then demand effects will affect the user cost of capital via effects on capital goods prices. So it may be difficult to separate the cost of capital and output influences, particularly as multicollinearity may blur the precise estimation of the output and user cost parameters.

A more severe problem for OLS estimation techniques is the potential simultaneity between investment and its determinants. OLS procedures are justified by assuming that explanatory variables are non-stochastic or, at the very least, not contemporaneously correlated with the disturbance term. If the hypothesized determinants of investment are themselves endogenous, this condition is violated. For example, when investment is a determinant of output or the user cost of capital, the OLS estimates of the parameters on the user cost of capital and output will be biased. There are many potential sources of simultaneity: some authors argue that investment will affect the user cost of capital via its influence on interest rates (Abel, 1990) and multiplier effects will mean that investment affects output. Also, the autonomous shocks to investment (for example, technology shocks) captured in the disturbance term may also be correlated with output and the user cost. Chirinko argues that this could account for significant output and insignificant user cost terms. The appropriate remedy is to use 'instrumental variables' which can proxy the effects of the endogenous variables. However, it is often difficult to find suitable instruments because it may be difficult to identify the structural parameters determing the relationships between investment and other variables; the parameters on instrumental variables may have many interpretations depending upon the instruments selected (Chirinko, 1993).

Conclusion

In this chapter we have shown that the estimation of putty-clay models has been only partially successful. The volume of literature on the testing of putty-clay models is vast and tends to support putty-clay models over flexible accelerator and putty-putty models. It is generally agreed that the influence of quantity variables (specifically output) on investment is greater than the influence of the user cost of capital. Most studies have confirmed an output elasticity approaching one (Chirinko, 1993; Hay and Morris, 1991). But there is little agreement about the magnitude of the responsiveness of the capital stock to changes in the user cost of capital, except that there is some consensus that the lags on user cost are longer than on output. Estimates of the elasticity of substitution have varied considerably. Estimates of close to -1 have been documented by Jorgenson *et al.* but estimates of not much more than zero have been documented by Bean. Problems have emerged with the identification of the lag structures, and even the most sophisticated putty-clay models, whilst they may fit the historical data, have poor predictive power (Hay and Morris, 1991). All these findings indicate that there is little consistent evidence to support Jorgenson's model and its refinements.

Whilst there is agreement that putty-clay models have not performed well empirically, assessing the findings is complicated. It is difficult to judge whether the poor performance of empirical models reflects either an inappropriate theoretical model or the empirical difficulties that arise in measuring complex reality. The contradictory findings outlined in this chapter may reflect, not that neo-classical theory is completely misguided, but instead that empirical difficulties, for example the existence of heterogeneous firms, externalities in production and aggregation problems, mean that aggregate models of investment cannot be properly tested. In addition, there is some agreement that issues of rationality and expectations formation were not properly addressed in putty-clay models. So the next stage in the development of investment theory involved a more rigorous attempt to capture the dynamics of irreversible investment decision-making in a world of uncertainty.

In assessing these developments, two common threads connect the different approaches to analyzing investment under uncertainty. There are two possible reactions by fixed asset investors facing uncertainty: they may form expectations of the future in essence anticipating future events in spite of uncertainty and/or they may modify their decisions in response to uncertainty. From the late 1970s onwards, models of aggregate investment behaviour focus on the first type of reaction: expectations were quantified by incorporating a rational expectations assumption into a model of optimal investment decisions and positive adjustment costs. These expectational hypotheses were included explicitly in the representative firm's optimization problem. The other development was the explicit treatment of uncertainty within models of investment by examining the independent effect of uncertainty on investment decisions. Both approaches maintained the basic rationality assumption implicit within Jorgenson's model: i.e. that of the rational, optimizing economic agent. These two approaches are assessed in the following two chapters.

Chapter summary

1. In this chapter, the theoretical differences between accelerator and Jorgensonian models are explained in terms of the elasticity of factor substitution (σ): i.e. the responsiveness of factor inputs to relative factor costs. For investment models, the relative factor cost is measured as the user cost of capital.
2. Accelerator models assume that production processes are fixed as if in clay: i.e. capital–labour ratios do not change because firms cannot respond quickly to changes in relative factor costs; the technology underlying production processes (including the capital labour ratio) is fixed, determined by past investment decisions. In these models the elasticity of substitution is equal to zero and output growth is the important determinant of investment decisions. Accelerator models are sometimes referred to as clay-clay models.
3. Jorgenson's neo-classical model incorporates the assumption that production processes are more like putty: i.e. factors of production can respond very flexibly to changes in relative factor costs – with an elasticity of factor substitution of one. This is because capital goods are homogeneous and past investment decisions do not constrain future investment decisions. Jorgensonian models are referred to as putty-putty models.

Chapter summary continued

4. Hybrids of these models are called putty-clay models. Putty-clay models allow that production processes are like putty *ex ante*, i.e. in the planning stage and in the long-run, but like clay *ex post*, i.e. once the capital stock is in place and in the short-run. So these models predict an elasticity of substitution less than one but greater than zero. They also predict that adjustment to changes in the user cost of capital will be more sluggish than in putty models and so the lags on the user cost of capital will be longer than the lags on output.
5. In the 1960s and 1970s, a large number of economists were analyzing the relative merits of putty and clay models. The econometric assessment of these three groups of models was achieved by assessing the merits of the models independently, for example, by estimating elasticities of factor substitution and the different lag lengths on output versus the user cost of capital.
6. The empirical performance of putty-clay models has been mixed. Whilst most evidence suggests that investment responds to output growth, there was no agreement about the magnitude of the elasticity of factor substitution. Estimates ranging from close to zero to close to one have been proposed. This unsatisfactory empirical performance, together with the theoretical problems noted in Chapter 6, meant that the emphasis in mainstream investment research shifted towards different modelling strategies in the 1980s and 1990s. These further developments are outlined in the next two chapters.

Revision questions

1. Why are Keynesian investment models sometimes referred to as clay models and why are neo-classical models sometimes referred to as putty models?
2. Why are factor proportions fixed in accelerator models of investment?
3. What are putty-clay models?
4. Explain two ways in which relatively sluggish responses to changes in the user cost of capital can be captured in empirical versions of putty-clay models.
5. From the 1970s onwards, why did attention shift from the analysis of putty-clay models?

8 Adjustment costs and *q* theory

Introduction 93
Adjustment costs in investment models 94
Modelling rational expectations in *q* theories 99
Conclusion 106
Chapter summary 107
Revision questions 108

As shown in the preceding chapters, early neo-classical and accelerator models dealt with uncertainty in an unsatisfactory way, super-imposing distributed lag structures on top of essentially static models in order to capture expectations of the future. Quite apart from the estimation problems that accompany the use of distributed lag structures to capture the different causes of investment lags, Jorgenson's critics argued that these refinements lacked the theoretical basis that an explicit behavioural assumption about rationality provides. In response, *q* models of dynamic optimization were formulated by incorporating uncertainty directly: expectations appear explicitly in the firm's optimization problem and can be linked directly to underlying assumptions about technology and expectations. A key problem for the empirical estimation of these models is that expectations of the future are unobservable but some solutions to this problem are outlined in this chapter, the most influential of which is probably Brainard and Tobin's *q* approach, in which expectations are captured using Stock Market data. Other solutions discussed include the 'transformation' and 'direct forecasting' approaches identified by Chirinko (1993). The outcome of empirical work on adjustment cost models, whilst more encouraging than results from the estimation of Jorgenson's theory, were still empirically disappointing, but did pave the way for real options models of investment, outlined in Chapter 9.

Introduction

As explained in Chapters 5 to 7, Jorgenson's neo-classical model of investment was originally formulated assuming static expectations. However, investment is forward-looking behaviour and so expectations and uncertainty about the future will be crucial determinants of investment decisions. Refinements to Jorgenson's model generally incorporated expectations in an *ad hoc* way, using distributed lag structures. This approach was widely criticized as lacking proper theoretical foundations. Subsequently, orthodox theories of investment adopted two approaches to describing investors' responses to the future: expectational assumptions were explicitly incorporated into firms' optimization problems and/or uncertainty was introduced as an independent influence. This chapter addresses the first of these approaches, as presented in *q* theories of investment. However, problems remained. Identifying the roles played by expectations and uncertainty in aggregate investment models is a complex exercise: first, because it is difficult, if not impossible, to quantify expectations and uncertainty; and second, because investment is the outcome of the interaction of so many influences operating over a number of periods.

In *q* theories, investment is described as a process of 'dynamic optimization': investors are assumed to maximize the present value of all future net benefits arising from their investment decisions. Most *q* theories were developed combining the rational expectations hypothesis (REH) with this dynamic optimization approach. The REH was originally associated with Muth (1961). Although it takes many forms, it is generally understood to describe economic agents forming subjective expectations of the future in a very rational way. It assumes that agents are forward-looking, make complete use of all current information and do not make systematic errors in their expectations. Non-systematic mistakes are not ruled out but agents learn from their mistakes and will not make the same mistake twice. So, according to the REH, subjective expectations will, on average, correspond with an objectively determined reality. The REH approach assumes that expectations-formation takes place in a world of quantifiable uncertainty or Knightian risk and so investment decisions are modelled using a mathematical approach.

As explained in Chapters 5 and 6, in Jorgenson's simple model, adjustment to a new desired capital stock takes place instantaneously and investment decisions are assumed to be reversible. However, if adjustment is instantaneous and costless, then the rate of investment per unit time will be undefined (Haavelmo, 1960; Junankar, 1972; Lerner, 1944): it may take almost any value depending upon the specific assumptions made about the rate of adjustment to optimal capital stock implicit in the lag structure super-imposed onto the model. In *q* approaches, this theoretical difficulty is resolved with the introduction of adjustment costs. By assuming that the integration of new equipment into the firm's production process imposes adjustment and installation costs upon the firm, investment will be defined at the point where the benefits of further investment are balanced by increasing costs of adjustment.[1] This insight forms the basis of the *q* models discussed in this chapter.

Adjustment costs in investment models

Adjustment costs are incorporated into theories of investment decision-making in one of two forms, either as external adjustment costs and/or as internal adjustment costs.

External adjustment costs

External adjustment costs reflect factors associated with whole industries and/or the macroeconomy rather than one individual firm. Eisner and Strotz (1963) assume that external adjustment costs are strictly convex (i.e. they are increasing at an increasing rate as investment increases) and non-negative. They are external to the firm, reflecting an upward-sloping supply curve in capital goods industries. Given the existence of these costs, the adjustment to a new desired capital stock will not be instantaneous but instead will be spread over a number of periods. However, Nickell (1978) argues that external adjustment costs may not be strictly convex if the supply price of capital goods does not rise with increasing investment by an individual firm. Furthermore, fixed costs of expansion may fall per unit of investment; thus it is possible to invest too slowly as well as too quickly, in which case investment models will still be undefined. Lumpiness in capital goods will mean that the capital stock may jump in response to changes in its determinants because in this way average installation costs will be minimized. Similarly, the capital stock may not respond to small changes in its determinants because the fixed costs involved in adjustment are too great to justify the potential gains (Nickell, 1978). There will be sluggish adjustment to changes in the optimal capital stock whilst cautious, risk-averse investors facing irreversible investment decisions decide whether or not changes in their environment are ephemeral.

Internal adjustment costs

Internal adjustment costs reflect factors affecting an individual firm and result from disruptions to the production process, for example as new capital goods are broken-in and workers are re-trained. This imposes additional labour costs because more labour is required to 'bolt-down' new equipment and because of limitations on managerial time (Chirinko, 1993; Hay and Morris, 1991; Nickell, 1978). All these factors drive a wedge between the cost of uninstalled and installed capital. As in Eisner and Strotz's approach, adjustment costs are assumed to be convex in investment: i.e. they increase at an increasing rate as investment increases.

Lucas (1976) points out that the installation of new equipment is costly and introduces the adjustment costs of capital installation. He presents these adjustment costs as output forgone in the process of installing capital and this adjustment is disproportionately costly: as investment increases, adjustment costs increase. In other words there will be a convex relationship between the rate of investment and adjustment costs. This convexity is illustrated in Figure 8.1, which also shows that convexity ensures a unique solution for the investment

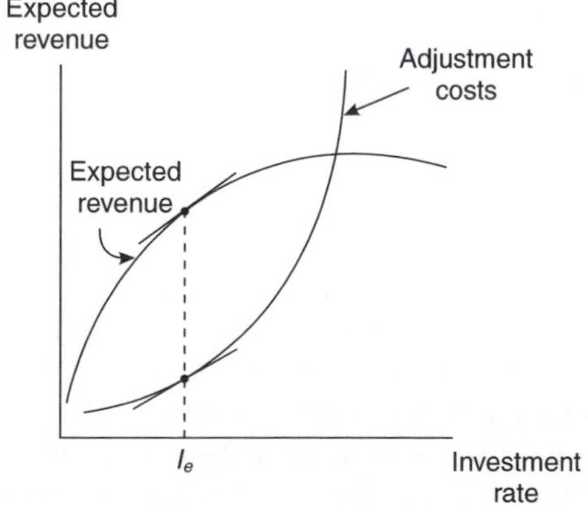

Figure 8.1 Adjustment costs and investment

rate (I_e), when the marginal benefits of investment (in terms of increasing expected revenues) are balanced by the marginal costs of adjustment. This occurs at I_e i.e. when the slopes of the revenue and adjustment cost curves are equal.

Scarth (1988) points out that within a model incorporating a quadratic adjustment cost function, investment has only three time paths consistent with the analysis of investment described above: it can approach either $+\infty$, $-\infty$ or I_e where $I_e = \delta K^* =$ replacement investment, the steady state. Scarth argues that firms want investment activity to be the same every period because adjustment costs increase with increasing investment (given his adjustment cost assumption). Therefore whilst investment varies, adjustment costs can be reduced by cutting investment in high investment periods and increasing it in low investment periods. These adjustment cost savings will be maximized when investment is the same in all periods assuming no lumpiness in capital goods.

Adjustment and installation costs in *q* theory

These internal adjustment costs are of particular importance to Abel's (1980; 1983; 1990) *q* theory of investment because the problem of an undefined rate of investment is resolved by incorporating internal adjustment costs explicitly into firms' optimization problems. Abel argues that, to minimize adjustment costs, firms tend to smooth investment according to their future expectations of factor prices and the value of output. Abel also makes a distinction between stock and flow oriented approaches to specification of investment equations. He argues that stock adjustment approaches, such as Jorgenson's model, are not valid because they describe investment as a process of adjustment towards a capital stock that is optimal only in one period; this ignores the forward-looking behaviour of rational investors. Instead, Abel argues that a flow-oriented *q* approach is more defensible because it explains the rate of investment directly as a result of the balancing, over an infinite time horizon, the marginal benefits of investment and the increasing marginal costs of increasing investment.

In formulating his model, Abel follows Lucas in defining internal adjustment costs as the output losses that arise in adapting to new investments. The value of a firm's investment and employment activities is described in much the same way as in Jorgenson's model but an additional adjustment cost term is incorporated. Adjustment costs are increasing in investment but decreasing as the capital stock increases. The production function is a function of inputs of labour and capital and a stochastic (random) technology shock. Firms aim to maximize their expected cash flow with respect to investment given these constraints. Marginal q (q_M) is defined as the 'shadow price' of capital and captures the marginal benefits of investment over an infinite time horizon. It is equal to the discounted sum of 'spot' marginal revenue products of investment. The marginal costs of investment are the sum of the sunk purchase and adjustment costs associated with investment.

This sort of formulation of q theory, describing firms maximizing the value of their production and investment activities, is outlined in Box 8.1. This optimisation decision will involve two sets of conditions: one relating to the maintenance of the existing capital stock and the other relating to the marginal benefits and costs of new investments. Overall, the net benefits from maintaining the existing capital stock come via three sources, which are also captured in Jorgenson's concept of the user cost of capital:

1. the capital gain (or loss) from increments to the marginal value of capital (q);
2. the opportunity cost in terms of lost interest from financial investment for each unit (in value terms) of retained capital; and
3. depreciation of the existing capital stock.

However, in contrast to Jorgenson's theory, Abel shows that *new* investments impose additional costs to the ones outlined above, i.e. adjustment and installation costs. Overall, the firm will be maximizing its value when *all* these marginal benefits and marginal costs of production and investment are equalized. As shown in Box 8.1, the optimal *investment* rate will be reached when:

1. the marginal productivity of *new* capital is equal to net marginal capital costs (i.e. marginal installation/adjustment costs of capital, interest costs and depreciation, net of capital gains);
2. the marginal value of new investments in terms of future expected output is equal to the marginal cost of new investments (i.e. the price of capital goods plus marginal installation costs of investment).

So the key difference between Jorgensonian and q models comes in the inclusion of installation/adjustment costs. To derive the optimal investment path, installation costs must be specified. Once these adjustment costs are defined, as explained in Box 8.1, the investment rate is described as a function of q and capital goods prices.

The optimization rule resulting from q models is the dynamic equivalent of Jorgenson's marginalist decision rule of equating the marginal benefits and costs of investing. When these marginal benefits and marginal costs are in balance, the firm is maximizing profits over an infinite time horizon. In other words, an increase in the optimal capital stock as a result of investment will lead to an increase in future output but this will be balanced by an increase in the marginal adjustment cost. The rate of investment will rise until the higher marginal return on investment is exactly counter-balanced by the higher marginal adjustment costs.

If the restrictive assumptions incorporated within this model are allowed, this approach has many advantages over the putty and clay models described in Chapters 4–7. Investment is not a function of the divergence between the current

Box 8.1 Adjustment cost models

In adjustment cost theories, as for Jorgensonian theories, the analysis begins with microfoundations: firms are assumed to maximize the value of their production and investment activities. The value of these production and investment activities (V) in a given period can be represented by the following:

$$V = Y(K, L) - wL - p_K I - C(I, K) + qI + (\dot{q} - rq - \partial)K$$

where $Y(K, L)$ is the value of output, K and L are inputs of capital and labour, w is the wage rate, p_K is the price of capital goods, I is gross investment, r is the real interest rate and δ is the depreciation rate, q is the shadow price of capital (i.e. marginal value of additional units of capital).

The key departure of q theory from Jorgenson's theory is in the inclusion of $C(I, K)$, which are the installation/adjustment costs of investment. These are increasing in investment and decreasing in capital. In Chirinko's (1993) description of q theories, adjustment costs are assumed to be quadratic in gross investment and linearly homogeneous in investment and capital, and affected by technology shocks. For example, adjustment costs can be described as follows:

$$C(I, K) = \frac{\alpha}{2}\left[\frac{I}{K} - \tau\right]^2 K$$

where τ is a random technology shock variable.

By maximizing V with respect to K and I it can be shown that:

$$C_I(I, K) = \alpha\left[\frac{I}{K} - \tau\right]$$

and the investment rate can be described as:

$$\frac{I}{K} = \frac{1}{\alpha}(q - p_K) + \tau$$

and the optimal capital stock. Delivery, adjustment, expectational, technological and other lags drop out of the optimization rule. Therefore, many of the problems associated with specifying the lag structure in capital stock adjustment models are resolved. In addition, the dynamics of expectations and technology are recognized explicitly and isolated within this specification. Error terms have a direct interpretation: they represent technology shocks.

Modelling rational expectations in *q* theories

Whilst adjustment cost versions of *q* theory present a theoretical solution to the problem of explaining investment, an empirical difficulty remains. The solutions to these *q* models incorporate terms to describe expectations of the future but expectations of the future are unobservable. If these expectations cannot be quantified, then *q* theories cannot be captured empirically. However, Chirinko (1993) explains that there are a number of ways to incorporate rational expectations into investment models, including Brainard and Tobin's *q* approach, transformation and direct forecasting models.

Tobin's *q*

'Tobin's *q*' theories are based around Brainard and Tobin's (1968, 1977) insight that, although investors' judgements of marginal productivity of capital are unobservable, Stock Market valuations will act as a good proxy for the marginal benefits of investment. Following from Keynes's ideas about the role of the Stock Market as a signal of the value of investments, Brainard and Tobin argue that Stock Market capitalizations of firms can be balanced against the current replacement cost of capital stocks to get a measure of the incentive to invest. In this theory, two concepts of *q* are separated. Average *q* (q_A) is defined as the ratio of the market value of the firm and the current replacement cost of the firm's capital stock. Marginal *q* (q_M) represents the net present value of all future benefits from the increments to capital resources that constitute net investment. Hayashi (1982) shows that, given a number of restrictive assumptions (i.e. that product and factor markets are perfectly competitive, that production and adjustment cost technologies are linearly homogeneous and that the Modigliani–Miller assumption holds), q_M can be proxied by q_A. In this way unobservable expectations of the future profitability of investment activity, as captured by share prices, can be incorporated explicitly into *q* models of investment.

The result can be explained intuitively, using the following definition:

$$Q_A = \frac{MV}{CRC} \quad \text{and} \quad \mathrm{q_A} = \ln(Q_A)$$

where MV is the Stock Market capitalization of a firm's assets (share price multiplied by the number of shares) and CRC is the current replacement cost of the capital stock. Assuming an homogeneous capital stock, if an additional unit of capital increases the market value of a firm and this increase is greater than the cost of acquiring that marginal unit of capital (i.e. when q_M is greater than one), then the marginal benefits of investment exceed its costs and investment will take place. As more investment takes place, diminishing marginal returns ensure that the marginal benefits fall relative to marginal costs, until the two are equal, when q_M will equal 1. Thus q_M captures the incentive to invest and, when q_A is equal to q_M, q_A will give a *quantifiable measure* of this incentive to invest. So if the market capitalization of a firm exceeds the current replacement cost for the firm's capital stock, q_A will be greater than one. Assuming $q_A = q_M$, this will signal to the firm that the marginal gains from investment exceed the marginal costs of investment and net investment will take place. The actual capital stock will increase until its current replacement cost equals the market capitalization. At this point the capital stock will be at its optimal level and both q_A and q_M will be equal to unity.

In essence, this empirical device is based upon the 'efficient markets assumption': that asset prices, in this case share prices, fully reflect all available information, respond completely and instantaneously to news and therefore provide an indicator of rational agents' assessments of the fundamental value of firms: i.e. the discounted stream of expected future dividends. It follows that the true market value of a firm will be captured by the Stock Market capitalization. In other words, this model assumes that Stock Market valuations give an unbiased estimate of the future value of a firm's production and investment activities. If the efficient markets hypothesis holds, then investment decisions will be solely determined by contemporaneous q because all current, relevant information should be reflected in market valuations of a firm's assets.

By incorporating a representative agents hypothesis this model can be aggregated to provide a macroeconomic theory of investment in which the Stock Market capitalization of all listed companies is used to calculate aggregate average q as a measure of the aggregate incentive to invest.

The efficient markets hypothesis that underpins Brainard and Tobin's q is itself subject to widespread criticism as share prices often respond disproportionately to ephemeral factors, particularly in the short term, and (as Keynes pointed out) may reflect speculative decisions rather than well-informed judgements of a firm's expected future profitability. However, Chirinko (1993) argues that an advantage with Tobin's q theory is that it is not affected by unstable expectations parameters: expectations enter directly and explicitly through q_A and do not need to be incorporated separately. Past values of determinants are not needed to describe expectations and the data on the user cost of capital, which is notoriously difficult to collect, is not needed because the influence of all these variables should be captured by q_A and is assumed to be readily observable from Stock Market data.

Tobin's *q*: empirical evidence

Tobin's q models do capture a significant relationship between q and investment although econometric problems emerge. Jenkinson (1981), in an analysis of UK quarterly investment between 1967 and 1976, finds that q is a significant determinant of investment and that q models provide a better explanation of investment than the simple accelerator model. Oulton (1981) analyzed investment by UK industrial and commercial companies using quarterly data from 1960 to 1977. He found that q_A is an important determinant of investment and that it out-performs other variables in explaining investment. Malkiel, von Furstenberg and Watson (1979) found that the deviations in q_A from its average level are a significant determinant of investment. Grunfeld (1960) found that q_A has greater explanatory power than current or lagged profits. By contrast, von Furstenberg (1977), using a distributed lag investment model, found that q is an insignificant determinant of investment in the USA. Similarly, Clark's (1979) distributed lag q model of equipment investment in the USA does not perform well, and persistently under-estimates actual investment. Studies by Summers (1981), Blanchard and Wyplosz (1981) and Hayashi (1982) gave low R^2s and tended to be characterized by strong positive residual serial correlation (Abel, 1990; Chirinko, 1993). For the UK, Baddeley (1996) found that Tobin's q models did contribute explanatory power independently to that contributed by accelerator theory; however q models were characterized by significant serial correlation in the residuals. Abel (1990) also notes that q models are often characterized by a large, unexplained and serially correlated error terms. Chirinko (1993) argues that this conflict between results reflects the fact that earlier models performed better because they included other explanatory variables. For example, Engle and Foley (1975) show that q is a significant determinant of investment but they introduce extra variables and lags on these variables on an *ad hoc* basis. This approach is inconsistent with the intellectual foundation of q theory because, as explained above, if the efficient markets hypothesis is true, then q should capture all available information relevant to investment decisions. However, there are justifications for augmenting q models, as explained below.

Problems with Tobin's *q*

Empirical problems reflect a number of more specific difficulties that can be separated into three broad categories: mismeasurement of components of q_A; divergences between q_A and q_M; and the role of additional variables in q models.

Mismeasurement of components of q_A

Abel (1980) remarks that the Stock Market measures the value of a firm, not its physical capital, but it is the latter that will determine expectations about the future value of investments. Financial asset prices may not be a reliable indicator of future cash flows because there may be differentials, reflecting investor sentiment, between market value and the fundamentals determining the value of a firm's capital stock. If investment decisions are based on fundamentals, then the investor sentiment component of the market value will invalidate q theory.

The divorce of management and ownership means that shareholders may not be that concerned with long-run profitability. Whilst managers may worry about share prices if they intend to raise further funds using the Stock Market, generally shareholders are more likely to focus on short-run speculative gains and outwitting the market than managers. So short-run fluctuations in the stock market valuation of a firm will not be a good proxy for management's expectations of a firm's future value (Keynes, 1936, pp. 151–5). Also, even if share prices do reflect shareholders' expectations of the present value of prospective cash flow from a firm's capital stock over an infinite time horizon, managers may hold a different view of that value and it is the managers' expectations which matter: managers make the decisions about investment.

Mismeasurement of the current replacement cost of the capital stock may also lead to a systematic bias in the calculation of q. Measurement assuming 'straight-line'depreciation methods will be inaccurate because major structural shifts (for example, the rapid rise in energy prices in the 1970s and the computing revolution in 1980s) can make a significant proportion of the capital stock obsolete. This accelerated depreciation will not be captured if straight-line depreciation methods are used and the replacement value of the capital stock will be over-estimated.

In addition, the current replacement cost of the capital stock will not reflect the value of intangible investments, such as components of R&D expenditure, investments in training of staff and the implementation of new business processes. This measurement problem has had a particular impact in recent years because of the substantial intangible investments that have accompanied the growth of the 'New Economy', particularly those investments associated with computerization. To a lesser extent this problem will affect Stock Market capitalizations as well: whilst share prices are more likely to reflect the value of intangible investments (at least to the extent that investors are rational enough to recognize the contributions that these intangible investments might make), only the true value of companies *listed* on stock exchanges will be captured. The value of intangible assets for the large number of new, unlisted firms will still be missing from Stock Market capitalizations (Yang and Brynjolfsson, 2001). As will be seen in Chapter 13, the omission of the substantial intangible investments accompanying the IT revolution will mean that the current replacement cost, and to a lesser extent market capitalizations, will not properly reflect the benefits and costs of firms' investment activities in the aggregate. Capital stock measurement problems may also arise because of difficulties measuring the impact of taxes of the value of the capital stock.

Despite these problems, Chirinko (1993) asserts that it is unlikely that capital stock mismeasurement is a crucial problem for q theory because the greatest variability in q comes from its numerator. Furthermore, he asserts there is little evidence that the problems with q theory can be attributed solely to problems of mismeasurement of q, either due to capital stock mismeasurement or investor sentiment creating market value mismeasurement.

Divergences between average q and marginal q

As explained above, Tobin's q theory of investment is based upon the equality of q_M and q_A but there may be important divergences between q_M and q_A. In monopolistic situations, where there are non-constant returns to scale and endogenous prices, q_M is often less than q_A (Chirinko, 1993, p. 1890). If inputs of labour are allowed to vary, the marginal productivity of capital (MP_K) will only be *proportional* to the average productivity (AP_k) and therefore q_A will only be proportional to q_M. Hayashi (1982) finds that measured q_A and q_M do move together closely but he emphasizes that this does not necessarily mean that q_A is a good proxy for q_M. Abel (1980) notes that q_M depends on *ex ante* values of future marginal profitability. However, q_A only gives a measure of *ex post* average profitability. This is reflected in the fact that while investment is the most volatile component of aggregate demand, it is not as volatile as q_A, suggesting that responses to fluctuations in q_A are somewhat muted.

Attempts have been made to assess models that abandon the restrictive assumptions implicit in the theoretical literature. For example, Hayashi estimates investment models based upon measures of q_M but these models are characterized by the same problems as q_A models. He therefore concludes that the empirical shortcomings of q approaches are not due to the fact that q_A is an inadequate proxy for q_M (Hayashi, 1982, p. 222).

The role of additional variables in q models

As discussed in the preceding section, in the empirical estimation of q models many studies have found that q models suffer from serially correlated residuals. In addition, seemingly extraneous variables such as lagged dependent variables, lagged q_A and quantity variables (such as liquidity and output), are highly significant when included within q models. Chirinko argues that:

> The *ex post* rationalisations [associated with including additional variables] are wholly inappropriate in the context of explicit models, which require that all assumptions enter prior to the characterisation of the optimal investment policy. When incorporated into the optimization problem, the resulting specifications bear little resemblance to the estimated equations. (Chirinko, 1993, p. 1892)

So it is important to separate the reasons for including additional variables in empirical estimations of q theory and to only include those additional variables that are theoretically justified. It appears that the additional variables included in empirical specifications of q theory can be separated into two broad categories: those variables which can be incorporated *a priori* into a theoretical specification of q to allow a loosening of some of the strict theoretical assumptions underlying traditional q models; and those which have been included on an *ad hoc* basis, with no theoretical justification. One of the key advantages of q models over Jorgenson's model is that they incorporate expectations explicitly. To then introduce additional variables without justification undermines one of the key virtues of the approach.

The legitimate additions that can be incorporated into a theoretical specification of q are variables that capture the existence of imperfect competition, heterogeneous capital stocks and heterogeneous production functions. Hayashi (1982) and Chirinko and Fazzari (1988) show that, by incorporating a price elasticity of demand and heterogeneity parameter into the theoretical specification of q, output as a proportion of capital stock is a justifiable inclusion in q models. However, as Chirinko (1993) argues, a structural interpretation of the parameters in a q model incorporating output as a proportion of capital stock is problematic.

The presence of lagged q_A within an investment model is not inconsistent with the theoretical specification of q because investment is subject to delivery lags and only decision lags should be redundant within a q approach. In a world of delivery lags, a given investment expenditure in one period may reflect investment decisions over many periods and therefore various lags on q will be important.

However, no theoretical justification exists for the inclusion of factors that, if q theory is correct, should be captured by the Stock Market valuation of the firm. The prime examples are liquidity when used a measure of financial constraints and capacity utilization when used as a measure of cyclical factors. In both these cases it could be expected that financial constraints on investment decision-making and cyclical factors would be captured by the Stock Market valuation of firms if the efficient markets hypothesis is true. As Chirinko (1993) argues:

> the theoretical basis for inserting variables representing finance constraints has been absent . . . it is not necessarily the case that liquidity should appear in a q invesment equation. Even though financial market frictions impinge on the firm, q is a forward-looking variable capturing the ramifications of these constraints on all the firm's decisions . . . q capitalises the impact of some or all finance constraints . . . [So] it remains uncertain whether significant liquidity . . . variables are capturing a structural element . . . missing in the investment equation or are merely reflecting general misspecification. (Chirinko, 1993, pp. 1892–4)

So, overall, it is sometimes justifiable to include lagged qs and output variables in empirical specifications of q but it is not theoretically justifiable to include liquidity and other measures of financial constraints. In conclusion: there is a general consensus that q theory, on its own, does not provide a good empirical basis for the analysis of investment expenditure. Chirinko concludes that:

> Thus, neither mismeasured components of q_t nor the restrictiveness of the conditions permitting q_t to proxy for [expectations] appear to be responsible for the shortcomings [of empirical applications of q theory]. Given the direct treatment of expectations, the poor empirical performance of q models is disappointing.
> (Chirinko, 1993, pp. 1891–3)

Transformation and direct forecasting models

As noted above, the major empirical problem for the dynamic adjustment cost models presented in this chapter lies in relating the unobservable discounted value of expected future earnings from investments to observable variables. Anderson argues that, because marginal adjustment costs are not an observable variable, 'theoretical work on adjustment costs has offered little in terms of tractable restrictions in empirical models' (Anderson, 1981, p. 92). Chirinko describes two alternative sets of rational expectations solutions to the problem of incorporating expectations explicitly into investment models that have some advantages over the Tobin approach. First, 'transformation' models, incorporating a perfect foresight assumption (that expectations are, on average, equal to subsequent realizations); and second, 'direct forecasting' models, which assume that agents use their knowledge of the underlying stochastic process to forecast future revenues from investments.

Transformation models

Abel (1980) argues that the use of market data in Tobin's q models as a proxy for profit expectations is not appropriate. Therefore, he develops a different approach to capturing the shadow price of capital by substituting actual values for expected values using a rational expectations assumption of perfect foresight: he assumes that expectations are equal to realized values plus an additive, random error term. Thus a rational expectations hypothesis of perfect foresight is combined with the optimization rules described above. He uses instrumental variables (IVs) to capture the shadow price of capital and selects the actual values of the investment rate in the next period as one of the instruments. In other words, Abel uses lead values of marginal profitability rather than lagged values as instruments, arguing that lagged values will be correlated with the disturbance term and so will lead to inconsistent estimates of the parameters. Problems emerge as described by Garber and King (1983) who argue that serially correlated technology shocks will invalidate most IVs. There is also a problem in finding good instruments as most candidates for instruments tend to be correlated with the residuals in the model and therefore will produce inconsistent IV estimates.

Generally, transformation models are estimated in conjunction with other constraints from the optimization process. There is a wide variation in the estimates of price and output elasticities in these models (Chirinko, 1993, pp.1894–5). Using US data to estimate transformation models, Abel (1980) finds elasticities of the investment rate with respect to q_M of between 0.58 and 1.11. Pindyck and Rotemberg (1983a), using annual data for the USA, find that capital is highly responsive to changes in capital goods prices within q models, with a long-run price elasticity of −2.93, and to changes in output, with elasticity of 1.48. As with the putty-clay models of investment discussed in Chapter 7, there seems to be little consistency in the estimated elasticities from the transformation versions of q. Whilst these models do perform well in terms of well-specified regressions, this success may be a reflection of the other variables included within the models. However, perhaps these additional variables help overcome some of the difficulties, for example, emerging from the heterogeneity of firms and production externalities, inherent in the use of aggregate adjustment cost models.

Direct forecasting models

Direct forecasting versions of adjustment cost models incorporate an assumption of rational expectations in which economic agents form rational forecasts of q_M based on some function of past spot marginal revenue products of a capital good. The results from the estimation of direct forecasting models are variable. Messe (1980) found insignificant coefficients. Abel and Blanchard (1986) in their analysis of investment in the USA found that the elasticity of investment in response to changes in current and lagged expected future profitability was small, varying between 0.1 and 0.3. They also estimated very large adjustment cost parameters and their models were characterized by serially correlated residuals and significant coefficients on output, liquidity and lagged expected future profitability. Many other direct forecasting models are also characterized by substantial residual serial correlation suggesting that adjustment cost technology does not account for all the relevant dynamics (Chirinko, 1993). These problems are very similar to those found in Tobin's q models.

Another problem with direct forecasting approaches is that the estimated coefficients from the models are an amalgam of many parameters, just as in Jorgenson's model and its refinements. Other problems are that the relationship between past and expected future marginal profitability is assumed to be stable over time and this may not be the case in reality. If the steady-state capital stock changes with the arrival of new information, then the optimal investment path will be unstable and this will lead to instability in the estimated coefficients (Chirinko, 1993). In booms, expectations of the future will be over-optimistic and in slumps, expectations will be over-pessimistic. However, in direct forecasting models, forecasts of the expected future profitability of investments will tend to be similar over time and thus may not capture cyclical changes in investment expenditure.

Conclusion

The performance of rational expectations adjustment cost models of investment has been mixed. Whilst transformation models perform best empirically, they do not give an intuitively plausible decision rule that can be adapted by real-world investors because real-world investors do not possess perfect foresight. The basis of Tobin's q models and direct forecasting models is more intuitively plausible and empirically tractable but these models do not perform well empirically and tend to be characterized by problems of serial correlation. In addition, direct forecasting models do not solve the problem of separating the different dynamic aspects of the investment process and in this sense are subject to the same criticisms directed at the putty-clay models, discussed in Chapter 7.

A more fundamental problem with these rational expectations approaches to the specification of investment models comes in identifying the reasons for their empirical failure. Are the empirical results from these models poor because the REH is wrong or because the assumption of profit maximizing behaviour is wrong? These models incorporate the REH without directly testing REH for its validity. There is no escape from this because we cannot know the probability distributions that are supposed to describe rational agents' expectations formation, so we can only *assume* that agents form expectations rationally. Although experimental psychology may provide some answers, the results here are also contradictory. For example, evidence in support of the rational expectations assertion is provided by laboratory experiments (Dwyer *et al.*, 1993); and Biais *et al.* (2002), who find that psychological traits, such as over-confidence, affect behaviour and performance in financial markets. Financial investors suffer from 'winner's curse' with overly confident subjects earning lower profits. Dittrich, Gueth and Maciejovsky (2001) find that, in psychological experiments, investor behaviour is characterized by overconfidence, particularly as task complexity increases. Aiginger (1987) argues that there are 'striking divergences' between investors' reported expectations and rational expectations forecasts. This evidence suggests that the rational expectations hypothesis and associated efficient markets hypothesis that underlie Tobin's q theory are misplaced in reality.

Also, whilst the models discussed in this chapter are built on rational expectations assumptions, there may be alternative interpretations of the results reached. For example, a significant q could be interpreted as confirming q approaches based on rational expectations, but it could also be interpreted as confirming empirically Keynes's insights about the relationships between fixed investment, the Stock Market and uncertainty, as discussed in Chapter 3. These interpretative difficulties can be addressed by comparing different empirical models using model comparison techniques. A comparative empirical analysis of q models is presented in Chapter 12.

Chapter summary

1. The q theories of investment developed as a response to some of the difficulties and restrictive assumptions embedded within Jorgenson's neoclassical model of investment. Jorgenson's theory assumed instantaneous and costless capital stock adjustment but this led to an undefined rate of investment. In addition, Jorgenson did not capture expectations formation in a theoretically rigorous way.
2. In q theories, adjustment costs are introduced to generate a model in which the rate of investment over time is defined. Adjustment costs can take one of two forms: external and internal adjustment costs. External adjustment costs reflect factors affecting industries and/or the macroeconomy; internal adjustment costs reflect factors affecting an individual firm.

Chapter summary continued

3. Adjustment cost versions of q theory incorporate expectational assumptions explicitly into their models by adopting a rational expectations hypothesis (REH). The REH is the assumption that agents make full use of all available information and do not make systematic mistakes, meaning that on average their subjective expectations will coincide with some objective probability distribution of outcomes. The q theorists combine the REH with the assumption that rational investors will maximize the net benefits over time of their production and investment activities. When these assumptions are combined, the optimal investment path will be determined by marginal q, q_M, where q_M is defined as the shadow price of capital: i.e. the discounted sum of 'spot' marginal revenue products from an investment.
4. An empirical problem for adjustment cost theories comes in capturing rational expectations because expectations are inherently unobservable. There are solutions to this problem, the most influential of which is described within Tobin's q models of investment. Other solutions include modelling rational expectations using transformation and 'direct forecasting' approaches.
5. Tobin's q models are based upon the insight that, given a number of restrictive assumptions, q_M (the shadow price of capital) will be equal to q_A (average q, the market capitalization of a firm relative to the current replacement cost of its capital stock).
6. There are a number of limitations to the adjustment cost approaches and whilst the empirical evidence is more encouraging than the empirical evidence about Jorgenson's model, adjustment cost models are often characterized by econometric problems such as serial correlation. This could be a sign that empirical specifications of the theory are omitting important influences. Some orthodox theorists have attributed these limitations to a neglect of uncertainty. The role of uncertainty in orthodox models of investment is discussed in the following chapter.

Revision questions

1. What are the relationships between q theory and Jorgenson's theory?
2. What is q?
3. How is q theory used to address some of the limitations of the putty-clay models, as analyzed in Chapter 7?
4. What are some of the problems surrounding the empirical estimation of q models?

9 Uncertainty and investment

Introduction	110
Some theoretical issues	111
Real options theories of investment under uncertainty	114
Empirical investigations of investment under uncertainty	117
Conclusion	122
Chapter summary	122
Revision questions	123

As seen in the preceding chapters, Jorgenson's model did not perform well empirically and the *q* theorists attempted to resolve some of the problems within Jorgenson's theory by incorporating rational expectations and adjustment costs explicitly into their models of firms' optimizing behaviour. While the empirical performance of *q* theories was generally superior to that of Jorgensonian models, there were still signs that something was missing from these theories, either because the expectations assumptions embedded within these models did not properly capture the influences of uncertainty and/or because the basic assumptions underlying a model of profit maximizing investors were empirically fallible. In this chapter, the influence of uncertainty within orthodox models of investment is investigated. These models are based upon the insight that, in a world of irreversible investment, there are benefits in waiting to acquire more information about the likely success of investments. This insight can be incorporated into models of rational optimization to give a 'real options' theory of fixed asset investment, such as the theory developed by Dixit and Pindyck (1994). These models are based upon the insight that exercising an option to invest involves opportunity costs and these opportunity costs will rise as uncertainty increases the value of waiting for further information. So, on balance, there will be a negative relationship between investment and uncertainty.

Introduction

Early orthodox theorists tended to simplify the relationship between uncertainty and investment by assuming that all future possibilities will be captured in agents' rational expectations. For example, Lucas and Prescott's 1971 article 'Investment under Uncertainty' describes rational expectations formation by investors facing uncertainty, without assessing the independent influence of uncertainty. This approach neglects the complicated interrelationships between expectations and uncertainty: whilst expectations are formed because of uncertainty about the future, uncertainty will have a quite separate influence as well because it will affect the perceived reliability of expectations. To use Keynes's (1921) statistical analogy, rational conduct will be driven not only by judgements of probable outcomes but also by the *weight* placed on these judgements of probability.[1] As uncertainty increases and confidence decreases, rational agents will place less trust in their expectations.

The independent role of uncertainty in the determination of investment, always a crucial aspect of Keynes's investment theory, has more recently become the focus of orthodox investment theory. This shifting focus reflects the poor performance of neo-classical empirical models of investment based on assumptions of rational and adaptive expectations. However, the broad nature of mainstream orthodox analyses of investment under uncertainty remains the same and the assumptions associated with rational forward-looking, optimizing economic agents are retained in the analyses of investment under uncertainty described in this chapter.

Some theoretical issues

The orthodox investigation of the relationship between investment and uncertainty began with the initially counter-intuitive assertion that investment and uncertainty will be positively related. For example, Abel, 1983; Hartman, 1972; Pindyck, 1982; Roberts and Weitzman, 1987; and Sakellaris, 1994 postulated a positive relationship between investment and uncertainty for perfectly competitive firms facing completely reversible investment decisions. Nickell (1978) notes that assertions about the positive relationship between investment and uncertainty centre on the hypothesis that higher expected profits are an inducement to take greater risks in expansion, assuming risk-neutrality. Therefore, firms will undergo larger increases in capacity in response to uncertain demand if high profits are expected because they have nothing to lose if they can reverse their investment decisions quickly (Nickell, 1978, p. 74). Pindyck (1993) suggests that, as uncertainty increases, there is an increased desire for the increased flexibility which larger capital stocks and faster rates of investment allow: a larger capital stock will mean that output can vary more widely meaning that the firm can take advantage of unanticipated increases in output prices. Similarly, Manne (1961) argues that if firms need the capacity to cope with random increases in demand, capacity will be added in larger increments when demand uncertainty increases. Oi (1961), Hartman (1972, 1976) and Abel (1983) argue that if labour can be adjusted more easily than the fixed capital stock, then capital goods price fluctuations will lead to a change in the capital–labour ratio in excess of the change in the marginal revenue product of capital. For example, if capital prices fall and so the relative cost of labour rises, with a workforce which is more flexible than the capital stock, the fall in labour will exceed the rise in capital and the capital–labour ratio will increase requiring an increased rate of investment. So increased variability in wages/output prices will lead to increased investment. It is the flexibility of labour compared with capital in a world of reversible investments that leads to the positive relationship between investment and uncertainty (Leahy and Whited, 1995).

Irreversible investment

Uncertainty will dampen investment activity only if investments are irreversible. Assuming asset specificity, investment involves sunk costs and so on a microeconomic scale net disinvestment is limited because 'second hand' markets for investment goods are poor. So without the sale of assets gross disinvestment is constrained to be equal to the amount of depreciation. On a macroeconomic scale, unless firms are prepared to destroy their existing capital, disinvestment in excess of depreciation is impossible. This inability to reverse investment decisions imposes additional costs on investors if there is an adverse change in circumstances. Investors will accordingly be more cautious in the face of down-side uncertainty.

Dixit and Pindyck (1994) develop those points and argue that leeway over the timing of investment has a profound effect on the investment process when investment is irreversible and involves sunk costs. Sunk costs arise not only because de-installation is costly but also because capital goods have a very limited resale value. A large proportion of investment purchases involve sunk costs because many investments are industry or firm specific. If demand conditions change, then other firms within a given industry will be unwilling to buy second-hand capital goods because they face the same demand conditions as the seller of the capital goods. In non-competitive markets, highly specific capital goods have no resale value because they are of no use to other businesses.

Waiting for information

Once irreversible investment is introduced, a negative correlation between investment and uncertainty seems more likely. For example, Viner (1931) argues that, because investment is irreversible, it pays firms to wait for more accurate information before deciding about what size of plant to build. He argues that this result holds even for risk-neutral firms. Cukierman (1980) argues that risk-averse investors facing irreversible investment decisions and increased uncertainty will require and acquire more information about future demand conditions before they decide to invest. However, although they will delay investment they will not necessarily cancel investment plans altogether. The length of time devoted to collecting information, the 'optimal waiting period', will increase as the variance of expected rates of return increases. Cuikerman relates this result to the precision of information. A decrease in the precision of information about the future potential of investments will have ambiguous effects. The overall value of information will decrease because uncertainty will muffle the information and therefore there will be less incentive to wait for more information before investing. However, it takes more time to accumulate enough relevant information. On balance the latter effect predominates and therefore the optimal waiting period will increase under uncertainty.

Bernanke (1983) argues that investment decisions are divided into decisions about how much to invest and decisions about the timing of investment. Irreversible investment means that investment timing decisions are made which balance the extra returns from an early commitment to an investment project against the benefits, in terms of increased probability of making the right decision, of waiting for more information about the project. Increased uncertainty will increase the return to waiting for more information in order to avoid the consequences of adverse changes in demand conditions. Bernanke argues that investment:

> is not a purposeful adjustment of stocks to a lower level, investor behaviour in recession is better described as a cautious probing, an avoidance of commitment until longer run states of both the national economy and the investor's own fortunes are better known. There is a general perception of low points in the cycle as times of

> low 'confidence', a fact that [the accelerator theory of investment] is inadequate to explain. (Bernanke, 1983, p. 86)

Therefore, according to Bernanke, investment is very sensitive to changes in expectations about the rate of arrival of information and thus to changes in confidence in the economy.

Bernanke also elaborates on the 'bad news' principle of irreversible investment: investment is sensitive to 'down-side' uncertainty, and this promotes caution. Negative shocks have asymmetrically large effects on investment: they are not offset when good news arrives because the greater dispersion of possible outcomes both good and bad under increased uncertainty increases noise and thereby encourages investors to wait until signals are clearer, increasing the optimal information search time. This result is a reflection of irreversible investment. Even non-specific capital goods may involve large sunk costs if Akerlof's (1970) 'lemons principle' applies to the second-hand market for capital goods.[2]

Arrow (1968) argues that difficulties of resale of capital goods in second-hand markets lead to myopic 'optimal' investment policies because firms do not take account of the fact that they can only resell capital goods at prices well below the purchase price. The limitations imposed by irreversible investment may also be compounded by institutional and governmental regulations.

Aggregate uncertainty versus idiosyncratic uncertainty

Bernanke points out that whilst the law of large numbers may suggest that firm fluctuations will balance out in the aggregate, aggregate uncertainty will have an additional independent influence. Lucas (1976) also highlights the role of uncertainty in driving business cycles in his discussion of endogenous uncertainty. Lucas argues that signals about the current state of demand are imprecisely perceived by businesses. Firms cannot separate transitory fluctuations from permanent fluctuations in demand and therefore will delay investment whilst they decide about the true state of the economy. Reduced investment in one period is reflected in a lower aggregate demand in that period. The decrease in economic activity is perceived as a sign of ensuing recession by other firms and these firms will reduce their demands for inputs etc. in response. Therefore what might have been an intrinsically transitory fluctuation leads to a persistent downward fluctuation with investment as the propagating mechanism.

Pindyck (1993) also distinguishes between the effects of aggregate or industry-wide uncertainty and 'idiosyncratic uncertainty': i.e. uncertainty that only affects the individual firm. He argues that the positive effect of uncertainty on investment will only hold for idiosyncratic uncertainty. Pindyck allows Caballero's (1991) result: for firms facing an infinitely elastic demand curve and idiosyncratic uncertainty the opportunity cost of irreversible investment approaches zero. However, Pindyck argues that the same result will not necessarily hold for industry-wide demand uncertainty, where price and industry output are determined endogenously and investment is irreversible, because any positive benefits of uncertainty will be moderated if an increase in demand encourages the entry of new firms into the industry. During a boom this limits price increases and therefore limits increases in marginal profitability for existing firms, in turn limiting the potential benefits of positive demand uncertainty for incumbent firms. On the other hand, during a slump, if investment is irreversible and firms cannot sell their excess capacity in the face of *falls* in demand, there is no mechanism to prevent falls in prices in response to adverse demand shocks. An asymmetric relationship between investment and uncertainty emerges: increases in profitability in response to uncertainty are limited during booms by entry of new firms but decreases in profitability are not similarly limited during slumps. The net effect of uncertainty will be to depress investment.

Real options theories of investment under uncertainty

Developing these ideas, Pindyck (1988, 1991, 1993) and Dixit and Pindyck (1994) developed their influential 'real options' approach to investment under uncertainty. They argue that uncertainty has counter-balancing effects on investment: irreversibility will lead to decreased investment under uncertainty but the desire for increased flexibility as described by Hartman and others will promote increased investment under uncertainty. The net outcome depends on which effect predominates.

Following Cukierman's (1980) ideas about optimal waiting periods, Dixit and Pindyck argue that the ability to delay investment will have an effect on investment decisions. As explained above, benefits of delay include the ability to acquire more information about the investment and, if demand falls, avoid problems of excess capacity. Costs of delaying investment include forgone cash flows and risk of entry by other firms. Following Bernanke, Dixit and Pindyck emphasize a 'bad news' principle of investment and show that downward, rather than upward, movements in output prices and profits will drive the incentive to hold onto options to invest. Pindyck (1988, 1991) and Dixit and Pindyck (1994) argue that investors will incorporate these benefits and costs into their optimization problem. They compare investment decisions to financial call options: i.e. options to buy financial assets. The option to invest has a value that includes the value of future investment opportunities that can exploit a firm's existing capacity, skills, technology and market position. Increased uncertainty increases the value of retaining the option to invest because waiting for more information is desirable. Therefore whilst the firm will hold less capital as uncertainty increases, the market value of *existing* capital will be greater, reflecting the value of *future* options to invest. On the other hand, *exercising* an option to invest involves an opportunity cost not only of the sunk costs of irreversible investment but also of the costs implicit in not being able to invest at some, possibly more favourable, future point or, on the other hand, of regretting investment decisions in the future. There are also costs involved in abandoning the opportunity to collect more information. The wedge between the value of the option and the internal rate of return can also be negative: for sequential investments, starting on a project by exercising an option to invest may have value because it may allow the release of further information about the future success of projects and therefore should be undertaken even if NPV of the project overall is negative (Roberts and Weitzman, 1987). Overall, the alternatives facing a firm are not to invest now or never. Once postponement of investment decisions is recognized as a possibility, the standard NPV rules do not apply unless the opportunity cost of exercising the option to invest is fully accounted for in NPV calculations.

Using real options principles in practice

Real options approaches are used in judging investment opportunities facing real-world firms, for example, in the oil and mining industries. In Box 9.1, Dixit and Pindyck's theory is illustrated with an application of their principles to an example of oil production.

Pindyck (1991) argues that, in practice, optimal investment rules such as NPV should be modified to advocate investment only when the value of exercising the investment option is greater than the purchase and installation cost plus the value of retaining the option. Similarly, Bertola (1989) argues that the marginal profitability needed to trigger investment under uncertainty is greater than the conventional user cost of capital. The opportunity cost of investment is highly sensitive to uncertainty about the future value of investments and therefore changes in the economic conditions that affect the risks of investment will have a profound effect, often larger than the effect of interest rate changes. Pindyck and Solimano (1993) argue that uncertainty drives a wedge between the direct cost of an investment and its net present value (NPV). This will increase the critical value at which it is optimal to exercise an option to invest.

Dixit and Pindyck (1994) argue that the use of NPV investment appraisal techniques without recognizing the opportunity cost of exercising options to invest will encourage over-investment. The existence of opportunity costs of exercising investment options may explain why real-world firms use hurdle rates of return generally three to four times the cost of capital; even allowing for differences in risk, hurdle rates are generally high relative to the unadjusted cost of capital.[3] McDonald and Siegel (1986), assuming lumpy investments and risk- averse investors, demonstrate that it is optimal to defer investment until present value is up to double the investment cost.

Box 9.1 Applying real options principles in practice

Real options principles are used by some real-world firms, for example, in the oil and mining industries where the sunk costs of irreversible investments are large. Following Dixit and Pindyck (1994), the technique can be illustrated by comparing the appraisal of an investment project using conventional *NPV* (explained in Chapter 2) versus NPV techniques adjusted for the value of retaining an option to invest. As explained on p. 12, the present value (*NPV*) of an infinite stream returns is calculated as follows, where *C* is the cost, *R* is the annual revenue (assumed here to be constant) and *r* is the discount rate:

$$NPV = \frac{R(1+r)}{r} - C$$

The example of oil production

An oil production company is thinking of building a new refinery, which will cost US$300 million to build and will produce 1 million barrels of oil per year. The price of oil is $25 per barrel. The accountant uses a 6 per cent discount rate to assess the present value of future returns. She assumes that the refinery will deliver oil indefinitely and that the price of a barrel of oil will not change once the project has begun. The present value of returns from the new refinery will be about $442 million if the refinery is built today. So, using conventional techniques, the NPV will be $142 million, i.e. $442 m revenue minus $300 m construction cost. But this approach assumes that firms are facing the decision to invest either now or never. In fact, these are not the only alternatives. Another possibility is to wait.

If the accountant recognizes that exercising the option to invest has a value and that she can wait to decide, she will adopt a different approach. She assumes that there are two possibilities for the future: by the time the new refinery is built, oil prices will have either gone up to $30 per barrel or gone down to $20. The accountant estimates that the probability of each of these outcomes is 50 per cent. In other words (to keep things simple) the expected price of oil tomorrow is $25, i.e. the same as today. The accountant decides to wait and see what happens to oil prices and she'll only invest in the new refinery if oil prices rise to $30 per barrel tomorrow. If prices fall she'll abandon the project. If she does this, she will not incur any costs today and may be able to exploit the price rises tomorrow so her adjusted *NPV* will be calculated as:

$$NPV = 0.5\left[\frac{R(1+r)}{r} - \frac{C}{1+r}\right]$$

In this case, there is a 50 per cent chance of a price increase in which case the present value of revenue will have increased to $530 million because of the oil price rise and the construction cost will have fallen to $283 m in present value terms. So when she recognizes that the option to invest has a value, the accountant calculates a *NPV* of $123.5 million. The difference between her first and second calculations is the cost of exercising the option to invest – i.e. $18.5 million in this example. Given this additional information, the accountant decides to wait for a year, to see what happens to prices, before deciding whether or not to make the investment in a new refinery.

Box 9.1 continued

Sequencing of investment projects

For the oil industry, these issues are complicated even further by the fact that not only does oil production involve large sunk costs, it also requires careful sequencing of investment stages. First, oil reserves must be found and so money is spent on oil exploration projects. Once oil is found, wells and pipelines must be built. Therefore, oil producers will face a 'sequential option' problem; they have a new option to invest each time an investment stage is finished (Dixit and Pindyck, 1994).

Ingersoll and Ross (1992) argue that the value of retaining investment options means that investment will only take place when interest rate is below a critical level that is a lot less than the internal rate of return. The wedge between this critical level and the internal rate of return increases as the volatility of interest rates increases but the effect will be ambiguous because a lowered critical interest rate implies a lower discount rate and this will raise the present value of future income from current investments and so lower the opportunity cost of exercising an option to invest.

Driver and Temple (1999) explain that real option theories can be extended to take account, not only of irreversible investment decisions, but also of constraints on a firm's expansion. In assessing the value of an option to invest, firms will also judge the negative consequences of facing increases in demand that cannot be exploited. However, as will be seen in Chapter 13, developments in the 'New Economy', particularly new inventory control methods allow businesses to respond more quickly to changes in current economic conditions. So the expansion constraints described by Driver and Temple are likely to be less substantial for today's firms.

Empirical investigations of investment under uncertainty

The existing orthodox literature on the effect of uncertainty on macro-economic investment is largely theoretical because the models constructed are difficult to translate into well-specified empirical models. So the empirical evidence about the relationship between investment and uncertainty is a-theoretical because uncertainty variables are usually introduced into empirical models on an *ad hoc* basis, via some measure of the spread of output, prices or expert forecasts. Generally in these empirical specifications, an increased spread or variance is assumed to proxy uncertainty. (Given the a-theoretical nature of the *empirical* evidence, the findings outlined below include investigations from a range of theoretical perspectives.)

Leahy and Whited (1995) analyze the investment decisions of 772 US manufacturing firms between 1981 and 1987. They measure the relative effect of aggregate or industry-wide uncertainty (measured as the variance of asset returns) and the idiosyncratic risk embedded in CAPM (Capital Asset Pricing Model), measuring the covariance between asset returns of a given firm and the returns in the market as a whole. They argue that the positive effects of uncertainty on investment will be dominated by negative effects and, on balance, increased uncertainty will lead to decreased investment. They estimate the effects of aggregate uncertainty on investment by incorporating uncertainty variables super-imposed on top of a *q* model. They find that the coefficient on uncertainty is negative but insignificant at a 5 per cent significance level. However, they argue that uncertainty may also affect investment via *q* because the uncertainty variable is insignificant in models that include *q* but is significant in models that exclude *q* and because the variance of asset returns is also highly correlated with *q*. Leahy and Whited also found a positive but insignificant relationship between the investment rate and CAPM. Therefore, they conclude that there is no evidence that firm-specific risk affects *ex post* investment.

Caballero and Pindyck (1992) argue that uncertainty has its effect on investment indirectly via the trigger/hurdle rate of return for investment. They analyze data on 20 US manufacturing sub-sectors from 1958–86 and calculate the standard deviations of marginal profitability in the 20 sectors to measure aggregate uncertainty and in 443 sub-sectors as a proxy for idiosyncratic uncertainty. They find that the standard deviations in the sub-sectors were two to three times standard deviations in the broad sectors and assert that idiosyncratic uncertainty exceeds aggregate uncertainty. They estimated partial elasticities, of the trigger rate of return in response to an increase in aggregate uncertainty, of 0.12 to 0.18. Therefore, they conclude, in agreement with Leahy and Whited, that it is systemic, economy-wide uncertainty that affects the trigger rate of return.

Pindyck and Solimano (1993) develop Caballero and Pindyck's result but relax the assumption of homogeneous firms. They allow that heterogeneous firms face different threshold rates of return. They confirm the positive relationship between uncertainty and trigger/threshold rates of return. They also assess the relationship between investment and uncertainty for panel data on 29 countries in three sub-periods: 1962–71; 1972–80; 1981–9. Again they measure uncertainty as the standard deviation of marginal profitability and they regress the investment rate on this uncertainty variable. They find a negative relationship between uncertainty and investment for their full sample of countries. They also attempt to explain the volatility of marginal profitability in terms of economic and political uncertainty by including changes in inflation, real exchange rates and real interest rates and various political variables (including the probabilities of change in government, assassinations, crisis, strikes, riots, revolutions and constitutional change). They found that the major influence on the volatility of investment was the standard deviation of changes in inflation and argue that political uncertainty has little impact on the volatility of marginal profitability and investment. They use this result to argue that the focus of government policies encouraging investment should be the control of inflation.

Pindyck and Solimano also ran time-series regressions using annual data from 1960–90 for the 30 countries in their sample. They split their sample into high inflation and low inflation countries arguing that high, volatile inflation may indicate a lack of government control. Policies in high inflation countries will be perceived as risky and unsustainable and as a consequence firms will abandon/delay their investment decisions. For both low inflation OECD countries and high inflation developing countries they find that only the level of inflation has significant negative impact on investment. They argue that this result may reflect the fact that the standard deviations of inflation, the real exchange rate and the level of inflation are highly correlated. They conclude that increased volatility increases the trigger rate of return on investment and thus leads to a decrease in investment spending in the short-run. However, the long-run effects are unclear. They also emphasize that their results may reflect the restrictive assumptions of their model and the small sample of countries used. They also acknowledge that instability may affect different types of investment in different ways and that it is difficult to measure and interpret instability because of its complexity.

Price (1995) models the impact of uncertainty on investment in the UK manufacturing sector using quarterly data from 1963–94 and incorporating an error correction mechanism to separate short-run dynamics from long-run equilibrium. He measures uncertainty as the conditional variance of output. He relates long-run investment to capacity utilization, interest rates and uncertainty. He finds that real interest rates are not significantly related to investment even when included with up to four lags (using quarterly data). He also finds that uncertainty is significantly correlated with investment only if the variance of output exceeds some critical level. He estimates a long-run responsiveness of investment with respect to uncertainty of about 60 per cent but argues that slow dynamics in aggregate investment (reflecting delivery lags and adjustment costs) prevent dramatic collapses in investment in response to uncertainty. He concludes that uncertainty slows the process of adjustment, affecting both the level of investment and the adjustment to equilibrium. (His results must be qualified by the fact that there is some evidence of autocorrelation at a 5 per cent significance level, possibly indicating model misspecification.)

Acemoglu (1993) devises an accelerator model of investment but with a rational expectations interpretation of the influence of output on investment given imperfect information. He argues that output acts as a signal to rational investors about the activity of other investors in the economy. Aggregate investment will create positive externalities: for example, technological externalities, spill-overs from training, learning by doing, innovation and aggregate demand externalities. These external economies will make it more desirable for individual firms to follow the crowd when deciding about investments and herd behaviour results, reflecting the fact that fixed investors learn from each other. However, aggregate investment is not easily observable and rational agents will learn to deduce current investment from other variables. Output data is more readily available and more reliable than investment data and investors will extract information about current investment from output. Thus as output increases investment will increase. If output is more volatile and noisy, the extraction of a signal about investment from the data on output becomes more difficult, uncertainty will increase and investment will be delayed. Similarly, as noise decreases, signal extraction will become more accurate and whilst the initial response of investment to decreased noise in output will be cautious, as evidence accumulates, investment will increase.

Acemoglu analyzes US quarterly data from 1965–89 and UK quarterly data from 1965–90 using various lags. He finds that, for the USA, output Granger-causes investment and investment Granger-causes output; and for the UK, that output Granger-causes investment but that there is no reverse effect. He measures uncertainty as the conditional variance of output and finds that the variance of output has significant negative effects on investment in the UK, although there are positive but insignificant effects on investment for some lag structures. In the USA the effects are insignificant. Acemoglu (1993) concludes that the predictive power of output falls as its variance increases and argues that this gives evidence in support of his learning explanation of accelerator theory.

Federer (1993) assesses the hypothesis that conflicting news encourages agents to wait for extra information. Ferderer proxies uncertainty by creating a forecaster discord variable, derived from the standard deviations of growth, unemployment, short-term and long-term interest rates and inflation forecasts from the US Blue Chip survey. Ferderer builds two models of investment based on the models of Barro (1990) and Clark (1979). Barro uses lagged values of real stock price returns to explain investment. Clark uses lagged real GNP and real corporate bond interest rates as explanatory variables. Federer regresses these two models using US annual data from 1978–91. The results from Federer's estimation of Barro's model suggest that lagged stock returns have positive but insignificant effects on investment; this contrasts with Barro's own results. The parameter on lagged forecaster discord is negative and significant in most models although inflation rate discord is insignificant. Industrial production forecaster discord is significant. For the Clark model, lagged real GNP growth is positive and significant and real interest rates are insignificant. Coefficients on forecaster discord are negative, with industrial production and interest rate uncertainty having the most significant effects. The effects of forecaster discord are robust across both types of model and the relative importance of the different types of discord is consistent. Real uncertainty (industrial production and short-term interest rate uncertainty) has the most significant impact on investment. This result conflicts with that of

Pindyck and Solimano (1993), who found that inflation uncertainty had the most crucial impact on investment.[4]

Driver and Moreton (1992a, pp. 112–37; 1992b) and Temple, Driver and Urga (2001) argue that uncertainty deters investment because of risk-aversion, technological non-linearities, probable costs of unsold production and dynamic considerations. They adopt a putty-clay approach, following King (1972), in which total production costs are minimized subject to a target for output. They argue that investment can be specified as a function of required new capital, relative factor prices and profits.[5] Driver and Moreton argue that uncertainty will depress and smooth the optimal capacity adjustment path and that there will be a long-run effect of demand uncertainty on the capital–output ratio and therefore investment.

Driver and Moreton run regressions for UK manufacturing investment in plant and machinery between 1978Q4 and 1987Q4. Uncertainty is captured using the standard deviations of a range of year-ahead forecasts of output growth and inflation from 12 forecasting teams, as reported in *The Investor's Chronicle*. All coefficients were significant and of the expected sign and the influences of output uncertainty and inflation uncertainty were strongly negative. Driver and Moreton find that output uncertainty has the greater effect. They estimate a long-run elasticity of investment with respect to uncertainty of –0.15. These findings confirm Price's result that uncertainty affects long-run investment and does not merely increase the likelihood of delaying investment decisions. These results confirm Federer's results rather than Pindyck and Solimano's in suggesting that real uncertainty has a greater influence on investment activity than price/inflation uncertainty.

Alvarez and Koskela (2002) assess the impact of interest rate volatility as a measure of uncertainty. They also assess the impact of revenue variability on irreversible investment projects. They argue that whether or not interest rate changes encourage or discourage investment will depend upon whether or not the prevailing interest rate is above or below its long-run steady state value. They also find an interactive effect for the different types of uncertainty with revenue volatility reinforcing interest rate volatility and vice versa.

Judging the theoretical implications of all these empirical results is problematic because the finding of negative relationships between investment and uncertainty is essentially a-theoretical: both mainstream and Post Keynesian economists predict this result and a problem emerges in separating the empirical findings from the theoretical under-pinnings. As was explained in Chapter 6, conceptions of uncertainty differ radically between mainstream analyses and Post Keynesian analyses, the latter being grounded in a world of unquantifiable Knightian uncertainty rather than quantifiable risk. Driver and Temple (1999) and Aiginger (1987) argue that the empirical evidence does seem to favour models set in a world of quantifiable uncertainty over a Post Keynesian approach, although they do acknowledge that limits on rationality and the importance of conventional behaviours both need to be properly addressed in mainstream investment models. Driver and Temple (1999) also admit that it is difficult to apply real options theory to macroeconomic investment because real-world businesses are operating in a world of imperfect competition. In this sense the macroeconomic evidence in favour of real options theories over Post Keynesian theories is limited. So, ultimately, the jury is still out when it comes to judging the relative merits of mainstream versus Post Keynesian empirical analyses of investment under uncertainty.

Conclusion

In terms of recent developments within the analysis of fixed asset investment, it seems that there is some consensus that uncertainty will have a depressing effect on investment, even in a world of perfectly rational agents. This result evolves from a further modification of the broad maximizing approach adopted within Jorgenson's model. In the real world, investment decisions are irreversible. Even strongly rational agents will respond in quite a different way in a world in which investment decisions represent a commitment over a substantial period of time that cannot easily be reversed. In such a world, even rational investors will respond negatively to uncertainty. In this sense there has been theoretical convergence in the recognition that uncertainty deters investment activity. However, whilst the negative uncertainty effect is and always has been essential to Keynes's and Post Keynesian approaches, in many orthodox approaches uncertainty is introduced into investment models on an *ad hoc* basis, in much the same way that expectations were introduced *ad hoc* into Jorgenson's model. This does not help to resolve theoretical disputes about the relative merits of rational optimizing approaches versus Keynesian approaches because the uncertainty result can be captured in a range of theoretical models. The Post Keynesians adopt quite a different approach to their analysis of investment in the face of uncertainty and these approaches are discussed in the following chapter.

Chapter summary

1. In the 1980s, in response to the empirical limitations of Jorgensonian and *q* theories of investment, mainstream empirical research shifted to an analysis of the relationship between investment and uncertainty.
2. Real options cost theorists, for example, Dixit and Pindyck (1994), postulate a negative relationship between investment and uncertainty, assuming irreversible investment. They argue that investment decisions are like financial call options and exercising the option to invest involves opportunity costs. These opportunity costs arise because there are benefits in waiting for more information before deciding whether or not to invest.
3. Uncertainty is important within these theories because, with uncertainty, more information is valuable and so the benefits of waiting are likely to increase. So uncertainty usually increases the opportunity cost of exercising an option to invest. In real options theories, a 'bad news principle' operates: if investments are irreversible, then the possibility of bad news drives the incentive to wait.

Chapter summary continued

4. Standard approaches to the use of NPV as an investment appraisal technique are misleading according to the options theorists because investors are not facing a decision between investing now or never. Instead, investors are assumed to have control over the timing of their investment decisions and so they should be calculating NPVs to describe each possibility as far as the timing of investments is concerned. The options cost theorists argue that using standard NPV techniques that do not take account of the opportunity costs involved in exercising options to invest will lead to over-investment.
5. The empirical evidence from the estimation of real options models of investment confirms the hypothesis that uncertainty depresses investment but this finding is essentially a-theoretical because the Post Keynesian theorists also emphasize the negative relationship between uncertainty and fixed asset investment.

Revision questions

1. Although most economists argue that there will be a negative relationship between investment and uncertainty, some economists have argued that a positive relationship is also possible. How do these economists defend their assertion that these may be some positive relationship between investment and uncertainty?
2. What are the opportunity costs associated with making a decision to invest?
3. Why do the options cost theorists argue that the timing of investment decisions is important?
4. How are net present value (NPV) investment appraisal rules affected by the presence of uncertainty?
5. Explain how a negative relationship between investment and uncertainty can be explained by the options cost theorists?
6. Why is the finding of a negative relationship between investment and uncertainty theoretically limited?

10 Post Keynesian analyses of investment

Introduction 125
Limits on rationality in Post Keynesian analyses 126
Post Keynesian analyses of money and finance 127
Conclusion 133
Chapter summary 133
Revision questions 134

The neo-classical and other orthodox theories of investment outlined so far are based upon the assumption that fixed investors are well-informed profit maximizers. Investors behave in mechanical ways and a number of assumptions are used to describe human behaviour: i.e. that people form rational expectations, that uncertainty is measurable and that macroeconomic relationships can be described by aggregating the microeconomic behaviour of firms and individuals. This aggregation process is based upon an assumption of 'methodological individualism': the assumption that the macroeconomy can be described atomistically by describing its constituent microeconomic parts. These simplifying assumptions allow the creation of a logically coherent theory that can be analyzed mathematically and is relatively easy to understand – being based essentially on the insight that people balance marginal benefits and marginal costs. However, orthodox theories are criticized by Post Keynesian theorists because they do not seem to fit well with observations of real-world investor behaviour. Post Keynesians argue that a completely different approach to investment theory is needed if investor behaviour is to be properly understood. In this chapter, some Post Keynesian theories of investment are outlined. Following Keynes, Post Keynesians incorporate quite different understandings of human behaviour because they do not believe that investors are rational profit maximizers. The influence of uncertainty is always central but, again, it is not treated in the same way as described in Chapter 9. Overall, Post Keynesians argue that uncertainty about the future is inherently unmeasurable and this means that psychological forces, for example, animal spirits and herd instincts, will have strong influences on investment activity.

Introduction

As described in Chapters 4–9, orthodox theories of investment incorporate a wide range of assumptions that are often criticized as unrealistic. Economists such as Friedman (1953) and Hahn (1973*a*, 1973*b*, 1985) adopt a range of defences for this lack of realism in orthodox theory: for example, that orthodox models are justifiable abstractions that illuminate our understanding of reality; that they provide a 'benchmark' to work towards; that they have predictive power. However, the Post Keynesian economists argue that the unrealism of these assumptions invalidates orthodox theory. They argue that a completely different approach to investment theory is needed, based upon fundamentally different understandings of the nature of human economic decision-making to those seen in orthodox theory. Because the Post Keynesians tend to avoid simplifying assumptions, there is no simple theoretical backbone to the range of ideas described. This means that the literature cannot easily be summarized. So in this chapter, a few key Post Keynesian debates relevant to investment theory are summarized including analyses of uncertainty and expectations; and the role of money, finance, savings, profits and the Stock Market.[1]

Limits on rationality in Post Keynesian analyses

One possible reason for the mixed empirical performance of many orthodox empirical models of investment is that the rationality assumptions of optimizing behaviour and rational expectations are unrealistic. Simon (1979) distinguishes between the conceptions of rationality seen in neo-classical models and alternative models by separating the concepts of substantive rationality and procedural rationality. The investors described in Jorgenson's model, *q* theory and real options approaches are substantively rational: they form quantifiable expectations of the future and operate objectively to maximize profits given the constraints that they face. Simon (1979) argues that orthodox descriptions of 'substantively rational' goal-oriented, optimizing behaviour may be inappropriate to the analysis of many aspects of economic decision-making. Alternative Post Keynesian approaches to the description of rational decision-making allow 'procedurally rational' behaviour, or behaviour which is the result of 'appropriate deliberation' rather than precise mathematical calculation. This view of rationality may be more appropriate to the analysis of economic phenomena such as investment activity. Adopting Simon's insight, this section summarizes some Post Keynesian approaches to the modelling of investment, many of which incorporate assumptions of procedurally rather than substantively rational investment. They follow from the approach adopted by Keynes in his analyses of rationality, expectations and investment in *A Treatise on Probability* (1921), *The General Theory of Employment, Interest and Money* (1936) and 'The General Theory of Employment' (1937).

Rather than focusing on profit maximizing behaviour by rational investors, Post Keynesian analyses focus on the profound impacts of uncertainty in a non-deterministic world. Given Keynes's emphasis on psychological factors, a number of Post Keynesian economists have attempted to assess the rationality of investor behaviour within Keynes's analysis but this has proved to be a complex task. As explained in Chapter 3, Keynes believed that conventional behaviour, i.e. following the crowd, propels a lot of investor behaviour. Keynes argues that conventions may be rational, non-rational or irrational depending on the nature of belief determining behaviour. If people adopt conventions because they realize that others may have more information or because they believe that money can be made from following the crowd, then that is probably reasonable if not rational behaviour.[2] But if people adopt conventions on a whim then that is likely to be non-rational or irrational. However, Keynes's conventions cannot be easily understood in terms of individual rationality because they reflect the overlap between individual and aggregate behaviour, where aggregate behaviour affects individual behaviour and vice versa.[3] Keynes observes that it is not rational for one individual to believe, in isolation, that the current situation can be projected into the future but given that outcomes are determined by the aggregate behaviour, a conventional belief in the current situation as a guide to the future does have a reasonable basis.[4]

A range of views exists among Post Keynesians about Keynes's view about investors' capacity for rational behaviour.[5] Bateman (1990); Dow and Dow (1985); Gerrard (1994); Littleboy (1990); Meeks (1991); O'Donnell (1989, 1991b); and Skidelsky (1992) argue that there is continuity in the development of Keynes's understanding of rational behaviour between his early work on probability and rational belief as elucidated in *A Treatise on Probability* (TP) and his later ideas, e.g. as outlined in *The General Theory* (GT). These economists argue that, in terms of Keynes's theory of rationality developed in TP, the economic behaviour described in Keynes's GT is rational, given lack of information about the future. In contrast, Mini (1990), Shackle (1955, 1967, 1972) and Winslow (1986) emphasize the subjectivism of economic behaviour and, to them, Keynes presents the volatile characteristics of the economy as the result of irrationality, viciousness and destructiveness (Mini, 1990).

A further group of interpretations occupies the middle ground between the polar emphasis on rational calculation versus irrational animal spirits. Carabelli (1988), Colander and Guthrie (1980), Crotty (1992), Davidson (1965, 1978, 1991a), Howitt (1996), Lawson (1981, 1985, 1995), Littleboy (1990), Minsky (1975, 1986), Robinson (1979) and Runde (1991, 1996) argue that, in GT, the expectations and the conventions that determine them are sensible and reasonable rather than strictly rational or irrational. Robinson (1979) views Keynes's conventions as non-rational and Littleboy (1990, p. 34) argues that 'conventional behaviour lies between two extremes, the fully rational and the fully irrational'. Conventions are not the same as customs/habits. They emerge from rational, purpose-oriented behaviour under uncertainty and promote coherent behaviour (Littleboy, 1990, p. 271). According to Crotty (1992), social conventions 'create' and 'imagine' the missing data which links the logical chain connecting data to decisions.

Post Keynesian analyses of money and finance

Some Post Keynesians have moved beyond the interpretation of Keynes's key insights in GT and TP by developing Keynes's style of analysis. For example, a second strand in the Post Keynesian literature on investment has focused on developing Keynes's analysis of the importance of money and finance in a world of uncertainty and in particular the problems that emerge from financial constraints on investment decisions. These refinements of Keynes's approach form an alternative to the Modigliani–Miller assumption, which was described in Chapter 6.[6] To recap: Modigliani and Miller (1958) showed that in a world of perfect capital markets, the costs of different forms of financing will be the same for all firms in a given risk category. Their implication was that the form of financing used by firms has no impact on the cost of finance and so financing choices do not affect investment decisions.

Post Keynesians reacted against this approach in arguing that money plays a crucial role given the existence of uncertainty. Following Keynes (1937) they argue that, in an uncertain world, money is a barometer of our distrust of our own calculations and conventions. Keynes argued that money exerts its effect on investment decisions in two ways: first, via interest rates – which are determined by the interaction of liquidity preferences (demand for money) and the supply of money;[7] and second, via the 'business motive' (or 'finance motive') (Davidson 1965). Keynes describes this finance motive as a component of the transactions demand for money and it includes businesses' demand for cash in order to bridge the interval between incurring costs and receiving revenues. Keynes points out that investors do not have an unlimited command over money and therefore investment is affected not only by general business confidence but also the state of credit: i.e. the willingness of banks to lend. Collapses in equity prices precipitate slumps by weakening the state of credit and the willingness of financial institutions to lend to potential investors. Either a collapse in the state of credit or in the state of confidence is sufficient for economic activity to collapse but a recovery in both is required for investment to recover. Therefore, financial factors will be a crucial determinant of the cycle.

So in contrast to the Modigliani–Miller approach of financing neutrality, Post Keynesian theorists argue that the availability of finance is a crucial constraint on investment decision-making and both the supply and price of money are endogenously determined, created by developments within the economy rather than external forces. This means that capitalist systems are characterized by inherent instability as uncertainty in one sector spreads so easily through the macroeconomy. For example, Harcourt and Sardoni (1995) argue that imbalances between finance capital and industrial capital are the sources of crisis and instability. Also, Davidson (1978) argues that because money is an uncertainty barometer, the speculative demand for finance will increase in times of uncertainty. Liquid reserves give decision-makers time to think, to interpret market signals and to meet existing commitments before making decisions (Davidson, 1965, 1978, 1980). If the money supply is created endogenously, i.e. within the system, to satisfy business demands for liquidity, instability within the system will spread to deter lenders. The consequent decrease in liquidity in the private sector will limit firms' ability to exploit investment opportunities. Consequently, aggregate output and employment will decline (Davidson, 1978).

Kalecki on profits and corporate savings

Michal Kalecki also introduced some of these issues in his analyses of macroeconomy. Both Kalecki and Keynes were writing at similar times, with similar insights. Kalecki (1943) argued that one way in which financing constraints will affect capital accumulation (net investment) decisions is via profits. Profits will determine firms' ability to invest in the future. However, the relationship is complex because a double-sided relationship exists between capital accumulation and profits: profits will finance investments but actual investment expenditure will lead to capital accumulation (i.e. will augment the capital stock) creating expected profits for the future. Joan Robinson (1964*b*) developed these ideas, illustrating the double-sided relationship between capital accumulation and profits. But she argued that it will not be a stable relation and will be changing all the time because of volatile animal spirits.

Kalecki (1943) focuses on the role of profits and savings to investment financing decisions and argues that the rate of investment is increasing in gross corporate savings, decreasing in the rate of change in capital stock and increasing in the rate of change in profits. So Kalecki constructed the following model to describe investment:

$$D = aS + b\frac{\Delta P}{\Delta t} - c\frac{\Delta K}{\Delta t} + d$$

where D is the rate of investment, S is gross savings, $\Delta P/\Delta t$ is the rate of change in profits, $\Delta K/\Delta t$ is the rate of change in capital stock and d is a deterministic trend.[8]

This model is consistent with Kalecki's earlier insight that the availability of finance is a crucial constraint on investment decision-making and, like the Post Keynesian theories outlined above, contrasts with the financing neutrality assumption of Modigliani–Miller. Kalecki's (1937*b*) 'principle of increasing risk' describes the effects of debt and declining liquidity on borrowing costs and businesses' willingness to invest. In booms, more investment decisions take place and, because fixed investment must be financed, debts build up at the same time. Although output and employment rise as a result of this increasing economic activity, the stock of debt becomes increasingly risky and as the increasing debt build-up becomes unsustainable, lenders start to increase the risk premia that they attach to their lending rates. This has a depressing effect on new investments. Kalecki (1937*b*) argues that the more entrepreneurs have to rely on outside finance rather than their own capital, the greater will be the level of risk involved with investments, so firms' own corporate savings will be a less risky and cheaper source of funds with crucial impacts on investment decision.

Similarly, Mahdavi, Sohrabian and Kholdy (1994) argue that sources of internal funds are a more crucial constraint on investment activity than external funds. The volume of internal funds not only determines a business's ability to raise more funds but also cushions them against adverse developments. As businesses' ratios of debt to equity rise, both lender's and borrower's risk will increase. The increased borrower's risk will be translated into an increased discount rate and a decreased demand price of capital. The increased lender's risk will be manifested in increased costs of borrowing.

Stegman (1982, 1983) captures some of these influences by allowing for the effects of changes in corporate profitability on investment, within an accelerator framework. In his models profitability is tested as a constraint, rather than a conventional explanatory variable, using the techniques of 'switching regressions'. Stegman finds that his switching regression, allowing profitability constraints, out-performs a conventional accelerator specification.

Minksy's financial fragility hypothesis

Ideas about the importance of money and finance to real investment decisions are also developed by Minsky (1978, 1986). Palley (2001) argues that Minsky provides a 'weak' alternative to the neo-classical specifications of *q* theory outlined in Chapter 8. Minsky disagrees with the 'efficient markets hypothesis': that asset prices reflect the fundamental value of expected future returns from assets. Instead, Minsky agrees with Keynes that Stock Market activity reflects attempts to outwit the crowd rather than make accurate judgements of the demand price of capital. In this way, Minsky states that changes in equity prices do not signal much about the expected profitability of a firm in the long-term. However, Stock Market changes do affect the cost of capital. When stock markets are doing well and equity prices are high relative to output prices, investment will be buoyant and the costs of external financing will be low. In contrast, when equity prices are low, the costs of external financing will be high and investment will be depressed.

Minsky also builds upon Kalecki's ideas, for example the 'principle of increasing risk', in explaining the role played by endogenous money and finance in propelling bubbles and crises. Minsky argues that the banking system, in its ability to create money, holds the key to boosting investment. The interaction of financial factors determining investment decisions generates endogenous instability, i.e. instability that feeds upon itself, and this contrasts with the orthodox approaches outlined in Chapter 9 which essentially assume that uncertainty is an exogenous force.

Minsky asserts that conventional theory cannot explain financial crisis – first, because of its emphasis on the role of markets in generating full employment and second, because the role of endogenous money in capitalist economies is not fully explained in orthodox theory. Minsky builds upon Keynes's analysis of inefficient and perverse endogenous market processes and upon Keynes's insight that the state of credit can have as much influence on investment decisions as the state of confidence.

Minsky argues that lending institutions respond to general economic confidence when making their decisions. The banking system, in its ability to create money, holds the key to boosting investment. This interaction of the state of confidence and the state of credit amplifies deviations and these deviations spread throughout the macroeconomy. The resulting interdependencies between markets mean that an equilibrium position is not easily reached.

Minsky also reinforces the earlier Post Keynesian and Kaleckian insights that just as profits determine investment so investment determines profits. Current investment determines the ability of businesses to finance their debts in the future because it adds to the capital stock that eventually generates profits. Minsky argues that, in reaching equilibrium, short-run expectations of profits must be in line with financed investment and profit flows must be sufficient to meet debt obligations. So profits will affect the long-run expectations of businesses and provide the crucial dynamic link within a capitalist system. It is the expectation of future profit that makes debt financing possible but these future profits will only emerge if investment continues in the future. So Minsky describes profits as the carrot and the stick that make capitalism work.

These ideas are incorporated in Minsky's (1986) 'financial fragility hypothesis'. In this theory, Minsky reiterates that finance and investment are interdependent and exert crucial influences on the development of the business cycle. Minsky's theory is based upon the insight that there are three basic types of 'financial posture' that together make up the debt structure underlying the financing of investment decisions: hedge finance, speculative finance and Ponzi finance. These different forms of financing involve different levels of risks for both the borrowers and lenders because they are funding investment projects with differing spreads of expected returns.

Hedge finance

Hedge finance is the relatively risk-free financing of investment decisions and finances safe investments. It is the sort of lending that is relatively secure because it is used to fund investments for which the cash flows accruing from past investments exceed cash flow commitments (i.e. for the repayment of borrowings) so the expected present value of hedge finance units is positive for finite interest rates.

Speculative finance

Speculative financing is more risky than hedge financing because it finances investment for which the short-term cash flows expected from sales exceed the short-term interest costs of debt, and expected long-term cash flows are enough to allow the repayment of the money borrowed. So speculative financing, whilst more risky than hedge financing, is sustainable as long as economic conditions remain stable.

Ponzi finance

The riskiest fixed investments are financed via Ponzi finance units. Ponzi financing is in essence a gamble, based on a hope of profit bonanzas in the *future*. But current cash flows fall short of both interest costs of debt and repayment commitments. So holders of Ponzi finance in effect expect increasing cash flows only in the future and are *hoping* that these will enable them to repay their debts. Some of the dot.com companies of the late 1990s were financed in this way, such as boo.com.

The mixture of these three types of financing unit will change according to the state of expectations and the history of the economy. In stable times, there will be a decline in the precautionary and speculative demand for money as uncertainty is less prevalent. The fall in demand for money promotes declines in interest rates and these will lead to a rise in the demand price of capital assets. The demand price of capital (i.e. the present value of expected future revenues – defined in Chapter 3) will rise because the present value of future expected cash flows has risen as a result of the falling interest rate. There will be a portfolio shift towards speculative and Ponzi finance units and banks will endogenously create money in response to these boom conditions. However, this over-optimism encourages excessive reliance on debt financing. When businesses realize that their ability to service their debt is falling, they will also recognize the increasing risk of their investment plans and they will start to worry about spending more money on new investment projects. As investment takes place, profits increase but this encourages not just further investment but also rises in the price of capital assets. As inflationary pressures develop, the banking system will respond to rising uncertainty by constraining the supply of finance. The consequent increasing inelasticity in the supply of finance will be accompanied by increasingly inelastic demand for finance, reflecting the fact that some investment projects are already in process and future stages of investment and investment financing cannot easily be abandoned. This combination of inelastic demand and supply for finance leads to rapid increases in short-term interest rates.

In addition, as the proportion of speculative and Ponzi units dominates, the economy becomes increasingly sensitive to interest rate variations thus pushing a proportion of investment projects into unsustainable Ponzi finance units. This promotes increasingly rapid rises in short-term interest rates, in turn leading to rises in long-term interest rates. The rise in interest rates will lead to a fall in investment and as profits are driven by investment, profits will start to fall. The financial crisis is under way. Interest rates and borrowing costs rise, reflecting increasing risk premia as well as imbalances between the supply of and demand for money. Falling profits fuel falling investment. The fall in profits also means that the ability to service debts falls: hedge finance units become speculative finance units; speculative finance units become Ponzi finance units. The holders of Ponzi debt are forced to sell assets to meet payments but as the price of assets has fallen, so the ability to avoid default is constrained. Revenues from production will fall as assets are sold. Furthermore, 'present value reversals' will take place as rising interests lead to falls in the demand price of capital because the present value of future revenues will fall. This in turn contributes to further falls in investment and profits. In the end, the ability even to meet payments on relatively safe hedge finance units is reduced. The overall level of default increases, compounding financial instability.

So, according to Minsky, the seeds of of financial crisis are sown during euphoric, expansionary phases. It is during periods of tranquillity that the price of holding money declines. And this is when capital asset prices, the demand price of capital and investment increase and portfolios shift towards Ponzi and speculative units. But it is this portfolio shift that contributes to the financial crises characterizing the end of boom phases.

Minsky concludes that during phases of crisis and deflation, endogenous market processes are inefficient and perverse and so capitalist economies need robust financial institutions (such as a strong central bank) to guide finance and investment and to reduce the sensitivity of aggregate investment to the vagaries of private sector financing of investment projects.

Conclusion

Within Post Keynesian analyses, uncertainty, profits and finance play key roles in the determination of investment decisions. However, in contrast to the uncertainty models analyzed in Chapter 8, in Post Keynesian models, agents are not fully rational. Uncertainty limits both the availability of accurate information and the ability to act rationally. So businesses will use a range of devices, such as following the crowd and adopting conventional behaviour, in formulating their investment decisions. Post Keynesian models are grounded in a world of uncertainty; money and finance are essential to understanding investment activity. The banking system can create money endogenously and not all sources of financing are equal. This also means that profits will be central to investment decision-making. The conclusion from these models is that capitalist systems will be characterized by a lot of instability. Markets will not necessarily work effectively to secure an adequate or appropriate volume of investment activity and thus governments must play a key role in moderating uncertainty, for example, by controlling speculative forces, and in encouraging investors to look to the long-term.

Chapter summary

1. The Post Keynesian economists adopt an alternative approach to investment theory to the orthodox theorists. They argue that the assumptions of rational expectations and profit maximization do not illuminate the real processes that determine investment in the real world.
2. Post Keynesian alternatives to orthodox theories of investment tend to focus on limits to rationality, the importance of profits and the effects of money and finance on investment activity.

Chapter summary continued

3. Simon distinguishes between concepts of rationality seen in orthodox versus alternative models. In the orthodox literature, investors are described as being 'substantively rational': i.e. they are maximizing an objective, measurable function, subject to given constraints. In contrast, in Post Keynesian analysis, investors are generally 'procedurally rational'. They are using 'appropriate deliberation' when deciding about investments: i.e. they are acting reasonably.
4. Post Keynesians believe that reality cannot be described by fixed, immutable constants. The existence of unmeasurable uncertainty means that it is difficult, if not impossible, to quantify expectations of the future and so psychological factors will exert key influences on aggregate investment activity. Herd behaviours, feedback effects and deviation-amplifying tendencies suggest that describing macroeconomic behaviour by aggregating microeconomic relationships, via a representative agents hypothesis, will be of limited use.
5. Another group of Post Keynesian theorists focus on the role of profits as a crucial form of financing for fixed asset investments. These concepts build upon Kalecki's ideas about the role of profits as well as upon Keynes's ideas. The association between profits and investment is complex in these analyses because there is a double-sided relationship between capital accumulation (net investment) and profits: profits finance investment and investments, by augmenting the capital stock, create profits in the future. However, these relationships are not necessarily stable because they are propelled by volatile animal spirits and so may be shifting all the time.
6. Other Post Keynesian theories focus on the role of endogenous money and finance (i.e. money created within the system in response to economic developments). Lending institutions will respond to buoyant conditions by lending more money but they will withdraw money when they think that financial crisis is imminent.
7. Some of these ideas form the basis of Minsky's financial fragility hypothesis. Minsky's theory is based upon the insight that there are three basic types of 'financial posture' that together make up the debt structure that finances investment decisions: hedge finance, speculative finance and Ponzi finance. Fixed asset investment projects are dependent upon all these forms of finance but in boom phases excessive risks are taken with lending and borrowing encouraging portfolio shifts towards risky Ponzi units. As these risks are recognized and rising interest rates result, the process of investment will be destabilized and economies will head into recession, unless governments intervene.

Revision questions

1. What are the key differences between the descriptions of human behaviour seen in Post Keynesian analysis and those in Jorgenson's analysis?
2. How are the theories of Keynes and Kalecki connected?

3. Which of Keynes's insights (as outlined in Chapter 3) re-surface in Minsky's financial fragility hypothesis?
4. What do Post Keynesians mean when they assert that money is created endogenously? Explain how money may be created endogenously.
5. What parallels exist between Post Keynesian investment theories and the orthodox theories outlined in Chapters 4–9.

Part III

Testing the Theories

11 Comparing Jorgenson's model and accelerator theory: evidence from the UK 139

12 Uncertainty in competing models of investment: evidence from the USA 149

Introduction

As the theoretical sections illustrated, there are key areas of disagreement amongst economists about the determinants of investment behaviour. Which of these theories is most illuminating? In comparing theories, a number of issues are important, such as the extent to which a theory illuminates our understanding of the real world, the logical consistency of a theory and the extent to which theoretical models can be used to predict economic behaviour. Mankiw (1989) argues that the relative virtues of divergent approaches can be understood in terms of their 'internal consistency' versus 'external consistency'. Neo-classical theory is internally consistent because all the pieces of the theory hang together in a logical way: it is built up from basic axioms or principles to give a logical result. The problem is that neo-classical theory is not so good at capturing real events: it lacks external consistency. Post Keynesian theories suffer from the opposite problem: they evolve out of observing the real world and so often possess a great deal of external consistency. But critics argue that if Post Keynesian theories emerge just from observation of the world, they must be *ad hoc* generalizations and not necessarily internally consistent constructions with logical underpinnings.

What does the empirical evidence suggest? Are relative factor costs important, as argued by the neo-classical theorists? Or are the accelerator theorists right that output growth is the sole determinant of investment behaviour? Does Stock Market information provide an important signal about the future potential of investments, as argued by the *q* theorists? If so, how do rational investors use this information? How important is uncertainty? All these are questions that an examination of purely theoretical information can never resolve. A good way to start however to resolve some of these debates is to have a look at the data; the following two chapters analyze US and UK investment data in an attempt to establish which of the theoretical ideas presented in the theoretical chapters have more empirical support.

11 Comparing Jorgenson's model and accelerator theory: evidence from the UK

The theoretical models 140
Estimation procedures 141
Empirical findings 142
Model comparison and non-nested hypothesis tests 145
Conclusion 146
Chapter summary 147
Data appendix 148

A number of models of investment have been presented in the previous chapters including the neo-classical, accelerator and *q* theories and Post Keynesian analyses of investment. So far, the econometric results from the application of orthodox models to real-world data has revealed a wide range of results although there is empirical agreement about a negative correlation between aggregate investment and measures of uncertainty. The aims of this chapter are first to provide a further test of the different approaches to investment analysis, focusing in particular on the estimation of accelerator and neo-classical models and second, to illustrate how basic econometric techniques can be used to test competing theoretical hypotheses.

The theoretical models

Accelerator theory

As described in Chapter 4, accelerator theorists postulate that investment will be a process of capital stock adjustment to a desired level, as dictated by a fixed capital–output ratio. In deciding about their desired capital stock, investors will proxy future profit expectations by looking at current and past levels of output and demand. In addition, they will moderate their investment decisions if the capital stock was under-utilized in the previous period. Simple specifications of accelerator models incorporate an implicit assumption that the capital adjustment process will take place over just one period of time. This limitation is addressed within flexible accelerator models. These introduce lags into the investment process to capture the delayed effects of investment decisions, for example, due to decision, financing, production, delivery, installation and adjustment lags. The incorporation of a distributed lag structure into accelerator models is also consistent with models of investment incorporating adaptive, extrapolative or regressive expectations. In this chapter, a flexible accelerator model of the following form was estimated:

$$i_{\mathrm{gt}} = \alpha + \sum_{n=0}^{8} \beta_n y_{t-n} + \sum_{n=0}^{8} \varphi_n CU_{t-n} + (\delta - 1)k_{t-1} + \varepsilon_t$$

where y is the natural log of output, i_{gt} is the natural log of gross investment, k_{t-1} is the natural log of the capital stock, CU is the index of capacity utilization and ε_{t} is a stochastic error term; α is the intercept, β_n and φ_n are the slope parameters on the y and CU variables and δ is the depreciation parameter.

Jorgenson's model

As discussed in Chapter 5, Jorgenson's neo-classical theory also represents investment as a process of adjustment to an optimal capital stock. But in neo-classical theory gross investment is determined not only by a scale effect but also by a relative factor cost effect. The scale effect is captured by the parameters on output, and the relative factor cost effect is captured by the parameters on C, the user cost of capital. Following Bischoff (1969), the investment model estimated here is described as a distributed lag function of C (the user cost of capital), y and lagged capital stock (K):

$$I_{\mathrm{gt}} = \alpha + \sum_{n=0}^{8} \mu_{cn} C_{t-n} + \sum_{n=0}^{8} \mu_{yn} y_{t-n} + \delta k_{t-1} + \varepsilon_t$$

Bischoff (1969), following Jorgenson, defines the post-tax user cost of capital as:

$$C = \left(\frac{p_K(r + \partial) - \dot{p}_K}{p_O} \right) \frac{(1 - \tau_c z)}{(1 - \tau_c)}$$

where p_O = price of output
p_K/p_O = relative price of capital goods
τ_c = marginal tax rate
r = Fisher's real interest rate captured by redemption yield minus inflation
δ = depreciation rate
z = capital depreciation allowance

For both sets of models, other variables were included within the regressions as well, including a measure of uncertainty (volatility in the FTSE All Share Index), a deterministic time trend and seasonal dummies. All these variables proved to be insignificantly different from zero. The insignificance of the uncertainty parameter was surprising given previous empirical findings (see Chapter 9) but it could be that the capacity utilization is picking up some of the effects of uncertainty.

Estimation procedures

The basic models

The basic models were estimated based on the classical linear regression model and the associated OLS techniques. The implementation of OLS estimation requires the satisfaction of various 'Gauss-Markov' assumptions about the properties of the disturbance terms that capture random elements in the models. Therefore, tests for serial correlation in the disturbances, incorrect functional form, heteroscedasticity, predictive failure, structural breaks, and non-stationarity of the dependent and explanatory variables were used to establish whether or not the OLS estimation of the models was justified.[1]

(Further information about these statistical techniques is summarized in the statistical appendix.)

Each model was estimated in two stages. First, after testing the variables for non-stationarity, a regression on logged levels was estimated and interpreted as describing the elasticities of manufacturing investment with respect to both the user cost of capital and output. The models were estimated using Koyck transformations and autoregressive distributed lag (ARDL) models (both in unrestricted form and by imposing a long-run elasticity of one: i.e. by allowing that changes in the user cost of capital and output lead to equiproportionate changes in investment). However, the results from these models were characterized by highly significant econometric problems, indicating possible model misspecification and/or other econometric problems. So, following Bischoff (1969), the models were estimated using lags of up to eight quarters. This style of analysis is vulnerable to the same 'ad-hockery' criticism as that aimed at early putty-clay models (as explained in Chapters 6 and 7) but the imposition of the lag structure does have some *a priori* backing in terms of Bischoff's (1969) evidence. Also, it seems unlikely that pure theory will give complete guidance about how long it takes for the sources of lags to work themselves through.

Once the lag structure was specified, a conventional specification search procedure was used following Hendry's 'top-down' approach. This approach involves testing-down from a model including all possibly relevant parameters to a parsimonious model structure (Gujarati, 1995, p. 485; Hendry and Mizon, 1978). Variables with insignificant t ratios are excluded from the models one by one. The t tests are used to test the null hypothesis that each parameter estimate is equal to zero. All excluded variables are then tested for joint significance using F tests of restrictions. The joint testing of significance of the various lags excluded from the distributed lag versions of the accelerator and neo-classical models is of particular importance because it may be that there is a high degree of multicollinearity between the different lags. Therefore the standard errors on the coefficients in the unrestricted models may be relatively large leading to insignficant t ratios and an increased probability of Type II error: i.e. of falsely retaining the null that the parameters are equal to zero.

Empirical findings

The accelerator models

The results from the estimation of accelerator models are outlined in Table 11.1. These findings indicate that the unrestricted accelerator model has a high degree of statistical explanatory power for UK manufacturing investment between 1958 and 1993. The unrestricted model captures 95.4 per cent of the variability in gross investment. However, while the model is well specified, the output terms are not highly significant and the only significant variables

Table 11.1 Results from the estimation of accelerator models

Dependent variable: Log of gross investment
Estimation period: 1972Q4 to 2001Q2

	Unrestricted model		*Restricted model*	
	Parameter Estimate	*t test [p value]*	*Parameter Estimate*	*t test [p value]*
Constant	0.372	0.787 [0.433]	0.512	1.602 [0.112]
$Investment_{t-1}$	0.920	19.82 [0.000]	0.944	25.74 [0.000]
Logged $output_t$	0.194	0.720 [0.473]	...	...
Logged $output_{t-1}$	−0.392	−1.030 [0.305]	...	...
Logged $output_{t-2}$	0.739	1.957 [0.053]	...	...
Logged $output_{t-3}$	−0.327	−0.920 [0.360]	...	...
Logged $output_{t-4}$	−0.361	−1.005 [0.318]	...	...
Logged $output_{t-5}$	0.201	0.557 [0.579]	...	...
Logged $output_{t-6}$	−0.060	−0.164 [0.870]	...	...
Logged $output_{t-7}$	−0.070	−0.192 [0.848]	...	...
Logged $output_{t-8}$	0.147	0.516 [0.607]	...	...
Capacity $utilization_t$	−0.0005	−0.558 [0.579]	−0.0019	−5.72 [0.000]
Capacity $utilization_{t-1}$	−0.001	−1.29 [0.199]	...	...
Capacity $utilization_{t-2}$	−0.0007	0.707 [0.482]	...	...
Capacity $utilization_{t-3}$	−0.0007	0.687 [0.494]	...	...
Capacity $utilization_{t-4}$	−0.002	−2.07 [0.041]	...	...
Capacity $utilization_{t-5}$	−0.0004	0.455 [0.650]	...	...
Capacity $utilization_{t-6}$	0.0008	0.723 [0.471]	0.0008	1.95 [0.054]
Capacity $utilization_{t-7}$	0.0002	0.232 [0.817]	...	...
Capacity $utilization_{t-8}$	0.0003	0.371 [0.712]	...	...
Logged capital $stock_{t-1}$	0.169	1.55 [0.124]	...	...
R^2 (adjusted)	0.954		0.958	
Diagnostic tests – probability values				
Serial correlation	0.366		0.226	
Functional form	0.391		0.303	
Heteroscedasticity	0.204		0.300	

remaining in the restricted version, i.e. the version excluding insignificant parameters, are some capacity utilization terms. These suggest that the net effect of decreasing capacity utilization operates to depress investment activity. This finding is consistent with the predictions of accelerator theory although the insignificance of the output parameters is not.

These results contrast with the analyses of Coen (1969) and Eisner and Nadiri (1968) for the US and Feldstein and Flemming (1971) and Bean (1981) for the UK. The difference in the findings may be explained by the fact that the estimation periods are very different. The other estimations were conducted in periods of relative economic stability (for example, Bean's estimation period was 1963–75 and the impact of the oil shocks may not yet have affected investment activity, given the lags that delay the implementation of investment decisions). In contrast, the estimation period used in this analysis was one of marked instability and covers periods of stagflation, debt crises, Stock Market instability, financial deregulation, exit from ERM and globalization, as well as rapid technological and structural changes in the macroeconomy, such as those that have accompanied the evolution of the 'New Economy'.[2]

Jorgenson's model

The results from the estimation of the preferred neo-classical models are recorded in Table 11.2. From the restricted model, the estimate of the long-run elasticity of investment with respect to the user cost of capital was very low at +0.091. It is also counter-intuitively signed (Jorgenson predicts a negative relationship between investment and the user cost of capital) though insignificantly different from zero at a 25 per cent significance level ($t = 1.04$ [$p = 0.298$]). The estimate of the long-run elasticity with respect to output is at least positively signed but it is very small at 0.007. This is insignificantly different from zero at an 80 per cent significance level ($t = 0.204$ [$p = 0.838$]).

Table 11.2 Results from the estimation of neo-classical models

Dependent variable: Log of gross investment
Estimation period: 1972Q4 to 2001Q2

	Unrestricted model		*Restricted model*	
	Parameter Estimate	*t test [p value]*	*Parameter Estimate*	*t test [p value]*
Constant	−1.64	−0.913 [0.364]	−1.19	−1.65 [0.102]
$Investment_{t-1}$	0.918	21.42 [0.000]	0.924	28.14 [0.000]
Logged $output_t$	0.2333	0.893 [0.374]	...	...
Logged $output_{t-1}$	−0.212	−0.595 [0.553]	...	...
Logged $output_{t-2}$	0.880	2.49 [0.015]	0.834	4.41 [0.000]
Logged $output_{t-3}$	−0.377	−1.0958 [0.276]	−0.422	−1.94 [0.54]
Logged $output_{t-4}$	−0.271	−0.781 [0.437]	...	...
Logged $output_{t-5}$	0.304	0.862 [0.391]	...	...
Logged $output_{t-6}$	−0.273	−0.760 [0.449]	...	...
Logged $output_{t-7}$	−0.2884	−0.793 [0.430]	−0.427	−3.97 [0.000]
Logged $output_{t-8}$	−0.053	−0.200 [0.842]	...	...
Logged user $cost_t$	0.009	0.169 [0.866]	...	...
Logged user $cost_{t-1}$	−0.076	−0.917 [0.362]	...	...
Logged user $cost_{t-2}$	0.140	1.666 [0.099]	...	...
Logged user $cost_{t-3}$	−0.150	−1.85 [0.068]	−0.067	−2.56 [0.012]
Logged user $cost_{t-4}$	0.0247	0.307 [0.759]	...	...
Logged user $cost_{t-5}$	0.0783	0.989 [0.325]	0.074	2.858 [0.005]
Logged user $cost_{t-6}$	0.0291	0.381 [0.704]	...	...
Logged user $cost_{t-7}$	−0.019	−0.257 [0.797]	...	...
Logged user $cost_{t-8}$	−0.026	−0.484 [0.630]	...	...
Logged capital $stock_{t-1}$	0.235	1.384 [0.170]	0.174	1.896 [0.061]
R^2 (adjusted)	0.954		0.959	
Diagnostic tests – probability values				
Serial correlation	0.095		0.283	
Functional form	0.431		0.418	
Heteroscedasticity	0.321		0.552	

So while the model seems econometrically well specified with a healthy-looking set of diagnostic tests, is not a theoretically consistent set of results.

Model comparison and non-nested hypothesis tests

The next stage of the econometric analysis was to compare the results from the preferred accelerator model with the results from the preferred neo-classical model. This was achieved by comparing the results from the various different models in two ways: first, by comparing both the explanatory power and diagnostic test results of the different models; and second, by using non-nested techniques to test different models against each other. These non-nested testing techniques included Cox, adjusted Cox, Wald, J, JA and F tests for model comparison. These tests allow the rejection of one, both or neither of the models and are based upon the assertion that a good model should capture the results from alternative models (Davidson and MacKinnon, 1981).

The probability values (p values) from the non-nested tests of alternative models against each other refer to tests of the null hypothesis that Model 1 contributes no significant additional explanatory power when imposed on top of Model 2. As explained in the Statistical Appendix, a low p value implies that H_0 should be rejected. In this case it will imply that Model 1 does contribute significant explanatory power independently of Model 2. The non-nested tests results in Table 11.3 indicate that both models possess independent explanatory power at relatively low significance levels.

The estimation of a hybrid model

The results from the accelerator and neo-classical models were not particularly revealing in terms of the estimated responses of investment to output and relative factor costs. And the non-nested tests revealed that each model contributed some explanatory power independently of the other model. Therefore, a hybrid model was estimated including up to eight lags on output, the user cost of capital and capacity utilization. The results from this model

Table 11.3 Non-nested test results, p values

	Model 1: Neo-classical *Model 2: Accelerator*	*Model 1: Accelerator* *Model 2: Neo-classical*
Cox test	0.002	0.002
Adjusted Cox test	0.010	0.026
Wald test	0.015	0.036
J test	0.014	0.004
JA test	0.015	0.101
Encompassing test	0.053	0.060

Table 11.4 Results from the estimation of the hybrid model

Dependent variable: Log of gross investment
Estimation period: 1972Q4 to 2001Q2

Variable	*Parameter Estimate*	*t test [p value]*
Constant	0.202	0.546 [0.586]
Investment_{t-1}	0.925	23.09 [0.000]
$\text{Logged output}_{t-2}$	0.271	2.27 [0.025]
$\text{Logged output}_{t-7}$	−0.175	−1.54 [0.125]
$\text{Logged user cost}_{t-3}$	−0.069	−2.61 [0.010]
$\text{Logged user cost}_{t-5}$	0.068	2.59 [0.011]
$\text{Capacity utilization}_{t}$	−0.001	−2.41 [0.018]
$\text{Capacity utilization}_{t-6}$	0.0006	1.32 [0.191]
R^2 (adjusted)	0.959	
Diagnostic tests – probability values		
Serial correlation	0.182	
Functional form	0.295	
Heteroscedasticity	0.220	

are outlined in Table 11.4. These results confirm that both theoretical approaches have merits in terms of explanatory power and that concentrating on one specification of investment models to the exclusion of others may lead to an omission of factors that are central to the determination of investment expenditure. The estimated parameters in the hybrid model indicate that the long-run elasticity of investment with respect to the user cost of capital is −0.013 which although small is at least negative although it is insignificantly different from zero at high significance levels (for a t test of H_0: long-run elasticity is equal to zero, $t = -0.305, p = 0.761$). The long-run elasticity of investment with respect to output is significantly different from zero and insignificantly different from one (for a t test of H_0: long-run elasticity is equal to one, $t = 0.308$). This result seems intuitively plausible in that it suggests that a 1 per cent increase in output will lead to a 1 per cent increase in investment. These results are consistent with the results from earlier estimations of putty-clay models, as outlined in Chapter 7. Investment responds elastically to changes in output but there is not much evidence of a strong, consistent relationship between investment and the user cost of capital. The results above therefore confirm the assertions about the empirical shortcomings of Jorgenson's model, discussed in Chapters 6 and 7.

Conclusion

This analysis of the neo-classical and accelerator models seems to raise more questions than it answers. Whilst the models appear to be econometrically well specified, the signs and significance of the coefficients do not seem to be consistent with any one group of theories. The accelerator models seem to out-perform neo-classical models in terms of plausible estimated parameters but the output terms in the unrestricted accelerator models are insignificant and the bulk of the explanatory power in those models was contributed by capacity utilization and the lagged dependent variable. For neo-classical models, some of the parameters were of counter-intuitive sign and/or insignificantly different from zero. The bulk of the explanatory power in the models is contributed by the lagged dependent variable and the lagged capital stock term. Uncertainty variables are insignificant, which seems surprising given previous econometric findings.

One of the problems with the estimation of these types of models, which may explain these unilluminating results, lies in specifying an appropriate lag structure. A range of lag structures was tried but the eight-quarter lag structure was the only one that did not create econometric problems. Overall, the best results were achieved from the estimation of a hybrid model that incorporated output, capacity utilization and user cost terms.

The results of this analysis confirm many previous findings, but for a later time period. They suggest that investment theory and analysis should continue to move beyond simple neo-classical and accelerator specifications to capture the more complicated factors that may depress investment activity in an uncertain world. This is particularly important given the environment of increasing uncertainty that has accompanied technological and structural changes in the last 20 or so years. Some of these issues are explored in the following chapter.

Chapter summary

1. As described in earlier chapters, accelerator theories are generally attributed with having superior explanatory power relative to Jorgenson's neo-classical model. The aim of this chapter is to see if this finding holds for UK gross investment quarterly data over the period 1972–2001.
2. A flexible accelerator model of gross investment is estimated, using output and capacity utilization variables and incorporating a distributed lag structure to capture investment lags and expectations formation. In addition, a neo-classical model of investment is estimated incorporating a measure of user cost of capital and output, again using a distributed lag structure following Bischoff's (1969) approach. The estimation of this model suggests that the long-run elasticity of investment with respect to the user cost of capital, is +0.091, which is very low and puzzlingly positive. But it is an estimate that is similar to the lower end of estimates mentioned in the literature on putty-clay models, as discussed in Chapter 7. For example, this estimate is comparable with Bean's (1989) estimate of 0.05.
3. The results from the estimation of the accelerator models suggest that accelerator models are characterized by a higher R^2: i.e. they capture the variance in gross investment more effectively than the neo-classical specifications. Even ignoring the econometric problems with the neo-classical specification, the insignificant estimate of the long-run elasticity with respect to the user cost of capital suggests that capital inputs are not

Chapter summary continued

particularly responsive to the relative factor cost of capital, as measured by the user cost of capital. In turn, this suggests that the elasticity of factor substitution is probably low. In addition, the accelerator specification is characterized by fewer significant econometric problems than the neo-classical specification.

4. The independent comparison of econometric models is inevitably subjective and so the two sets of models were tested against each other using model comparison and non-nested testing techniques. These tests suggest that both the accelerator and neo-classical specifications contribute some explanatory power independently of the other model. It seems that output, the user cost of capital and capacity utilization are all significant variables for this data set.
5. So a hybrid model was estimated incorporating the output, user cost and capacity utilization variables. This model captures nearly 96 per cent of the variability in gross investment and the diagnostic tests performed on the model were all insignificant at 10 per cent significance levels, suggesting that the model is generally well specified. However, the estimated long-run elasticity of investment to the user cost of capital is still very low (although it is negatively signed). These mixed results confirm previous empirical evidence and suggest that researchers should move beyond the estimation of accelerator and Jorgensonian models, for example, by trying to capture the effects of uncertainty more effectively.

Data appendix

Raw variables

Gross investment: Gross fixed capital formation in manufacturing (1990 prices): *Economic Trends Annual Supplement* (ETAS), ONS
Capacity utilization: CBI survey data on percentage of firms operating below capacity
Implicit price deflator for gross domestic fixed capital formation: ETAS, ONS
Manufacturing output (1990 prices): ETAS, ONS
Capital stock (manufacturing), constant prices: ETAS, ONS
Uncertainty: measured as the standard deviation in the FTSE All Share Index, for the three months of each quarter.

Components of user cost measure

Redemption yield: *Financial Statistics*, ONS
Corporate taxes and capital allowances: Institute for Fiscal Studies
Capital goods prices: Implicit price deflator for gross domestic fixed capital formation, ETAS, ONS
Output prices: GDP deflator at factor cost: ETAS, ONS

12 Uncertainty in competing models of investment: evidence from the USA

A recap on neo-classical theories of investment 150
A recap on Post Keynesian theory 152
The empirical analysis 153
Non-nested tests 156
Conclusion 157
Chapter summary 158
Data appendix 159

As explained in Chapter 8, Tobin's *q* models of investment are founded on the assumption that Stock Market valuations will provide information about the likely future prospects of firms. This approach revolves around an efficient markets assumption: that share prices fully reflect all available information about the likely future prospects of firms and so rational investors can look to the Stock Market in assessing the potential future value of investments. As explained in Chapter 9, the influence of uncertainty is generally captured in orthodox analysis by super-imposing uncertainty variables on top of *q* models. Keynes and Post Keynesian analysts also argue that the Stock Market will influence investment but Post Keynesian analyses tend to focus on the role of speculative activity as a destabilizing force that exacerbates uncertainty. As discussed in Chapter 8, the real options theorists have confirmed empirically the hypothesis that uncertainty will depress investment but this negative correlation is also consistent with Post Keynesian theory. In other words, the finding of this negative relationship does not in itself provide evidence about the relative merits of competing investment theories.

The aim of this chapter is to assess the relative empirical merits of the two sets of theories after controlling for the influence of uncertainty. In the first part of this chapter, the development of orthodox ideas about the role of Stock Markets is re-introduced; then some key Post Keynesian analyses of the relationship between investment, finance, uncertainty and cyclical instability are summarized. These theoretical issues are analyzed empirically for the USA from 1970–98, by comparing the empirical performance of orthodox *q* theory versus Keynesian/Kaleckian models of investment. Post Keynesian/Kaleckian models and *q* models were estimated both with and without uncertainty variables. The models were then tested against one another using non-nested testing procedures in order to assess the relative empirical merits of the divergent approaches.

A recap on neo-classical theories of investment

In early neo-classical theory, factors such as uncertainty, speculation and Stock Market activity do not play much of a role. As described in Chapter 5, in Jorgenson's (1963) model, investment is described as a process of adjustment to an optimal capital stock. Gross investment is determined by a scale effect and a relative factor cost effect. The scale effect is captured by output and the relative factor cost effect is captured by the user cost of capital. The size of the effect of changes in the user cost of capital is captured by the elasticity of substitution of capital for labour in response to a change in factor prices. Assuming that the previous period's capital stock is not at its optimal level, gross investment can be described as a function of the user cost of capital, output and the lagged capital stock. The empirical estimation of standard Jorgensonian/neo-classical models of investment has been largely unsuccessful and these models are invariably characterized by poor predictive power and econometric problems. These findings were confirmed in Chapter 11.

In addition, the theoretical interpretation of neo-classical investment models has been blurred by the complexity of forces affecting the lag structure of investment.[1] Whilst empirical specifications of accelerator models have performed somewhat better, these models have been criticized because of *ad hoc* specifications, particularly of lag structures. Also, as aggregate investment is a component of aggregate expenditure, it is not particularly illuminating or surprising to find that there is a strong correlation between investment and output/expenditure.

Tobin's *q* models

As explained in Chapter 7, one of the problems with Jorgenson's theory was that it is essentially static and does not incorporate explicit assumptions about rationality and expectations. So the orthodox reaction to the empirical difficulties with Jorgensonian models was the marriage of rational expectations hypotheses with the Jorgensonian marginalist, maximizing approach. The most predominant of these are the rational expectations versions of Tobin's *q* theory.[2] In Tobin's *q* theories Stock Market information is assumed to be a proxy for rational agents' expectations of the future profitability of investments (Abel 1980, 1983, 1990). As explained in Chapter 8, incentives to invest are captured by the market valuation of firms' assets relative to the current replacement cost of firms' capital stocks. Aggregation of the basic relationship between marginal benefits and costs of incremental investment proceeds in two stages. First, for the individual firm, the average *q* (the natural log of the ratio of a firm's market capitalization to the current replacement cost of its individual capital stock) is assumed to approximate marginal *q* (the marginal value of increments to a firm's capital stock relative to the marginal costs of those increments). Second, the individual firm relationship is aggregated to an industry-wide and macroeconomic scale by incorporating a representative agents hypothesis. In essence, this approach is justified by the efficient markets hypothesis and various restrictive assumptions about the specification of the production function.

As explained in Chapter 8, in *q* theories the investment rate is a function of capital goods prices (p_k) and average *q* (q_A). In this chapter this approach is simplified by looking at the relationship between investment and *q*, capital goods prices and the capital stock. The following model is estimated:

$$i_t = \alpha + \lambda i_{t-1} + \beta_1 k_t + \beta_2 k_{t-1} + \gamma_1 q_t + \gamma_2 q_{t-1} + \eta_1 p_{kt} + \eta_2 p_{kt-1} + \varphi CU_t + \delta VOL_t + \theta TO_t + \varepsilon_t$$

where i is the natural log of gross investment, k is the log of the capital stock, q is logged q_A, p_k is the price of capital goods (logged). Cyclical factors are captured via the inclusion of CU, a capacity utilization variable. Uncertainty is captured by looking at volatility in capital prices (VOL), measured as the standard deviation of capital goods prices. The effect of uncertainty in the stock market is captured including NYSE data on Stock Market turnover (TO).

A recap on Post Keynesian theory

In modelling real-world investment activity it is important to have a view about uncertainty because any description of expectations formation processes will necessarily depend upon assumptions about the nature of uncertainty. Whilst the neo-classical literature describes ways of quantifying the impacts of uncertainty at the microeconomic level (for example, in the real options theories outlined in Chapter 9), the influence of aggregate uncertainty, particularly if it generates feedback effects and herd behaviour, is difficult to incorporate into the fundamental axioms that form the microfoundations of neo-classical theory.[3]

In contrast, aggregate uncertainty has always been central to the Post Keynesian theories outlined in Chapter 10. In Keynes and in Post Keynesian literature, the destabilizing effects of uncertainty are communicated via financial channels and thus speculative and financial decisions have key effects on investment. As investment is the leading variable, this volatility and pessimism in investment activity translates into macroeconomic instability. The MEK is the major determinant of investment and a critical dynamic link in Keynes's analysis. Keynes (1936, 1937) argues that it is through the expectations that form part of the MEK that the future impinges on present activity. The influence of expectations and the state of confidence on the MEK means that it is the product of a mixture of subjective as well as objective influences. Liquidity preferences and the prospective yields of investments rest on insecure foundations and fluctuations in one are unlikely to be offset by fluctuations in the other. Factors that aggravate pessimism about prospective yields will also increase the propensity to hoard money and vice versa. Therefore the capitalist economic system will not be self-equilibrating. 'Uncontrolled', 'disobedient' business psychology and collapses in the state of confidence will mean that the MEK is insusceptible to control and purely monetary therapies will fail to raise investment. As Keynes emphasizes, 'it is the return of confidence, to speak in ordinary language, which is so insusceptible to control in an economy of individualistic capitalism' (Keynes, 1936, p. 317).

The Post Keynesian economists develop some of these insights in focusing on the role of uncertainty, conventional behaviour, attitudes towards money and the key role played by the availability of finance. For example, in constrast to the Modigliani–Miller theorem embedded in Jorgenson's analysis (that all sources of finance are equal) Kalecki (1954) argues that different forms of financing, internal and external, will have differential impacts on investment activity. In particular, profits and the availability of finance are central. Kalecki asserts that investment is determined as:

$$D = aS + b\frac{\Delta\Pi}{\Delta t} - c\frac{\Delta K}{\Delta t} + d$$

where D is the rate of investment decisions, S is gross savings, $\Delta\Pi/\Delta t$ is the rate of change in profits, $\Delta K/\Delta t$ is the rate of change in capital stock and d is a deterministic trend.

The Keynesian-Kaleckian model

In this chapter, a Kaleckian model is estimated, adapted with the inclusion of the uncertainty and cyclical factors defined in the previous section, to take account of some of Keynes's insights about the influence of uncertainty. So for the Kaleckian/Keynesian analysis, the following econometric specification is estimated:

$$i_t = \alpha + \lambda i_{t-1} + \beta_1 \Delta\Pi_t + \eta_1 \Delta k_t + \eta_2 \Delta k_{t-1} + \gamma_1 s_t + \gamma_2 s_{t-1} + \psi T + \varphi CU_t + \delta VOL_t + \theta TO_t + \varepsilon_t$$

where $\Delta\Pi$ is profits growth, Δk is growth in capital stock, s is the natural log of corporate savings, T is a deterministic time trend and CU, VOL and TO are as defined above.

This model is consistent with Keynes's and Kalecki's earlier insights that the availability of finance is a crucial constraint on investment decision-making. According to Keynes in *The General Theory of Employment, Interest and Money* (1936), the state of credit can have as much influence on investment decisions as the state of confidence. And according to Kalecki (1937b) as debts build up and liquidity declines, the willingness to invest by businesses declines accordingly. As businesses acquire more debt during expansionary phases, their ratios of debt to equity rise, risks will rise and the 'principle of increasing risk' will come into play. The increased borrower's risk will lead to increases in discount rates and decreases in the demand price of capital. Overall, the costs of borrowing will increase. So the availability of finance, particularly internal finance in the form of corporate savings, will have important effects on the cycle. Minsky (1986) argues that the banking system, because it creates money, is central to the health of business fixed investment. If the money is not created endogenously to meet business demands for liquidity, investment activity will fall away, and reverse multiplier effects will lead to concomittant declines in aggregate output and employment (Davidson, 1978).

The empirical analysis

The empirical analysis in this chapter aims to assess the relative predictive power of these Keynesian-Kaleckian approaches against mainstream q theory approaches. The analysis is conducted using US annual data from the period 1970–98. The analysis proceeds in three stages. The first stage involves the estimation of a Tobin's q model of investment; q models are then tested including cyclical and uncertainty variables.

The second stage is the estimation of a Keynesian-Kaleckian model of investment in which profits, debts and uncertainty play a key role. The third stage involves comparing the various models using non-nested testing procedures. The econometric procedures are explained in the statistical appendix.

Dickey Fuller (DF) and Augmented Dickey-Fuller (ADF) tests for non-stationarity were conducted and revealed that all the variables used in the models, apart from profits growth, are non-stationary. However, once the models had been estimated, further tests did reveal that the variables were co-integrated; the residuals were stationary in all models. Following Hendry's approach to econometric modelling, variables with insignificant t tests (of the null hypothesis that the parameter is equal to zero) were deleted but only after the t test results were confirmed by F versions of variable deletion tests, and only if no diagnostic problems were created by the variable's deletion.

In general, the models appear to be well specified econometrically. The tests for serial correlation (Breusch-Godfrey LM test), for incorrect functional form (Ramsey's RESET test) and for heteroscedasticity (LM test) were insignificant at 10 per cent apart from the functional form tests on the q models omitting uncertainty and cyclical factors.

The results from the q models are outlined in Tables 12.1 and 12.2. In models without uncertainty and cyclical factors, q was significant but the functional form test suggests a significant problem with the specification of the model. These two sets of findings may be explained if q is capturing aggregate uncertainty, for example, via the market capitalization term in the numerator of q. This interpretation would also explain the negative signs on

Table 12.1 Parameter estimates for q models without uncertainty

Dependent variable: Logged investment
Estimation period: 1970–98, annual data

	Unrestricted model		*Restricted model*	
	Parameter Estimate	*t test [p value]*	*Parameter Estimate*	*t test [p value]*
i_{t-1}	0.588	4.8 [0.000]	0.553	4.7 [0.000]
k_t	2.34	6.1 [0.000]	2.48	6.8 [0.000]
k_{t-1}	−2.17	−5.1 [0.000]	−2.26	−5.5 [0.000]
q_t	−0.027	−1.0 [0.321]	insignificant	
q_{t-1}	0.065	1.93 [0.065]	0.020	1.74 [0.094]
p_{kt}	−0.941	−2.1 [0.046]	−1.06	−2.5 [0.021]
p_{kt-1}	1.37	3.3 [0.001]	1.49	3.8 [0.001]
Intercept	0.636	0.64 [0.529]	0.514	0.52 [0.607]
Adjusted R^2	0.998		0.998	
Diagnostic tests – probability values				
Serial correlation	0.174		0.240	
Functional form	0.025		0.255	
Heteroscedasticity	0.677		0.838	

Table 12.2 Parameter estimates for *q* models with uncertainty

Dependent variable: Logged investment
Estimation period: 1970–98, annual data

	Unrestricted model		*Restricted model*	
	Parameter estimate	*t test [p value]*	*Parameter estimate*	*t test [p value]*
i_{t-1}	0.805	5.4 [0.000]	0.653	6.8 [0.000]
k_t	2.78	4.8 [0.000]	2.81	5.5 [0.000]
k_{t-1}	−2.59	−4.1 [0.001]	−2.57	−4.4 [0.000]
q_t	−0.012	−0.48 [0.633]	insignificant	
q_{t-1}	−0.014	−0.38 [0.711]	insignificant	
p_{kt}	−0.299	−0.57 [0.573]	insignificant	
p_{kt-1}	0.491	0.95 [0.353]	0.293	1.6 [0.117]
CU_t	0.006	1.98 [0.061]	0.006	2.8 [0.009]
VOL_t	−0.084	−2.9 [0.009]	−0.073	−4.0 [0.001]
TO_t	−0.162	−1.2 [0.238]	insignificant	
Intercept	−1.65	−1.4 [0.165]	−1.09	−1.2 [0.231]
Adjusted R^2	0.998		0.998	
Diagnostic tests – probability values				
Serial correlation	0.174		0.240	
Functional form	0.025		0.255	
Heteroscedasticity	0.677		0.838	

some of the *q* coefficients. This sort of evidence lends support to a Post Keynesian view of *q* as an indicator of aggregate uncertainty rather than rational forecasts of the future prospects for the current capital stock (a survey of these theories is outlined in Palley, 2001).

For the uncertainty models, the Stock Market turnover variable was insignificant as were current and lagged capital goods prices. However, lagged capital goods prices were retained because the deletion of this variable seemed to create significant functional form problems. In *q* models with uncertainty and cyclical factors, *q* was insignificant. Variable deletion F tests confirmed that the *q* variables were insignificant and so they were deleted from the final model.

Kaleckian model

The empirical specification of a basic Kaleckian model was constructed by regressing investment on profits growth, capital growth, savings and a deterministic time trend. Savings was captured using a net worth variable, where net worth is defined as the ratio of non-financial corporations' net worth to debt ratio. The results from the Kaleckian models and the Keynesian-Kaleckian model (the Kaleckian model with uncertainty variables included) are outlined in Table 12.3.

For the Kaleckian model without uncertainty variables, all the variables were significant at 5 per cent apart from the unlagged log of savings, which was

Table 12.3 Keynesian-Kaleckian models

Dependent variable: Logged investment
Estimation period: 1970–98, annual data

	Kaleckian model Unrestricted		*Kaleckian model Restricted*		*Keynesian-Kaleckian model*	
	Parameter Estimate	*t test [p value]*	*Parameter Estimate*	*t [p value]*	*Parameter Estimate*	*t [p value]*
Intercept	1.35	2.2 [0.040]	1.28	2.2 [0.039]	– 2.26	– 7.1 [0.000]
i_{t-1}	0.853	13.2 [0.000]	0.860	14.2 [0.000]	1.13	48.4 [0.000]
$\Delta\Pi_t$	0.122	1.9 [0.062]	0.130	2.2 [0.032]	0.108	2.6 [0.014]
ΔK_t	1.73	5.6 [0.000]	1.76	6.1 [0.000]	2.27	5.4 [0.000]
ΔK_{t-1}	−0.872	−3.0 [0.005]	−0.865	– 3.0 [0.005]	– 0.392	– 1.5 [0.142]
s_t	0.0242	0.36 [0.726]	insignificant		insignificant	
s_{t-1}	0.163	2.4 [0.020]	0.171	2.8 [0.010]	0.141	4.0 [0.000]
T	0.0150	2.4 [0.024]	0.0142	2.5 [0.020]	insignificant	
CU_t	...	...	...	...	0.007	3.6 [0.001]
VOL_t	...	...	...	...	– 0.072	– 4.0 [0.000]
TO_t	...	...	...	...	– 0.291	– 3.5 [0.002]
Adjusted R^2	0.99817		0.99822		0.99887	
Diagnostic tests – probability values						
Serial correlation	0.971		0.963		0.686	
Functional form	0.739		0.683		0.454	
Heteroscedasticity	0.575		0.633		0.511	

insignificant and deleted from the restricted version of the model. All the coefficients were of expected sign except the coefficient on the elasticity of investment with respect to current capital growth. Kalecki (1954) hypothesized a negative relationship between investment and capital growth but the estimated parameter on current capital growth is positive here. In other ways, the basic Kaleckian model seems to be well specified and seems to present a more coherent picture than the *q* models, for this data set at least.

For the Keynesian-Kaleckian model, the final restricted regression is also reported in Table 12.3. The variables were all of expected sign. The lagged capital growth parameter is insignificant but this variable was retained in this restricted model because its exclusion created significant signs of functional form problems. Its insignificance may reflect the fact that multicollinearity is widening the confidence intervals.

Non-nested tests

The non-nested test results are recorded in Table 12.4. As for Chapter 11, the probability values (p values) from the non-nested tests of alternative models against each other refer to tests of the null hypothesis that Model 1 contributes no significant additional explanatory power when imposed on top of Model 2. As explained in the Statistical Appendix, a low p value implies that H_0 should be rejected. This will imply that Model 1 does contribute significant additional explanatory power independently of Model 2.

Table 12.4 Non-nested tests, p values

Dependent variable: Logged gross investment		
Estimation period: 1970–98		
Excluding cyclical and uncertainty factors		
	Model 1: Kalecki *Model 2: q*	*Model 1: q* *Model 2: Kalecki*
Cox test	0.137	0.000
Adjusted Cox test	0.475	0.000
Wald test	0.499	0.001
J test	0.051	0.000
JA test	0.691	0.000
Encompassing test	0.053	0.006
Akaike's information criterion favours the *q* model (AIC = 3.3012)		
Including cyclical and uncertainty factors		
	Model 1: Kalecki *Model 2: q*	*Model 1: q* *Model 2: Kalecki*
Cox test	0.000	0.671
Adjusted Cox test	0.000	0.435
Wald test	0.005	0.407
J test	0.000	0.734
JA test	0.001	0.693
Encompassing test	0.019	0.971
Akaike's information criterion favours the Kaleckian model (AIC = –7.9737)		

The results from the non-nested tests indicate that *q* models appear to out-perform Kaleckian models when uncertainty and cyclical factors are ignored. However, as might be expected given the finding that the *q* variables are insignificant in models including cyclical/uncertainty factors, the Kaleckian models out-perform *q* theory in the non-nested tests when uncertainty and cyclical influences *are* included. As mentioned above, this seemingly inconsistent result may reflect the fact that *q* is in fact capturing investors' responses to uncertainty and/or movements in the business cycle, rather than rational judgements of the future worth of capital assets.

Conclusion

In Chapters 9 and 10, orthodox and Post Keynesian explanations for the negative relationship between investment and uncertainty were outlined. The aim of this chapter is to assess the relative empirical merits of these divergent theoretical approaches using US data. The empirical evidence presented here supports the generally widely supported finding that uncertainty depresses aggregate investment. Apart from that, the empirical findings are perhaps contradictory: when the models were estimated without the uncertainty and cyclical variables, the *q* models out-perform the Keynesian-Kaleckian models.

On the other hand, Tobin's *q* models were found to be empirically inferior to Keynesian-Kaleckian models when uncertainty and cyclical factors are allowed an influence within the model. This suggests that the two different models are, ironically, capturing much the same thing and so it is difficult to favour one model over the other on the basis of this evidence. However, it does also suggest that the Post Keynesian *q* approaches associated with Davidson and Minsky, that interpret *q* as a measure of instability, may have some empirical support.

Chapter summary

1. In Tobin's *q* models of investment, the Stock Market plays a key role because average *q* (q_A) provides a measure of the incentive to invest. Tobinś *q* theorists assert that, assuming an efficient markets hypothesis, share prices will capture all relevant information about the future prospects of firms and will adjust instantaneously to news. If this is true, q_A will capture all information relevant to a firm's future value and will provide a measure of the incentive to invest.
2. In real options theories, the empirical relationship between uncertainty and investment is captured by incorporating uncertainty variables on top of *q* models.
3. In Post Keynesian and Kaleckian theories of investment, the Stock Market will also act as a guide about the value of investment. However, the increases in liquidity allowed by the existence of modern Stock Markets will encourage speculation, contribute to uncertainty and thereby depress investment.
4. The empirical evidence about these different theories is assessed using annual USA data from 1970 to 1998. This evidence indicates that the Tobin's *q* model is superior to the Keynesian/Kaleckian model without uncertainty variables. However, once uncertainty is allowed, the Keynesian/Kaleckian model out-performs the Tobin's *q* specification.
5. Overall both sets of theories seem to be contributing some independent explanatory power suggesting that there are more parallels between these different theoretical approaches than is generally acknowledged. However, the empirical evidence presented in this chapter seems to support a Post Keynesian explanation of the influence of the Stock Market focusing on the destabilizing impacts of speculation, rather than an explanation of *q* as a measure of rational forecasts of the expected future value of firms' investment activities.

Data appendix

Capacity utilization:	Federal Reserve website
Industrial production:	Federal Reserve website
Federal effective interest rate:	Federal Reserve website
Stock Market turnover:	NYSE website
Gross investment:	Bureau of Economic Analysis, *Survey of Current Business*
Depreciation:	Bureau of Economic Analysis, *Survey of Current Business*
Capital Stock:	Bureau of Economic Analysis, *Survey of Current Business*
Price variables:	Bureau of Economic Analysis
GDP:	Bureau of Economic Analysis
Net worth ratios:	*Flow of Funds Accounts*, Federal Reserve
q:	From Tobin and Sommers, see 'Note on Rates of Return', *Survey of Current Business*

Part IV
Empirical Applications of Investment Principles

13 Computing investment in the New Economy: US evidence 163
14 Investment and development: a cross-sectional analysis 181
15 Residential investment: bubbles and crashes in the UK housing market, 1980–99 193

Introduction

The following section is included to demonstrate that the analysis of investment is not only important to the economic theorist; it can also illuminate everyday and topical real-world issues. Investment principles are relevant to many parts of economic life and can be applied to the analysis of economic development, technological change and housing markets, for example. In the following three chapters, these topics are examined with reference to the investment principles outlined in the theoretical chapters. Chapter 13 outlines how investment has evolved with the recent technological changes associated with the growing computerization of the economy; Chapter 14 examines the relationship between investment and economic development and Chapter 15 presents an analysis of housing investment.

13 Computing investment in the New Economy: US evidence

Introduction	164
The economic impacts of the IT revolution	167
Investment and the New Economy	168
Modelling innovation in computing investment	174
Conclusions and policy implications	177
Chapter summary	178
Data appendix	179

The aim of this chapter is to assess the relationship between investment and technological developments, using recent evidence about the development of the so-called 'New Economy', the knowledge-based economy that has evolved from innovations in particular from the IT and biotechnology sectors. The analysis will concentrate on computing investment in the USA. The USA has been chosen because of its global economic importance, its role as a leader in technical innovation and because some argue that a substantial proportion of US productivity improvement reflects the diffusion of computing technologies as well as the increasing efficiency of computing in terms of increasing computer speed and memory. An analysis of high-tech investments will illustrate that not only the magnitude but also the quality of the capital stock will affect productivity. The quality of the capital stock should be enhanced as new technological developments diffuse through economies.

In the first section of this chapter, some of the development of computerization is described and, in the second section, the economic impacts of the IT revolution are assessed. The New Economy that has evolved as a consequence of computerization has some unique characteristics that complicate the analysis of computing investments and these characteristics are analyzed in the third section. In the fourth section some of the theoretical ideas outlined in the theoretical chapter are re-introduced. These are then applied, in the fourth section, to an empirical analysis of computing investments. The aims of the empirical analysis are – first, to assess the usefulness of the theoretical ideas to the analysis of modern investment behaviour; and second, to assess some distinctive aspects of computing investment. The chapter concludes with a summary of the key findings and policy implications.

Introduction

There is no universally accepted definition of the New Economy but the term is generally used to refer to the development of new high-tech knowledge-based industries, particularly those associated with the IT (Information Technology) revolution. The New Economy can also be defined to include biotechnological developments but this chapter will concentrate on the impact of IT developments as these have been so profound and wide-reaching, particularly in financial sectors.

Widespread computerization of economic activity began in 1971 when Intel marketed its first microprocessor chip, allowing the development of powerful personal computers (PCs). During the 1970s, news of the innovations spread and new IT-related products and services evolved, starting with basic computerization of business activities (such as word-processing, spreadsheet and accounting packages); these technologies diffused affecting almost every aspect of modern economic life with innovations associated with computer networking, the Internet, mobile phone technologies and computer-based financial innovations (for example, Electronic Funds Transfer at Point of Sale [EFTPOS] and Automated Clearing House [ACH] systems). This diffusion of computer-related technologies was characterized by the rapid increases in the power of computers, reflected in exponential growth in transistor count.

Figure 13.1 illustrates that microprocessor transistor count rose from just above 1000 transistors per microprocessor in 1971 to close on 100 million transistors in 2001. This relationship between growth of transistors and growth of computing power is known as 'Moore's Law' and the doubling of microprocessor power every 18 months fostered rapid falls in the cost of computing equipment.

New IT innovations led to large increases in computing investments and Cecchetti (2002) estimates that annual growth in computer hardware inputs averaged 46 per cent rate of average annual growth in the second half of the 1990s. Yang and Brynjolfsson (2001) assert that computer-related investments, including investments in intangibles, accounted for about 10 per cent of GDP in the late 1990s. Figure 13.2 depicts investment in computing goods as a proportion of total fixed investments in equipment and software in the US. These data show that investment in computing now accounts for nearly 50 per cent of total investment in equipment and software; in 1959 it accounted for less than 15 per cent of total investment in equipment and software.

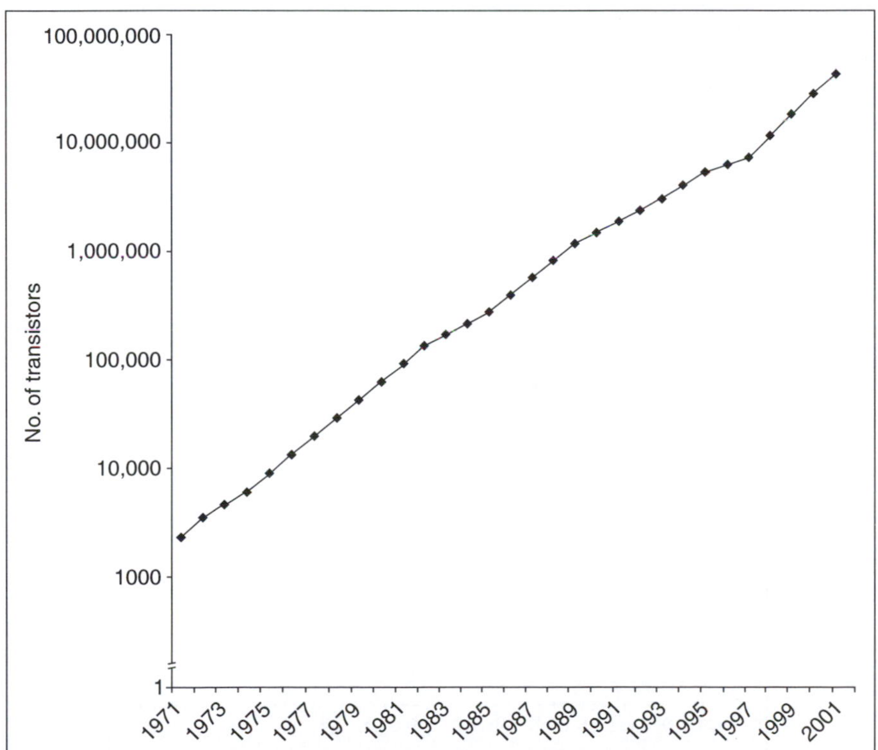

Figure 13.1 Growth in transistor count, logarithmic scale
Source: *Science and Technology Indicators*

A large proportion of computing investment was concentrated in the US service sector and finance, insurance and real estate (FIRE) companies invested particularly heavily in IT (Hobijn and Jovanovic, 2001). And computing investments have yielded good returns for innovative businesses; Yang and Brynjolfsson estimate that each additional US$1 spent on computer investments can foster $5–20 increases in firms' financial market valuations. Inevitably, the industries most closely involved with the innovation of high-tech products did particularly well and have experienced above average productivity growth in comparison with other older industries, when the contribution of intangible investments is taken into account (Carrado and Slifman, 1999; Jorgenson and Stiroh, 2000).

The IT revolution has also fostered an increase in overall research and development (R&D) expenditure, as innovations based round new IT technologies have spread. Real R&D capital has grown at a rate of 3.5 per cent per annum since 1990; R&D capital added 8 per cent to the stock of tangible fixed assets in 1999 (Landefeld and Fraumeni, 2000). And these figures are likely to be under-estimates because of the importance of intangible assets to investment in new technology.

Figure 13.2 Computing investment as a proportion of total investment
Source: *Bureau of Economic Analysis* (BEA)

The economic impacts of the IT revolution

In understanding the economic impacts of any technological revolution, it should be recognized that investment is both the source and consequence of technological change; investment takes place in response to technical innovations but in the process of investing in new types of plant, machinery and equipment, technological innovations diffuse through the economy and people learn about new innovations. This relationship between investment, technical innovation/ diffusion and macroeconomic activity is complicated and multifaceted.

Not all commentators agree about the revolutionary impact of the IT revolution. DeLong and Summers (2001) assert that the IT revolution is not an unique event. Nor is it qualitatively different from other technological revolutions, such as those accompanying the Industrial Revolution. Solow (1987) famously observed that computerization can be seen everywhere, except in the productivity statistics: between the 1970s and the 1990s, productivity slowed despite widespread computerization (this is known as 'Solow's computer paradox'). Though it should be noted that this paradox may reflect lags in investment decision-making, slow diffusion of innovations given the large adjustment costs accompanying adoption of innovative technologies and/or a measurement problem reflecting the neglect of intangible investments in conventional productivity statistics.

In contrast, Yang and Brynjolfsson (2001) argue that computerization is the most pervasive technological change this era. They argue that IT developments have promoted improved macroeconomic performance, culminating in large increases in productivity and growth in the 1990s, particularly in the USA. Landefeld and Fraumeni (2000) estimate that the contribution of high-tech products to real GDP growth in the USA between 1995 and 1999 was 24 per cent and difficulties measuring the impacts of high-tech investments mean that this is likely to be an under-estimate. The US Department of Commerce (1999) estimated that high-tech industry accounted for more than one third of GDP growth between 1995 and 1999. Gordon (2000) and Whelan (2000) also provide evidence about the impacts of the IT revolution on increasing trend growth rates in real-GDP and productivity. Increasing GDP growth has been accompanied by reduced volatility in GDP suggesting that IT innovations have promoted greater flexibility in the macroeconomy just as microeconomic innovations (for example, price comparison sites such as dealtime.com and kelkoo.com) have increased price transparency and and microeconomic flexibility.

IT developments have affected productivity and real wages as well. Plants using computer-aided manufacturing pay their workers two thirds more than traditional plants in the same industry (Dunne, 1991). The IT revolution has also promoted globalization, reflected in increasing trade in computers, semi-conductors and other high-tech goods. The stock of household wealth has risen in parallel: US household wealth doubled in the 1990s, reflecting increases in share prices – particularly in the IT sector, fostering income growth and growing consumer confidence (Landefeld and Fraumeni, 2000).

Of course a lot happened in 2000 and 2001 and following the NASDAQ crash in mid-2001, surplus computers stockpiled. Access to cheap finance had encouraged an unsustainable over-investment in computing resources (Cecchetti, 2002). But Cecchetti argues that, overall, the IT revolution has made economies naturally more resilient and flexible, for example, as new innovations in inventory control have allowed firms to respond quickly to changes in current economic conditions. He observes that the 2000–01 'mini-recession' in the USA was remarkably subdued and short-lived. It also seems that economies may have been more resilient in the aftermath of the September 2001 terrorist attacks than was initially predicted. US Bureau of Economic Analysis (BEA) data show that although US annual real GDP growth slowed to 1.7 per cent in the last quarter of 2001, real GDP growth the third quarter of 2002 is estimated to be 3.1%.

Investment and the New Economy

There are some distinctive forces affecting computing investments in the New Economy that do not necessarily affect traditional investments. These relate to externalities and network effects; inventory and replacement investment; measurement problems; intangible investments and venture capital funding.

Externalities and network effects complicate the analysis of investment in computing-related networks

Economists know well that not all the benefits and costs of economic activity are captured in prices; economic activity is affected by a wide range of externalities and this is particularly true for computing. Some of these externalities relate to the process of innovation. Negative externalities may exist if innovators destroy the value of their competitors' assets when they introduce new technologies. On the other hand, positive exernalities may exist with the diffusion of innovation. For example, investments in intangible assets (such as human capital investments, e.g. in training of staff) may have benefits for other firms (for example, if skilled workers move between jobs).

Network effects

A significant number of the externalities resulting from computerization relate to 'network externalities' or 'network effects'. A large proportion of modern computing technologies are tapping into computing networks of one sort or another, from fax machines, VCRs and local area networks (LANs) to the Internet and electronic payment systems. A positive network externality occurs when an increase in the number of users of a networked product increases the value of that product for other producers and/or consumers. If these positive network effects are ignored, then networked goods and services will be under-used at current prices and investment in networked products will be insufficient relative to the social optimum. However, there may be negative network effects, for example, those associated with the built-in obsolescence of certain types of software and hardware; this built-in obsolescence will be associated with excessive rates of replacement investment for computer goods (Cecchetti, 2002). The impacts on replacement investment are discussed in more detail below.

Also, if there are benefits in waiting to innovate, for example, if a firm is able to free-ride on an earlier entrant's network investments, then this will create a negative externality for the pioneering innovators and create a 'second mover advantage' for imitators (Glazer *et al.*, 2002; Katz and Shapiro, 1986). Negative network externalities may operate to deter innovative producers in new financial technologies. Gowrisankaran and Stavins (2002) present an analysis of investment in electronic payments systems. They observe that as pioneering innovators build up electronic payments systems, imitator firms free-ride on pioneers' networks, although, as electronic payment systems evolve, the pioneer firms nonetheless stand to gain from the wider acceptability of their facilities.

Computerization has led to decreases in inventory investment but increases in replacement investment

Replacement investment

Approximately 60 per cent of corporate IT budgets go towards product upgrades and the replacement of outdated equipment and software (Roach, 1998). This means that increasing investment is not necessarily accompanied by increases in the capital stock. As mentioned above, accelerated depreciation is exacerbated by what Cecchetti (2002) calls the 'dark side' of network externalities: with frequent product upgrades requiring increasingly powerful hardware, obsolescence is built-in to a large proportion of business hardware and software. Businesses are forced to replace their software and hardware more frequently than necessary in order to keep their computing resources up-to-date and in line with those used by customers, suppliers and competitors. Landefeld and Fraumeni (2000) show that the margin between GDP and net domestic product (NDP = GDP minus depreciation) has been widening as a consequence of this accelerated rate of depreciation and the accompanying increases in replacement investment. These increases in replacement investment are likely to impose unnecessary costs on modern businesses.

The accelerated rate of depreciation and replacement for computing equipment can be confirmed by examining data on the average ages of various types of equipment. The typical age of computing machinery, as captured by the median age of different types of computing equipment, is 1.7 years. Figure 13.3 shows the variation in average ages of various forms of equipment in the USA between 1978 and 2001. The average age of a typical piece of 'old economy' machinery, such as metal-working machinery, is considerably greater than the average age of two typical types of 'New Economy' equipment, i.e. mainframe computers and pre-packaged software. (The peaks in the average ages shown in Figure 13.3 may reflect lumpy investments and/or cyclical factors.) The differences in average ages are relatively stable throughout the 1990s suggesting that the differences reflect accelerated depreciation and not just that businesses are investing in these types of assets for the first time.

Inventory investment

In the mid-1980s, 'just-in-time' inventory control methods were developed allowing the computerized tracking of inventories through all stages from production to retail distribution. As a consequence, firms no longer have to store up large volumes of inventories because they can adjust their production relatively quickly in response to changes in demand (McConnell and Quiros, 2000). And decreases in inventory investment have made the US economy more resilient in the face of shocks. Inventory investment is the most volatile component of investment and investment is the most volatile component of GDP. So decreases in inventory investment have contributed to declining volatility in GDP during the 1990s, thus moderating the course of the trade cycle, reducing uncertainty, increasing growth rates and reducing inflationary pressures (Cecchetti, 2002).

Measuring the New Economy is constrained by data difficulties

The empirical analysis of developments in the New Economy is constrained by lack of data. This lack of data is exacerbated by the following problems:

1. As already noted, there is no commonly accepted definition of the New Economy although the term is generally used to refer to economic developments associated with the growth of high-tech, knowledge-based sectors of the economy. As these new technologies have diffused through the economy, economic processes and behaviours have changed in parallel.
2. Product categories for high-tech goods and services are not sufficiently detailed meaning that it is difficult to measure the impact of high-tech production on non-high-tech industries, for example, when using input-output data.
3. Conventional price indices do not capture quality improvements in computer goods and hedonic pricing methods for computing (which take

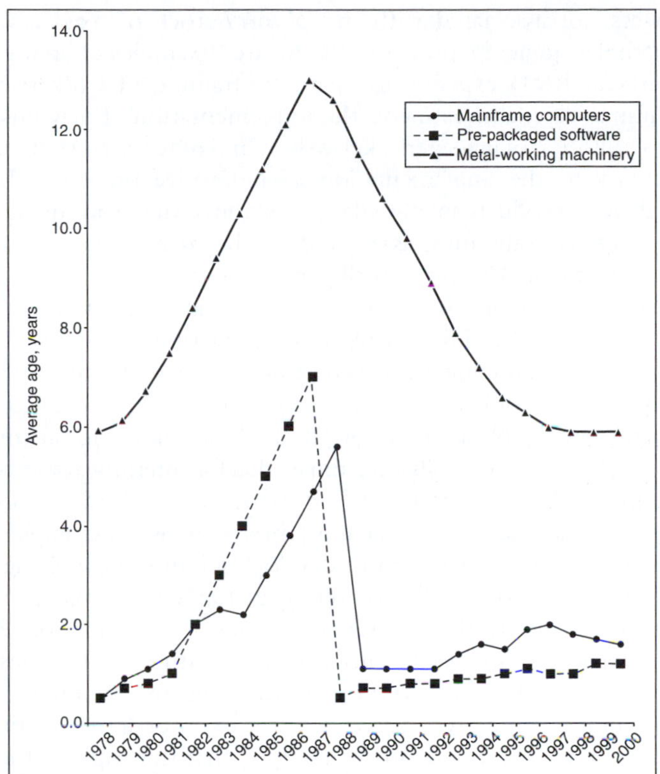

Figure 13.3 Average age of selected fixed assets, USA, 1978–2000
Source: *Bureau of Economic Analysis* (BEA)

into account the speed and memory of computer hardware and software) are not comprehensive, particularly outside the USA. This means that inflationary pressures in IT and telecommunications sectors are overestimated when conventional price indexes are used; conventional indices do not properly account for quality improvements in IT production. This measurement problem may also explain the surprisingly low productivity figures for high-tech industries, for example as noted by Solow (1987), when quality adjusted price indexes are used, the evidence reveals higher productivity growth in high-tech industries than the conventional statistics reveal (Jorgenson and Stiroh, 2000).

Measurement problems are exacerbated because New Economy investment involves many intangible assets

As companies innovate, a large proportion of their investment activity will involve intangible investments. As explained in Chapter 2, intangible assets are the assets not associated with the *physical* stock of fixed assets. These assets nonetheless generate profits in the future. Examples of intangible assets include parts of R&D expenditure, patents, training of workers and other forms of human capital investment, the implementation of new business processes, the acquisition of managerial know-how and other organizational changes complementary to the implementation of innovative processes. Investment in new high-tech products involves large-scale investment in intangible assets as well as tangible computing assets and so the *direct* benefits and costs of computing investment are only a small part of the story.

Yang and Brynjolfsson show that intangible investments are mathematically equivalent to the adjustment and installation costs associated with the introduction of new equipment. Whilst intangible assets are costly to create, they do yield a stream of benefits over time yet these costs are treated as current expenses and so intangible assets are not properly accounted for in conventional balance sheets. Yang and Brynjolfsson estimate that for enterprise resource planning (ERP) systems, the hardware costs involved average around US$1 million; but the internal and external costs of implementing these systems, for example – the large staffing budgets needed to pay staff to develop and implement changes, will be US $20 million. More typically for computing investments overall, the intangibles amount to about ten times the hardware cost (Yang and Brynjolfsson, 2001).

On a macroeconomic scale, growth accounting techniques exclude intangible investments and so the contribution of computer capital in national accounts is under-estimated, leading to an under-estimation of productivity growth overall. Some observers argue that this explains the apparent slowdown in productivity after 1973 despite widespread computerization. If the role of intangible investments had been properly accounted for, measured productivity would have risen since the 1970s (Hobijn and Jovanovic, 2001; Yang and Brynjolfsson, 2001).

The benefits of intangible investments *will* show up as future capital gains and Stock Markets may be amongst the first economic institutions to pick up the potential future benefits of innovative investments associated with the diffusion of computing technologies. Share prices and market capitalizations may rise in anticipation of the future profits generated from intangible investments. Initially, however, even Stock Markets will under-value because, until new firms launch themselves onto Stock Markets via initial public offerings (IPOs), aggregate market capitalizations will not fully reflect the present value of aggregate future dividends delivered by intangibles so a chunk of the future dividend yielding capital stock will be missing from aggregate market capitalizations (Hobijn and Jovanovic, 2001).

Venture capital funds are a crucial financing tool for new firms

Generally, new firms rather than old firms will have the flexibility to take advantage of new high-tech investments, both in terms of producing innovative goods and in terms of purchasing new high-tech equipment. For example, in an analysis of the the biotech sector, Darby and Zucker (2002) note that 512 of 700 biotech firms in their sample were new entrants. New firms are likely to be more prominent because old firms have a capital stock in place, consisting of machines of many vintages; existing firms may not be able or willing quickly to introduce new production techniques particularly as introducing new processes involves substantial intangible costs. For example, evidence suggests that computers displace white-collar workers and so staff in old firms, particularly managerial and non-production workers, may resist technological change (Hobijn and Jovanovic, 2001).

Hobijn and Jovanovic present empirical evidence to support their hypothesis that the IT revolution has adversely affected old firms. After allowing for the impact of mergers, they calculate the contribution to market capitalizations of firms existing in 1972 versus newer firms and find that the market capitalizations for the older firms did not increase by much between 1972 and 2000. In contrast, aggregate market capitalizations as a percentage of GDP almost doubled during the same period. So Hobijn and Jovanovic conclude that the source of new value is coming from new firms.

New entrants into the high-tech production sectors will be dependent upon venture capital funding as they will have limited financial resources of their own with which to develop and produce expensive high-tech products. It is difficult to over-estimate the importance of venture capital funding to developments in the New Economy, particularly the IT sector. Without venture capital funding the diffusion of new innovations would be strictly constrained; it seems unlikely that most traditionally conservative lenders would be prepared to take the risks involved in financing investment ventures when little or no concrete information exists about the potential future returns from innovative new investments. Venture capitalists operate by spreading their risks across a number of different innovative proposals, in the expectation that even if a small proportion of the investments deliver the goods, then these will be substantial enough to ensure profits. This is not to say that venture capitalists will invest in anything: market conditions, the usefulness and marketability of the potential products and the personal qualities of companies' business founders and/or star scientists are carefully assessed.

Developments in the computing industry had a profound impact on venture capital disbursements in the US in the late 1990s, as illustrated by Figure 13.4: the contribution to US venture capital disbursements of the computing sectors (covering computer hardware, communications and the Internet) rose rapidly between 1998 and 2000. Largely, this reflects Internet-related innovations: in 1999, 42 per cent of US venture capital disbursements were allocated to Internet-related businesses. And when the fact that total venture capital disbursements in the USA tripled between 1998 and 2000 is taken into account, the importance of the symbiotic relationship between venture capitalists and IT innovators becomes very clear.

Modelling innovation in computing investment

What is the relationship between investment, innovation and diffusion? How have recent innovations in the New Economy, particularly in the development of Internet-related goods, affected computing investment? According to many business cycle theorists, the relationship between innovation and investment is crucial in understanding economic fluctuations. Mensch (1979) argued that innovative phases are essential to the business cycle; when old technologies have outlived their potential the pressure for development of new basic innovations will propel economics out of recessions. Schumpeter (1911, 1939) argued that technological competition by oligopolistic firms generates a business cycle because the clustering of innovations creates 'bursts' of entrepreneurial and innovative activity. Initially, innovators make excess profits and, as they take factors and financing away from existing firms, prices increase, costs fall and profits rise. Rising profits foster 'bandwagon effects': herds of imitative entrepreneurs enter industries to exploit new innovations. The consequence is that profit margins fall as more and more people seek to exploit the diffusion of technological innovations. Downswings are the inevitable consequence of innovative upswings. The length of downswings is determined by the nature of new investments. If gestation lags are long and/or if investments are particularly 'lumpy', then the downswing will be prolonged.

These ideas can be incorporated into an empirical model of investment. In this section, the empirical evidence on the relationship between innovation and investment is assessed using US data on computing investment between 1980 and 2000. The model estimated is, in its basic formulation, a simplification of Bischoff's (1969) specification of Jorgenson's neo-classical investment model. In Jorgenson's model, investment activity is determined by the relative cost of investment goods (as measured by the user cost of capital) and expected future sales as captured by the value of current output. (For further details about Jorgenson's model see Chapters 5–7 and 11.) In addition, given the widespread theoretical agreement about the depressing effects of uncertainty, an aggregate uncertainty variable has been included (based on Stock Market volatility). Ideally, given the importance of adjustment / installation costs to new computing investments, the model would incorporate q but it would be difficult to calculate q for computing assets because market capitalizations capture the value of all investment goods and do not discriminate between different types of capital equipment. Also, a substantial proportion of US industry is unlisted.

Measuring innovation

Innovation is the process by which new technologies are developed into saleable new products. Measuring innovation is problematic because it has tangible and intangible aspects. R&D data were not used in this analysis

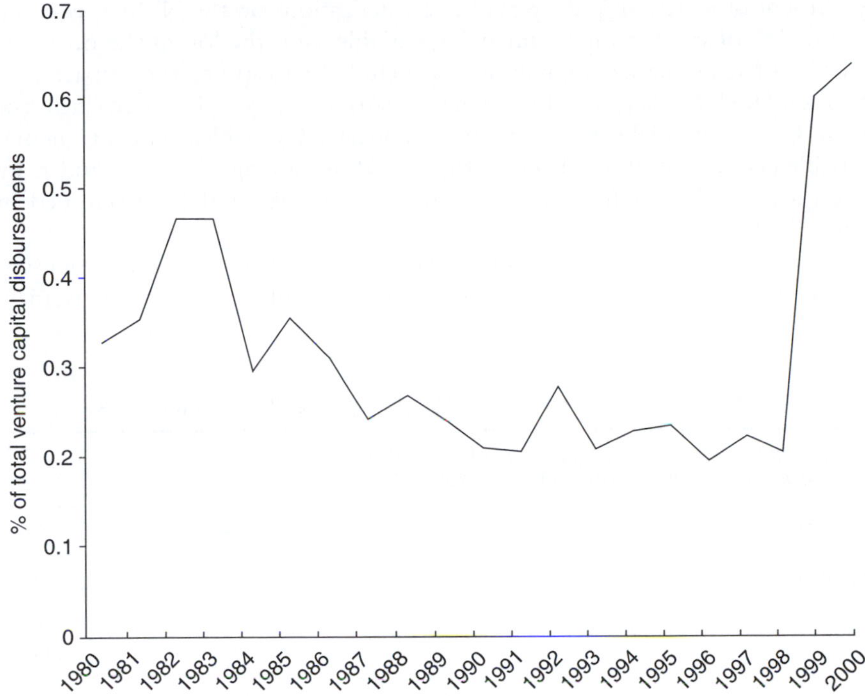

Figure 13.4 US venture capital disbursements to computer hardware, communications and the Internet

because a substantial proportion of R&D expenditure is not associated with product development and/or product launch. And Griliches (1979) argues that patent data is a better indicator of past R&D expenditure than of the process of innovation. Also, data on patents only capture the process of invention. A large proportion of patents, particularly in modern high-tech firms, are never used perhaps reflecting pressures to out-manoeuvre other firms. So innovation is proxied here by a transistor count variable, assuming that increasing microprocessor power will foster innovative opportunity in the computing industry. Also, assuming that innovative production is made possible by innovative financing, a venture capital finance variable has also been included.

To summarise: The following model was estimated:

$$i_{ct} = \alpha + \lambda i_{ct-1} + \beta_1 C_{ct-1} + \theta_1 \Delta \Upsilon_{t-1} + \eta vc_{t-1} + \mu tc_{t-1} + \varphi UNC_t + \gamma \mathrm{m_t} + \varepsilon_\mathrm{t}$$

where i_c is the natural log of investment in computing assets; C_c is the user cost of capital for computing assets; Δy_t is growth in aggregate output. *UNC* is uncertainty as measured by Stock Market volatility (i.e. the quarterly coefficient of variation of daily market capitalizations on the NYSE); *vc* is the natural log of venture capital financing variable; *m* is the log of the quarterly average of daily market capitalizations included to capture the impact of a buoyant Stock Market; *tc* is the log of transistor count; ε is the stochastic error term. Given potential simultaneity between the key variables, an instrumental variable (IV) approach has been incorporated by lagging C_c Δy, *vc* and *tc* by one quarter. The results from the estimation of this model are outlined in Table 13.1.

The results indicate that output growth has a positive effect on computing investment. The estimated parameter on the user cost of capital cost term is small,

Table 13.1 An estimation of computing investment in the USA

Dependent Variable: Natural log of computing investment
Estimation period (full sample): 1981Q3 to 1999Q4

Regressor	*Coefficient*	*t ratio*	*p value*
Intercept	1.74	5.014	0.000
i_{t-1}	0.758	16.50	0.000
C_{ct-1}	−0.0055	−2.41	0.019
Δy_t	0.580	4.87	0.000
vc_{t-1}	0.0087	2.97	0.004
UNC_t	−0.024	−2.53	0.014
m_t	0.0038	3.70	0.000
tc_{t-1}	0.0753	5.42	0.000
Adjusted R^2	0.99827		
Diagnostic tests – probability values			
Serial correlation	0.306		
Functional form	0.060		
Heteroscedasticity	0.003		

	Estimation Periods (split samples): 1981Q3 to 1987Q4		*1998Q1 to 1998Q4*	
Regressor	*Coefficient*	*t ratio [p value]*	*Coefficient*	*t ratio [p value]*
Intercept	3.02	2.25 [0.037]	2.98	4.09 [0.000]
i_{t-1}	0.673	7.05 [0.000]	0.586	6.32 [0.000]
C_{ct-1}	−0.00530	−1.13 [0.274]	−0.0001	−0.0156 [0.988]
Δy_t	0.770	3.53 [0.002]	0.382	1.69 [0.099]
vc_{t-1}	−0.0559	−0.714 [0.484]	0.0148	2.87 [0.007]
UNC_t	−0.0269	−0.430 [0.672]	−0.0335	−3.93 [0.000]
m_t	−0.0220	−0.407 [0.689]	0.00516	4.73 [0.000]
tc_{t-1}	0.129	2.19 [0.042]	0.131	4.97 [0.000]
Adjusted R^2	0.98560		0.99810	
Diagnostic tests – probability values				
Serial correlation	0.476		0.1323	
Functional form	0.026		0.956	
Heteroscedasticity	0.648		0.147	
Predictive failure	0.998		n/a	
Structural break	0.219		n/a	

though significant. Venture capital funding exerts a positive impact on computing investment suggesting that computing investment is responsive to increases in venture capital funding. The parameter on transistor count is also positive, suggesting that investors have responded to innovations made feasible by increasing computing power. The uncertainty variable suggests that there is a negative relationship between computing investment and volatility on the stock exchange.

The positive relationship between the average NYSE market capitalization and computing investment may imply that a buoyant Stock Market encourages computing investment if investors look to the Stock Market as an indicator of the aggregate state of confidence (though it could be that concomitant rises in both are just reflecting cyclical factors rather than an underlying causal relationship). It is interesting that this empirical model of computing investment does seem to deliver more plausible results than the models for aggregate investment described in the previous two chapters. This suggests that aggregation problems were at the root of the mixed empirical results described in Chapters 11 and 12.

The diagnostic tests indicate that there are problems with the estimation of the relationship over the period 1981Q3 and 1987Q4: the functional form and heteroscedasticity tests are significant at 6% and 0.3% respectively. A possible explanation for this can be seen when the sample is split into two: for the first period (1981Q3 to 1987Q4) the model does not work well and functional form problems are significant at 3% significance levels. However, for the latter period (1988Q1 to 1999Q4) the model works well: all the diagnostic tests are insignificant and the parameter values and signs are plausible and significant at 10% (apart from the user cost parameter). This suggests that a structural break occurred around 1987 and this would be consistent with the idea that it has taken firms a while to adapt their investment decisions to the arrival of new computing technologies.

In an attempt to model this possible structural break, a simple additive structural break dummy variable was introduced. But this created functional form problems significant at a 10% significance level as well as significant heteroscedasticity. This suggests that, if there is a structural break, it is complicated in form (possibly non-linear given the insignificant predictive failure and structural break tests for the full sample).

Conclusions and policy implications

Developments in the New Economy, particularly the evolution of the high-tech computing sector, have had wide-ranging impacts on macroeconomic activity, although it does seem that these effects have taken a while to work themselves through the economy. Some of the most significant impacts have been felt in inventory investment and replacement investment. Inventory investment has fallen because of more responsive inventory control techniques but replacement investment has risen, reflecting the accelerated rate of obsolescence with computing technologies. So in one sense, the IT revolution has had positive impacts, enhancing flexibility. On the other hand, the accelerated depreciation has probably added unnecessarily to the replacement investment costs facing modern businesses.

A policy question that emerges is the extent to which governments will be able effectively to implement macroeconomic stabilization policies in a world that can respond so quickly to changing conditions. If the Post Keynesians are right about the importance of conventional behaviour and herd instincts, it could be that the destabilizing forces of uncertainty and speculation will spread through the macroeconomy far more quickly with the increased speed of information processing allowed by computerization. In particular, the control of money supply and interest rates will become more difficult and this will have implications for investment activity, for example, as new electronic payment systems develop within deregulated financial markets (Baddeley, 2000). If the Post Keynesians are right about the destabilizing impacts of unfettered monetary and financial forces, the future for government policy looks particularly difficult.

In terms of other theoretical lessons from the analysis of computing investment, it does seem that it is easier to model investment at a more disaggregated level and the results from the econometric model presented in this chapter do seem to be more revealing than the results from the models presented in Chapters 11 and 12. However, it should be remembered that the econometric analysis presented here has not necessarily captured all the influences of intangible (and therefore not easily measurable) investments. Intangible investments are an integral component of investment in the New Economy and fuller analyses of their impacts are needed.

Chapter summary

1. The New Economy is the knowledge-based economy that has evolved as a consequence of various high-tech innovations, particularly in the IT sector.
2. Since the 1970s, computerization of the US economy has progressed at an exponential rate and has had profound implications for economic performance, for example, in terms of boosting economic growth and productivity. A large proportion of companies' investment budgets are now devoted to IT purchases.
3. Externalities and network effects complicate the analysis of investment in computing-related networks, such as the Internet.
4. Computerization has encouraged accelerated depreciation and replacement investment. Accelerated depreciation is one of the consequences of technological developments because new and substantially more powerful hardware and software products are produced all the time. Replacement investment costs may be excessively high creating negative network externalities. With frequent product upgrades requiring increasingly powerful

Chapter summary continued

hardware, obsolescence becomes built into a large proportion of relatively new business equipment. Businesses are forced to replace their software and hardware more frequently than necessary in order to keep their computing resources in line with those used by their customers, suppliers and competitors.

5. Computerization has led to decreases in inventory investment because innovations in inventory control have increased the resilience of modern economies in the face of shocks. 'Just-in-time' inventory control methods allow modern firms to limit their inventory investment and respond more quickly to changes the volatility of US GDP.
6. Measurement difficulties, for example, the limited coverage of price indexes for high-tech products, mean that empirically assessing the impact of investment in the New Economy is difficult. These measurement problems are exacerbated by the fact that a large proportion of New Economy investments involve intangible assets. The contribution of these intangible assets is not properly captured when conventional accounting methods are used.
7. New firms dominate in the production of innovative, high-tech goods. These firms will have limited financial backing of their own and so venture capitalists play a particularly important role in financing the process of innovation.
8. An empirical model of computing investment shows that, for computing investment in the USA from 1988 onwards, venture capital funding, transistor count and output growth all affect computing investment. However, the association between computing investment and these variables in an earlier period is far less clear, suggesting that a structural break occurred in the late 1980s.
9. The key policy implication from this chapter is that government control of investment activity and the macroeconomy is going to become increasingly difficult as computerization spreads and evolves.

Data appendix

I	Net investment in computing assets, US$ *US Bureau of Economic Analysis (BEA) website*
C	User cost of capital for computing investment (derived from BEA data)
Δy	Growth in US GDP *BEA*
UNC	Uncertainty, measured as the quarterly coefficient of variation in daily NYSE market capitalization *NYSE website*

m	Quarterly average of daily NYSE market capitalization *NYSE website*
tc	Natural log of transistor count *Science and Engineering Indicators, US National Science Board*
vc	Natural log of US venture capital disbursements to producers of computer hardware, communications and Internet *Science and Engineering Indicators, US National Science Board*

14 Investment and development: a cross-sectional analysis

Introduction	182
Investment convergence	183
Absolute β convergence models	183
Absolute gap convergence models	184
Conditional convergence models	184
The empirical analysis	184
Conclusion	190
Chapter summary	191
Data appendix	192

The empirical analyses covered so far in this book have concentrated on time-series analyses of investment in the USA and UK. But what is the experience in other countries? Have less developed countries (LDCs) been investing more rapidly to compensate for relative capital scarcity? Or does the evidence suggest that LDC economies are stagnant in terms of investment activity? In this chapter the investment performance of a cross-section of countries is assessed. In particular, the evidence about convergence in investment rates will be assessed over a sample of countries. Conditional and absolute convergence models are explained and some of the theoretical concepts outlined in earlier chapters are used as conditioning variables to capture the different investment convergence patterns. The resulting convergence models are analyzed using 1988–98 data from 47 different countries. In addition, dummy variables are used to capture the differences in convergence rates for LDCs and developed countries (DCs). The evidence presented indicates that investment rates in developing countries have been converging more rapidly than investment rates in DCs.

Introduction

Industrialization and modernization are two of the key goals emphasized by policy-makers in LDCs and investment activity is essential to these processes. The focus on industrialization reflects a belief that new investment will not only augment a limited capital stock but will also foster technology transfer as the technology embodied within new physical capital is introduced to an economy. It is thought that as economies are industrialized, the marginal productivity of labour will rise and real wages will increase accordingly. Production, output and employment opportunities will grow concomitantly. The net effects will include raised living standards and increased employment in the industrial sector. In addition, industrialization and modernization will promote global equality: if global investment patterns are converging as LDCs modernize and industrialize by adopting First World production techniques, then global productivity and incomes will be converging too.

However, the policy solution for promoting development is not as simple as it first appears. Dualism may limit the spread of modernization. If the benefits of industrialization are concentrated into the hands of the local elites and/or are harnessed by multinational corporations, then the linkages between different sectors of the economy will be limited and the benefits of investment growth will fail to spread and 'trickle down'. In addition, even if industrialization and investment do promote economic growth, it does not necessarily follow that more broadly based human development will improve in tandem, particularly if industrialization encourages the development of urban slums, in which case poverty and deprivation are more likely to increase rather than decrease. If the government supports industrialization at the expense of workers' rights then political freedoms will be constrained. For these and many other reasons, investment and industrialization are not unequivocally beneficial for LDCs. This raises two questions: are investment rates converging? If so, is this convergence promoting the process of development? This chapter aims to assess both of these two questions.

Investment convergence

In this chapter, conventional convergence models are used to examine the evolution of cross-sectional investment patterns. These convergence techniques are usually associated with empirical assessments of the neo-classical growth theories of Swan and Solow in which *savings* rates converge.[1] However, the empirical analysis in this chapter presents a contrasting analysis of macroeconomic patterns to that of neo-classical analysis – first, by looking at *investment* rates as the key determinant of economic potential; and second, by hypothesizing persistence rather than convergence in economic patterns.

Convergence models were developed to assess the neo-classical assertion that economies converge because markets act as effective equilibrating institutions in capitalist economies. The Post Keynesian approach contrasts with the theories of Solow and Swan in which savings rates are central to economic growth and investment has no independent role. In a Post Keynesian world, looking at *investment* is justified because *investment* is the leading economic variable. Post Keynesians believe that boosting investment directly will augment the capital stock and so is central in enhancing economic potential and fostering economic growth. Post Keynesians argue with the Solow-Swan emphasis on boosting savings because they believe that the 'paradox of thrift' will mean that boosting savings deters macroeconomic activity; that is savings are a leakage from the circular flow of income and so dampen the multiplier effects that magnify increases in aggregate demand. In a Post Keynesian world, markets do not equilibrate and so cross-sectional economic differences will tend to persist rather than converge, reflecting forces of path dependency and cumulative causation.

Absolute β convergence models

The simplest form of convergence is β convergence. Countries will be exhibiting β convergence if there is a negative relationship between where countries start and how quickly they change. For example: if Zimbabwe starts with low investment rate in 1988 but its investment grows more quickly than other countries in a sample over the period 1988–98, then this suggests that Zimbabwe is 'catching up' with the other countries, i.e. β convergence is taking place. However, if Zimbabwe starts with a low investment rate but its investment rate does not grow as quickly as other countries' investment rates, then this implies that Zimbabwe is being left behind, i.e. there is no β convergence. So, in essence, β convergence models assess whether or not there is a negative correlation between starting points and changes.

Absolute gap convergence models

The problem with β convergence models is that they do not capture the spread of observations across countries; they only capture mean reversion. This difficulty is resolved with models developed around the concept of σ convergence, where σ convergence implies a decreasing spread of observations as well as mean reversion. Baddeley, Martin and Tyler (1998), Barro and Sala-I-Martin (1995), Chatterji and Dewhurst (1996), show that σ convergence can be measured by analyzing cross-country differentials using 'gap convergence' models. In the context of the investment example, this involves calculating the gaps between each country's investment rate and the investment rate of a leader country. If there is a one-to-one relationship between a country's gap in 1998 and its gap in 1988, then this implies that inter-country differentials are persisting. For example, if Zimbabwian investment was less that Singaporean investment in 1988 and if this difference remains in 1998, then this implies persistence in international differentials.

Conditional convergence models

Absolute convergence models assess whether or not countries are converging onto one pattern. If the empirical evidence suggests no *absolute* convergence, this does not necessarily imply that there is no convergence at all. It could be that different groups of countries are moving on different paths and that these different paths will be determined by other economic variables. These differences can be captured by 'controlling' for the factors. In practice, this involves including additional explanatory variables into the convergence models to give conditional convergence models.

The empirical analysis

In this analysis, the first step involves assessing the degree of cross-country convergence by examining the evolution of cross-country investment rates (as a proportion of GDP) over time. Figure 14.1 plots growth in investment rates over the period 1988–98 against investment rates in 1988 for a cross-section of 47 DCs and LDCs. This chart does show a tendency for higher investment growth in LDCs than in the industrialized world. This suggests some degree of β convergence.

Figure 14.2 plots the standard deviations of investment rates across the sample of 47 countries for each year between 1988 and 1998. This chart shows some evidence of increasing spread across the countries sampled, at least until 1997. However, more rigorous tests are needed to establish whether these increases in spread are significant.

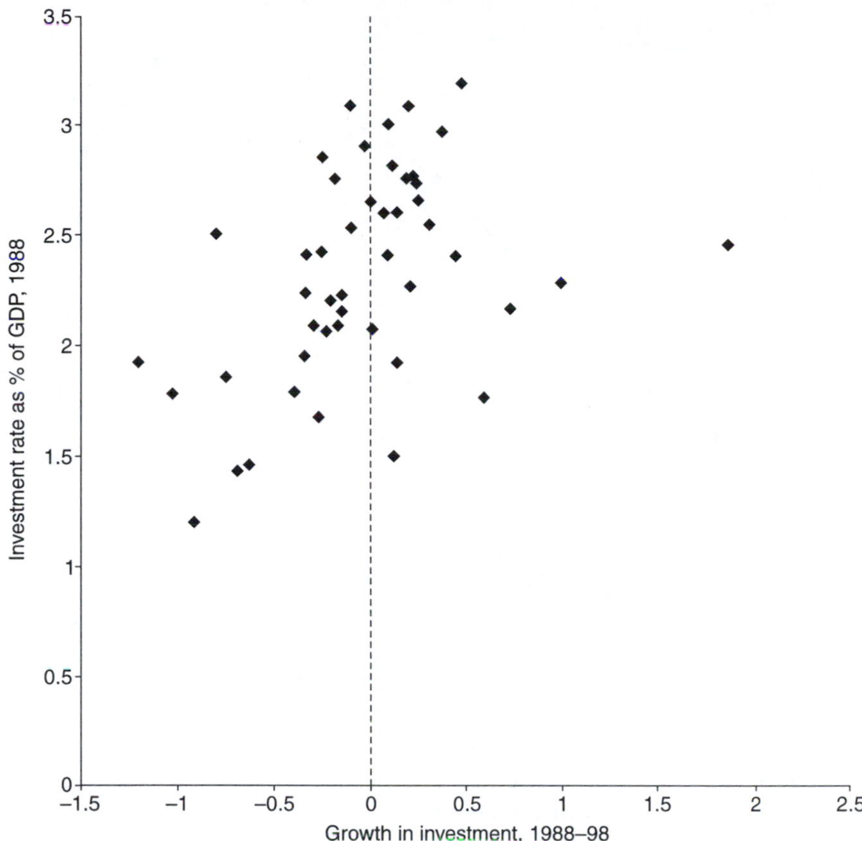

Figure 14.1 Growth in investment, 1988–98

To quantify these factors more objectively, the models of convergence outlined above were used to assess the extent of β and gap convergence across a sample of 47 countries over the period 1988–98. Both sets of convergence models were estimated in two forms: with and without additive and multiplicative dummy variables to capture differences in the intercept and slope parameters between DCs and LDCs.

Estimation of absolute convergence models

The empirical formulation of the models and hypotheses estimated in this chapter is summarized in Box 14.1. For both types of convergence model the null hypothesis tested is of persistence. The empirical results from the estimation of the absolute convergence models are outlined in Tables 14.1 and 14.2. These results indicate that there is both β and gap convergence in investment rates when all countries are treated together: the t tests on the H_0s give $t = -4.97$

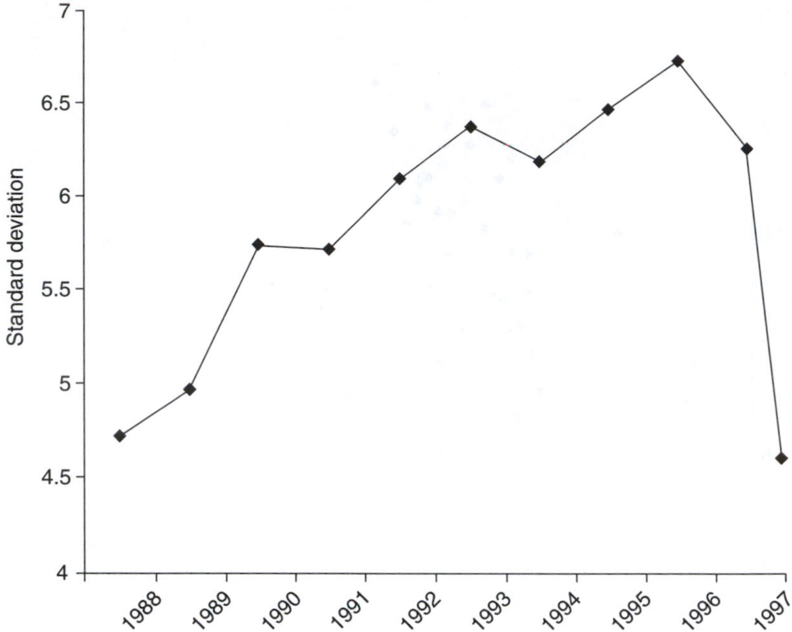

Figure 14.2 Standard deviation of investment rates, 1988–98

and −4.90 for β and gap-convergence respectively. However, the results are affected by the separation of the countries into developed and less-developed categories using dummy variables. These t tests reveal that there is evidence of significant convergence for the LDCs ($t = -5.64$ for β convergence and $t = -4.97$ for gap convergence). For the DCs the β convergence parameter is not significantly less than zero and the gap convergence parameter is not significantly less than one ($t = -1.41$ for β convergence and $t = -1.39$ for gap convergence), suggesting persistence. However, any interpretation of these results must be undertaken with caution: neither the β nor the gap convergence versions performed well econometrically: the models were characterized by heteroscedasticty and/or functional problems and these were significant even at 1 per cent signficiance levels.

These results are not entirely surprising as implicit within these models is an assumption either (in the first case) that all countries are moving on the same path as far as investment rates are concerned or (in the second case) that all DCs are moving on one path and all LDCs are following another. The latter assumption does seem to have more empirical validity in the sense that including the dummy variables reduces the extent of the functional form problems reflected in the diagnostic test statistics. Therefore, it seems more plausible to allow that the international patterns are affected by other variables and therefore conditional converence models were also estimated.

Box 14.1 Empirical convergence models

Absolute β convergence models

$$\Delta i_j = \alpha + \beta i_j + \epsilon_j$$
$$H_0:\ \beta = 0$$
$$H_1:\ \beta < 0$$

if $\beta < 0 \rightarrow \beta$ convergence; if $\beta = 0 \rightarrow$ persistence
i_j = *natural* log of investment rate, country j, 1998
$\Delta i_j \approx$ growth in investment rate, 1988–98, country j
ϵ_j = stochastic error term

Absolute gap convergence models

$$Gap_{98,j} = \phi + \lambda Gap_{88,j} + \upsilon_j$$

$H_0: |\lambda| = 1$ if $|\lambda| = 1 \rightarrow$ persistence
$H_1: |\lambda| < 1$ if $-1 < \lambda < 1 \rightarrow \sigma$ convergence

$Gap_{98,j}$ = The differential between country j's investment rate and the leader country investment rate, 1998
$Gap_{88,j}$ = The differential between country j's investment rate and the leader country's investment rate, 1988
υ_j = stochastic error term

Conditional convergence models

Conditional β convergence

$$\Delta i_j = \alpha + \beta i_j + \sum \theta_k X_{k,j} + \xi_j$$

Conditional gap convergence

$$Gap_{98,j} = \phi + \lambda Gap_{88,j} + \sum \theta_k X_{k,j} + \varpi_j$$

where:
θ_k = parameters on the conditioning explanatory variables
$X_{k,j}$ = conditioning explanatory variables
ξ_j = stochastic error term

Estimation of conditional convergence models

To capture some of the factors relevant to conditional convergence, the models include variables that might determine the volume of funds available for

Table 14.1 Absolute β convergence models

Dependent variable: Growth in investment rate, 1988–98
Sample: 47 countries

	Without dummy variables		*With dummy variables*	
	Parameter Estimate	*t ratio [p value]*	*Parameter Estimate*	*t ratio [p value]*
Constant	1.32	4.73 [0.000]	0.44	0.79 [0.432]
i	−0.57	−4.97 [0.000]	−0.32	−1.41 [0.166]
LDC dummy	...	...	1.15	1.87 [0.069]
LDC × i	...	...	−0.29	−1.13 [0.265]
R^2 (adjusted)	0.34		0.53	
Diagnostic tests – probability values				
Serial correlation	0.973		0.670	
Functional form	0.022		0.171	
Heteroscedasticity	0.059		0.049	

Table 14.2 Absolute gap convergence models

Dependent variable: Gap_{98}
Sample: 47 countries

	Parameter Estimate	*t ratio [p value]*	*Parameter Estimate*	*t ratio [p value]*
Constant	−0.72	−9.70 [0.000]	−0.92	−8.16 [0.000]
Gap_{88}*	0.43	−4.90 [0.000]	0.68	−1.39 [0.005]
LDC	...	...	0.37	2.69 [0.005]
LDC by Gap_{88}	...	...	−0.29	−1.13 [0.265]
R^2 (adjusted)	0.22		0.44	
Diagnostic tests – probability values				
Serial correlation	0.972		0.670	
Functional form	0.021		0.369	
Heteroscedasticity	0.184		0.801	

*t test is of H_0: $\lambda = 1$

investment. These variables are defined in the appendix to this chapter. The results from these models are outlined in Table 14.3 and Table 14.4. The β conditional convergence models are still characterized by significant econometric problems, in this case heteroscedasticity. This limits the validity of the results.

The estimation of the conditional gap convergence models with dummy variables revealed more encouraging results. These models did not suffer any econometric problems at significance levels up to about 20 per cent. The unrestricted model was 'tested down' by excluding insignificant variables one-by-one, starting with the most insignificant variable. Given the likelihood of multicollinearity the individual t tests of significance were supplemented with joint variable deletion tests of significance. These tests revealed that the additive dummy, the Human Development Index (HDI), real interest rate, market capitalization, exchange rate uncertainty, interest spread and Stock Market

Table 14.3 Conditional β convergence models

Dependent variable: Growth in investment rate, 1988–98
Sample: 47 countries

	Without dummy variables		*With dummy variables*	
	Parameter Estimate	*t ratio [p value]*	*Parameter Estimate*	*t ratio [p value]*
Constant	1.39	2.70 [0.010]	−0.09	−0.12 [0.905]
i	−0.68	−5.90 [0.000]	−0.32	−1.34 [0.190]
LDC	...	...	1.31	2.00 [0.053]
LDC by I	...	...	−0.40	−1.47 [0.151]
HDI	−0.34	−0.82 [0.419]	0.36	0.66 [0.511]
GDP growth	0.12	3.11 [0.004]	0.08	1.87 [0.069]
Interest rate	0.00	−0.32 [0.750]	0.00	−0.35 [0.728]
Volatility	0.00	0.83 [0.410]	0.00	0.56 [0.579]
Spread	0.02	1.11 [0.275]	0.01	0.58 [0.564]
Market				
Value	0.00	−0.42 [0.673]	0.00	−0.21 [0.833]
Volatility	0.00	−0.06 [0.954]	0.00	−0.04 [0.968]
R^2 (adjusted)	0.45		0.50	
Diagnostic tests – probability values				
Serial correlation	0.594		0.892	
Functional form	0.034		0.005	
Heteroscedasticity	0.095		0.737	

Table 14.4 Conditional gap convergence models – restricted versions

Dependent variable: Gap 98
Sample: 47 countries

	Without dummy variables		*With dummy variables*	
	Parameter Estimate	*t ratio [p value]*	*Parameter Estimate*	*t ratio [p value]*
Constant	−0.95	−2.07 [0.045]	−1.07	−7.63 [0.000]
Gap_{88}*	0.32	2.74 [0.003]	0.82	−0.907
LDC	...	...	...	...
LDC by Gap_{88}	...	...	−0.58	−2.89 [0.001]
HDI	−0.34	−0.82 [0.419]	...	...
GDP growth	0.12	3.11 [0.004]	0.1	3.14 [0.000]
Interest rate	0.00	−0.32 [0.750]	...	...
Volatility	0.00	0.83 [0.410]	...	...
Spread	0.02	1.11 [0.275]	...	...
Market value	0.00	−0.42 [0.673]	...	...
Volatility	0.00	−0.06 [0.954]	...	...
R^2 (adjusted)	0.34		0.46	
Diagnostic tests – probability values				
Serial correlation	0.594		0.801	
Functional form	0.030		0.316	
Heteroscedasticity	0.942		0.749	

*t test is of H_0: $\lambda = 1$

uncertainty variables were jointly insignificantly different from zero at an 80 per cent significance level: F(7.36) 0.41686 [p value = 0.885] – so these variables were excluded from the final regression.

As far as persistence is concerned, the results were not dissimilar from the absolute convergence findings. Results from the conditional β convergence models without dummies suggested convergence ($t = -5.9$) and with dummies: for LDCs suggested convergence ($t = -5.45$); for DCs suggested persistence ($t = -1.34$). The results from the gap convergence models without dummy variables suggested a rejection of the H_0 of persistence ($t = -5.87$) but with dummies, the final restricted version suggested convergence for LDCs ($t = -7.37$) and persistence for DCs ($t = -0.907$). The end result of this process gives the following gap convergence model as the preferred regression for this analysis:

$$\textit{For DCs}: \quad \text{Gap}_{98} = -1.07 + 0.82\text{Gap}_{88} + 0.1\text{GDP growth}$$
$$\textit{For LDCs}: \quad \text{Gap}_{98} = -1.07 - 0.24\text{Gap}_{88} + 0.1\text{GDP growth}$$

This suggests that there is persistence in the gaps between the investment rates across DCs. However, the gaps for LDCs are not exhibiting significant persistence. This confirms the evidence from the other convergence models which all suggested persistence rather than convergence in the investment performance for DCs but the opposite for LDCs. The other noteworthy finding is that GDP growth is significantly correlated with the gap in 1998. This finding may suggest some sort of catch-up mechanism, if below average countries experience more rapid output growth. In contrast, the other potential determinants of investment activity discussed in previous chapters are not significant variables within these models.

In terms of avenues for further research it should be noted that this analysis was conducted on a relatively small sample of data. Also, in the interest of simplicity and because of data constraints, these models were estimated using cross-sectional techniques. The limited degrees of freedom may reduce the reliability of these results suggesting that further research could concentrate on estimating these models over a larger number of countries and/or using panel data.

Conclusion

The results from the estimation of these models suggest that the pattern of investment rates across DCs versus LDCs is quite different. Certainly there is little evidence to support a neo-classical view that capitalist economies converge quickly. In addition, different countries are affected by different degrees of convergence, with more evidence of investment convergence in the LDCs than the DCs. The evidence also suggests that investment convergence is not absolute but is conditional upon other factors as well, particularly the rate of output growth. But it should be noted that the results may just be capturing simultaneity between the output growth and investment variables.

Chapter summary

1. This chapter presents a cross-sectional analysis of investment across developing and developed countries in order to assess the extent of international convergence in investment rates.
2. Two sorts of convergence models have been adapted to investment modelling: β and σ convergence models. β convergence models predict that convergence takes place when there is an inverse correlation between changes and starting values, i.e. when poorer countries grow faster than richer countries. σ convergence models predict that convergence will be reflected in a decreasing dispersion across countries. Following Chatterji and Dewhurst (1996), the latter can be captured statistically by examining the deviations in investment rates away from those of a leader country. If these deviations are stable over time, then there is persistence; if these deviations are diminishing over time, then there is convergence. β convergence models suffer from a number of limitations, reflected in the diagnostic statistics, and therefore the analysis of σ convergence using gap convergence models is preferred in this analysis.
3. The empirical analysis develops some of the theoretical ideas presented in earlier chapters in order to capture the different factors determining countries' investment rates. Factors assessed in the analysis included price, financial and demand variables. In addition, additive and multiplicative dummy variables are included to capture the differences in convergence rates between developing and developed countries.
4. The empirical results suggest that there has been conditional σ convergence. GDP growth both in itself and via its interaction with the development dummy variable was the only significant conditioning variable in the σ convergence analysis. The other interesting finding was that investment rates in LDCs appear to be converging more rapidly than investment rates in DCs.

Data appendix

Variable	Source
Investment rate (Investment ÷ GDP)	*World Development Indicators*, World Bank
Level of development (HDI – Human Development Indicator, 1995)	*World Development Indicators*
GDP growth (Average annual growth in GDP between 1988 and 1998)	*World Development Indicators*
Interest rate (Average annual real interest rate)	*World Development Indicators*
Volatility (Standard deviation of annual nominal exchange rate in US$)	*World Development Indicators*
Spread (Average difference between interest rate on loans vs savings)	*World Development Indicators*
Market value (Average Stock Market capitalization as a percentage of GDP)	*World Development Indicators*
Volatility (Standard deviation of annual Stock Market capitalization)	*World Development Indicators*
Gap_{98} (1998 differential between logged investment rate and rate for leader country, i.e. Singapore)	Derived
Gap_{88} (1988 differential)	Derived
LDC (An additive dummy = 0 for OECD countries, =1 for LDCs)	

Countries in analysis

Developed Countries
Australia, Austria, Belgium, Canada, Denmark, France, Germany, Greece, Italy, Japan, Netherlands, New Zealand, Norway, Portugal, Spain, Switzerland, UK and USA.

Less Developed Countries
Argentina, Bangladesh, Brazil, Chile, Colombia, Cote d'Ivoire, Egypt, Hong Kong, India, Indonesia, Israel, Jamaica, Jordan, Kenya, Malaysia, Mexico, Morocco, Nigeria, Pakistan, Philippines, Singapore, South Africa, Sri Lanka, Thailand, Trinidad and Tobago, Tunisia, Turkey, Venezuela and Zimbabwe.

15 Residential investment: bubbles and crashes in the UK housing market, 1980–99

Introduction	194
Theoretical considerations	194
Residential investment in the UK: the political and historical context	197
Empirical analysis	201
Conclusion	206
Chapter summary	207
Data appendix	208

The aim of this chapter is to show that the theoretical concepts presented in earlier chapters have applicability beyond business investment and can be applied to the investment decisions made by ordinary people buying new houses, i.e. residential investment. Understanding residential fixed investment is complicated by the fact that, unlike business fixed investment, housing investment combines the characteristics of production goods and consumption goods. Although residential investment does not augment future productive capacity and so does not, in itself, contribute to output and employment growth, its effects on the macroeconomy are far-reaching.

In the empirical parts of this chapter, UK residential investment between 1980 and 1999 is analyzed using both Jorgenson's neo-classical approach and a Minskian approach. The UK housing market experienced a great deal of instability from the 1980s onwards and so the empirical analysis will also focus on some of the economic and political forces that have destabilized UK residential investment in the last 30 years. In particular, the impacts of the financial deregulation and the consequent increases in liquidity in propelling housing investment bubbles and crashes will be assessed.

Introduction

Residential investment is the investment associated with the production and sale of new housing and it has significant impacts in the macroeconomy. Financial factors affect housing investment in just the same way as they affect business investment. For most consumers, house-buying decisions are coupled with the substantial financial decisions involved in getting a mortgage. This means that housing and financial markets are often interdependent. In addition, the state of the housing market will affect confidence and expectations in the macroeconomy more generally and, via wealth effects, changes in house prices will affect aggregate demand.

Developments in housing markets will also affect employment and unemployment via impacts on labour mobility: housing decisions affect people's ability to move and owners are more likely to be immobile. Private rental tends to be associated with a faster outflow from unemployment. Countries with fastest growth in home ownership in the 1980s and 1990s also had the fastest growth in unemployment (Oswald, 1997).

The housing market will have important implications for inequality because the interactions between the owner-occupied sector, private rental sector and the public rental sectors will have crucial impacts on poverty and homelessness. Therefore, an understanding of residential investment is as important to an understanding of the macroeconomy as is an understanding of business investment.

Theoretical considerations

Residential investment is an activity quite distinct from other forms of investment because houses are physical fixed assets that *do not* directly affect future productive capacity. Housing is a fixed investment asset and it represents future consumption. It contributes to householders' wealth and debt in the same way that non-residential investment adds to businesses' stock of assets and debt.

Complexity in housing markets is compounded by rigidities reflecting the fact that houses are heterogeneous goods: each house is unique in some way. Also, the buying and selling of houses does not operate in the same way as for most goods and assets: most of the time, housing transactions are simultaneously monopsonistic and monopolistic. Also, the supply of housing stock is inelastic in both the short-term and the long-term because of the lags involved with housing construction and because the supply of land is constrained, particularly in the UK. These supply lags exacerbate instability.

Both buyers and sellers of housing face information asymmetries: all sorts of information about the characteristics of a house can be concealed from potential buyers; sellers have limited information about the real intentions and financial position of potential buyers. Information asymmetries also affect mortgage lenders as they may have limited information about a mortgage borrower's true ability to meet financial obligations. These information asymmetries contribute to the substantial transactions costs associated with the UK housing market: for example, legal fees, survey and property search costs, property taxes and credit searches. The risks involved for both buyer and seller are particularly high in the UK because there may be a long lag between the decision to buy/sell and the signing of a legally binding agreement. The possibilities for reneging and gazumping further increase the riskiness of housing transactions.

Some theoretical lessons from business investment theory

In theory, residential investment (i.e. purchases of new houses) should be affected by the same factors that affect business investment, i.e. the marginal cost of housing relative to its marginal benefit. If so, Jorgenson's user cost of capital can be transported into an analysis of residential investment with minor modifications. All things being equal, the rate of return on housing investments will increase as house prices increase, will increase as the cost of the next best alternative increases (i.e. imputed rents) and will decrease as interest costs increase. Therefore, the user cost of housing will be:

$$c_h = \frac{p_h}{p_o}(\mu - \dot{p}_h - \rho)$$

And the rate of return on housing can be understood in similar terms as follows:

$$R = \frac{\dot{p}_h + \rho - \mu}{E}$$

where R is the rate of return on housing, p_h is the price of housing, p_o is the price of output, p_h is the expected capital gain in terms of house price inflation, ρ is the net imputed rent, μ is the mortgage interest cost and E is the proportion of equity held in the housing asset. 1/E is the 'gearing ratio', representing the proportion of the housing purchase that is 'geared-up' with borrowings. If a house purchase is financed solely by borrowing and if the capital gains accruing from house price rises together with net imputed rents exceed the interest costs, then the rate of return will be infinite. Conversely, if interest costs and capital losses exceed net imputed rent, then the rate of *loss* will be infinite. So gearing ratios will increase instability in the rate of returns on housing.

Financing constraints, even in the face of plentiful liquidity, will be a more substantial disincentive for residential investment than for business investment because of the risks involved in house purchases. Ordinary home-owners cannot personally escape the legal consequences of mortgage default and they do not have the option to float their houses on the stock exchange. This means that they must bear entirely the risks involved in their borrowing decisions and this is not the case for many business investors.

The affordability of housing, as captured by the ratio of disposable income to house prices, will also affect householders' decisions to invest in housing. As house prices rise and incomes fall, people will choose other forms of housing in preference to owner occupation and will wait to exercise their options to invest in housing. But the decision to buy a new house is not a smooth, continuous function of rates of return on housing and individuals do not behave atomistically with their housing (and mortgage) choices: residential investment will be affected by fashions and frenzies. For these reasons, it is difficult to scale up microeconomic relationships using demographic information because herd behaviour and speculative forces will mean that the housing investment whole is not just a sum of the individual parts. Expectations will play a key role and they are unlikely to be rationally based expectations because lack of information will mean that most house purchasers will be able to make only semi-rational forecasts of the likely future prospects of their residential investments. Adopting some of the insights from Keynes about conventional behaviour in the face of uncertainty: in an uncertain world, housing investors will not only look at their best judgements of the likely future path of their housing asset's value, they will also look to the valuations of other investors. If they realize that they do not have complete information, then it will be sensible to look at what others are doing before deciding how to value housing assets.

Minsky's insights about the nature of financial bubbles, as outlined in Chapter 10, can be applied to the housing market. Housing decisions are more often than not crucially dependent on the availability of mortgage financing and in times of stability and optimism, mortgage lenders will lend on favourable terms because of their positive expectations about the future prospects of the economy. As a housing boom builds up, this optimism will spread and mortgage lenders will take greater risks in their lending decisions moving from relatively safe mortgage conditions to more risky mortgage conditions (such as 100 per cent mortgages and larger multiples of borrowers' income). This will encourage self-propelling increases in house prices: the demand for residential investment will increase as liquidity builds up in mortgage markets and more mortgage financing becomes available on increasingly favourable terms. The boom phase will, initially at least, magnify itself. However, as mortgage rates start to rise, instability will creep in. When mortgage borrowers start to default on their mortgages, mortgage lenders will become more wary and the whole process will start to falter. The gathering instability will be exacerbated by house price falls: negative equity will develop for those borrowers whose mortgage commitments exceed the value of their houses and the extent of negative equity will be positively correlated with gearing ratios. So the housing market will be prone to the same speculative forces and frenzy effects that characterize other asset markets. But these frenzy effects will be exacerbated in housing markets because of the lumpiness of houses and the transactions costs associated with residential investment (Muellbauer and Murphy, 1997). This lumpiness means that people will have magnified incentives to respond to real and imaginary potential changes in the economic and political environment. For example, buyers will hurry into markets before prices rise but delay entry when house prices start to falter, or the market seems to be unstable.

These sorts of processes led to the boom-bust cycle in the UK housing market of the late 1980s and early 1990s and so, for the UK, this analysis of financial fragility has particular resonance. This is because inherent instability in housing and mortgage markets has been compounded by the three decades of political and social change following the election of Thatcher government in 1979.

Residential investment in the UK: the political and historical context

Residential investment is particularly important for the UK economy because there has been a large increase in owner occupation rates in the UK since World War II: in the early 1950s only 30 per cent of households owned their own homes and 52 per cent of households were in rental accommodation; in 1997, 67 per cent of people owned their own homes and 8 per cent were in rental accommodation. Throughout the 1990s about 65 per cent of UK households were living in their own home: a rate above the European average and considerably higher than some of the other EU leading countries, as shown in Table 15.1. For the UK, the greatest increases in home ownership since the 1980s have been for unskilled manual workers, reflecting council house sales as well as mortgage deregulation. In 1995, 43 per cent of unskilled manual workers owned their own homes whereas only 27 per cent owned

Table 15.1 Owner occupation rates in the OECD
percentage of households living in their own home, 1998

Rates up to 60%		*Rates above 60%*	
Switzerland	28	Canada	62
West Germany	40.5	USA	65.8
Sweden	60	Belgium	65
Netherlands	50.8	UK	67
Austria	55.7	Italy	75
Denmark	53.4	Australia	70
France	54	Spain	78
Japan	60	Ireland	80

Sources: UN Environment and Human Settlements Division, European Mortgage Federation

their own homes in 1981. For the professional classes, owner occupation rates remained stable over the period with rates of 87 per cent between 1981 and 1995.

Residential investment is also particularly complex in the UK because of the legal rigidities and lags involved in buying and selling houses. This complexity has been exacerbated by frequent policy changes affecting many aspects of housing decisions. The most substantial changes came after 1979, as encouraging home ownership became an essential element of the Thatcherite political agenda. The policy changes affected residential investment in three key ways: first, by altering the incentives to buy rather than rent; second, by affecting the supply of alternatives to owner occupation; and third, by affecting the availability and terms of mortgage lending.

Policies affecting incentives to buy houses

The volatile effects of financial deregulation on UK residential investment were exacerbated by changes in fiscal policy initiatives affecting incentives for home ownership. Some of the key policy changes are described in Table 15.2. The first of these changes came in 1983, when the Thatcher government introduced Mortgage Interest Relief at Source (MIRAS) in order to encourage increased rates of owner occupation. This policy gave tax breaks to mortgage holders and, by lowering the costs of mortgage financing, encouraged residential investment demand. However, just as the MIRAS tax break provided a financial incentive to own housing, changes to MIRAS changed incentives for residential investment. This was illustrated most profoundly in 1988 when MIRAS was restricted to one tax break per household. Before this time, groups of house-buyers could form house-buying cartels to fully exploit the tax break. The winding down of MIRAS to one household had a depressing effect because it reduced the incentives for home-owning but additional instability was created because of a delay between the announcement and implementation of the policy change. In the

Table 15.2 Policy changes affecting the housing market

Financial policy changes	
→ 1981	Substantial mortgage rationing
1981	Corset on bank lending abolished
1983	Building societies allowed to borrow from money markets
1985	Advent of centralized mortgage lenders
1986	Building Societies Act – Bank of England administration and guidance removed and building societies become self-regulating
Fiscal policy changes	
1983	Mortgage Interest Relief at Source (MIRAS) introduced
1988	MIRAS restricted to one per property with a £30,000 ceiling: policy announced in August and effected in September
1988	Community charge or "Poll tax" introduced to replace local rates
1992	Poll tax removed and Council tax introduced
1994	MIRAS ceiling reduced to 20%
1995	MIRAS ceiling reduced to 15%
1999	MIRAS ceiling reduced to 10%
2000	Withdrawal of MIRAS

intervening period, announcement effects took hold as house-buyers attempted to get into the housing market before MIRAS was restricted. This lack of co-ordination in the implementation of the policy created a mini housing boom. Instability was exacerbated by a further set of fiscal policy reversals (see Table 15.2). In 1988, the Community charge or Poll tax was introduced in place of the property-based rates. The replacement of a tax on home-owners with a non-property-based tax meant the effective relative price of home ownership decreased. Instability was fuelled by the reversal of this fiscal change in 1992 in response to political pressures.

Policies affecting alternatives to home ownership

Another set of factors that contributed to instability in the housing market was the change in public housing policy, reflecting a political drive towards increasing private ownership and limiting public expenditure on housing. At the same time that taxation changes were affecting incentives to own housing, the public housing stock was being sold off. Whilst the council house sales did generate windfall gains for local authorities, these local authorities were constrained in their ability to use proceeds from council house sales to build new homes so limited new housing construction was taking place. The supply of local authority housing was becoming increasingly limited and housing trusts and housing associations emerged as alternatives. Overall, these changes led to a decrease in the public housing stock. In 1981, there were 6.5 million units of social housing; by 1995 there were fewer than 5 million units. Public grants were cut from 90 per cent of new housing investment in 1988 to 55 per cent of new housing investment in 1995 (Hutton, 1996). So the public rental alternative to owner occupation was becoming increasingly constrained. At the same time, the supply of private sector rental accommodation was shrinking as rent controls decreased incentives to offer rental accommodation. Overall, housing alternatives were becoming more stark: if people could afford to buy their own council houses, then they could move into the owner-occupied sector; if they could not, then they were forced to join the lengthening waiting lists for council housing and suffer homelessness in the meantime.

Policies affecting mortgage lending

From 1981 onwards a series of policy changes associated with a more broadly based financial deregulation affected mortgage lending markets and this also had crucial impacts on residential investment activity in the UK. Until the 1980s, building societies were the sole mortgage lenders, but in 1981 banks entered the mortgage market. In 1985, other financial institutions also entered and in 1986 building societies became self-regulating. Other key changes included those in the sources of mortgage lending. Until the 1980s, building societies had relied on depositor savings to finance mortgage lending but from 1983 building societies were able to access money markets. By the 1990s, 40 per cent of building societies' mortgage lending was financed via the money market. All these policy initiatives led to large increases in the availability of mortgage finance, fuelling the demand for housing investments which in turn fuelled house price rises.

The increased availability of mortgage finance also meant that lenders took greater risks with their lending decisions in an attempt to attract customers: 100 per cent mortgages based on large multiples of borrowers' incomes were not uncommon. This meant that while house prices were rising, home-owners were enjoying very high rates of return on their housing purchases. Residential investments out-performed more liquid assets in a 'spectacular' way, generating frenzy effects that were further amplified by high gearing ratios. Muellbauer and Murphy (1997) argue that the housing boom of the 1980s cannot be explained by interest rate differences because real interest rates were not particularly low during the period of the 1980s housing boom. What was crucial was the extent of gearing: in the 1980s, financial deregulation allowed historically high gearing ratios, which meant that the rates of return on residential investments were very high despite relatively high real interest rates compared with the 1970s.

However, just as rates of return on investments are amplified by gearing in boom times, the losses are amplified in slump phases. For UK residential investment, financial instability started to creep into the mortgage lending market as interest rates rose in response to the inflationary consequences of the Lawson boom. A large number of borrowers held variable rate mortgages based on large multiples of their incomes and so had limited financial ability to adapt to interest rate rises. In addition, unemployment was rising throughout the 1980s and early 1990s. So job insecurity and unsustainable personal debt levels led to increased chances of default and repossession for individual borrowers. As instability set in, lenders abandoned their risky approach to mortgage lending.

Rises in unemployment compounded by rises in interest rates meant that more and more borrowers were forced into default. The extent of mortgage default translated into large increases in the number of repossessions of housing by mortgage lenders. In 1980 there were about 30,000 repossessions; in 1991 there were 75,000 – a rise of about 150 per cent. This intensified the pressures for house price falls. So mortgage lenders were facing erratic cash flows and they were forced into increasing financial stringency. Mortgages were no longer backed up with retail deposits by savers into building societies, so the traditional mortgage lenders, i.e. the building societies, were less able to cut costs during downturns simply by decreasing their interest payments to savers. The high gearing ratios meant that many home-owners were faced with negative equity as the price of their houses fell below the level of their mortgage commitments. All these financial pressures meant that the demand for residential investments fell away and the housing market fell into a protracted slump: in the early 1990s house prices fell, unusually, in nominal as well as real terms.

Empirical analysis

As described above, the boom-bust cycle in the UK housing market can be analyzed using Minksy's financial fragility hypothesis: lending risks undertaken during boom phases exacerbate instability in slump phases. The aim of the empirical analysis in this chapter is to assess the comparative performance of three sets of models in capturing the variability in UK new residential investment. The first model assessed is a Minskian model in which financial factors are central, the second is a Keynesian model in which both demand and financial factors are important and, finally, a neo-classical model based around the relative price of housing investments.

A Minskian bubble-crash model

The basic variable within the Minskian model is the availability of finance. In addition, multiplicative variables are included to assess the extent to which unstable forces are magnified during bubble and crash phases. Bubbles and crashes are defined as phases in which residential investors are propelled by herd behaviour with the consequence that upward spirals in house prices and transactions volumes build upon themselves. During crash phases, financial instability (captured in the residential housing market by number of repossessions) builds upon itself.

This gives the following model for residential investment (RI):

$$RI_t = \alpha + \lambda RI_{t-1} + \beta F_t + \gamma_1 \text{Boom}_t + \gamma_2 \text{Bubble}_t + \gamma_3 \text{Crash}_t + \phi t + \varepsilon_t$$

where F_t is the volume of mortgage lending, t is a deterministic trend and ε_t is a stochastic disturbance term. The lagged dependent variable was included to capture inertia within the residential investment market. The bubble variable was designed to capture the magnification of house price rises in the previous period. Similarly, the boom variable was designed to capture magnification of the impacts of transactions and the crash variable was designed to capture magnification in the impacts of repossessions. These bubble, boom and crash variables were calculated as the product of lagged new residential investment and house price inflation, the volume of housing transactions and number of repossessions respectively.[1] The results from the estimation of this model are outlined in Table 15.3. Adopting a 'top down' approach to estimation, all variables insignificant at 10 per cent were deleted from the model and, in case multicollinearity is compromising the power of t tests, the t tests were confirmed with F versions of variable deletion tests.

The resulting restricted model indicated that the regressors together accounted for 68 per cent of the variability in UK residential investment between 1980 and 1999. The diagnostic tests were insignificant at relatively high significance levels (of about 40 per cent and above), suggesting that the model is econometrically well specified. The elasticity of residential investment is positive and suggests that a 1 per cent rise in the availability of finance generates a rise in residential investment of just over 0.11 per cent. The signs

Table 15.3 Minskian bubble-crash models

Dependent variable: Residential investment, logged
Estimation period: 1980Q2 to 1999Q4

	With trend		*Without trend*	
	Parameter Estimate	*t ratio [p value]*	*Parameter Estimate*	*t ratio [p value]*
Constant	7.6673	8.6397 [0.000]	7.9462	9.1102 [0.000]
RI_{t-1}	−0.6574	−2.9028 [0.005]	−0.814	−4.0708 [0.000]
Lending	0.11124	2.7516 [0.007]	0.09379	2.4149 [0.018]
Boom	0.04764	4.3195 [0.000]	0.04043	4.0870 [0.000]
Bubble	0.03261	2.3309 [0.023]	0.04984	6.8699 [0.000]
Crash	−0.0065	−1.5349 [0.129]	−0.0072	−1.6888 [0.096]
Time trend	0.00206	1.4365 [0.155]	...	...
R^2 (adjusted)	0.66954		0.66473	
Diagnostic tests – probability values				
Serial correlation	0.458		0.184	
Functional form	0.959		0.673	
Heteroscedasticity	0.396		0.333	

on the bubble, boom and crash variables suggest that the effects of rising house prices, growing transactions volumes and rises in repossessions are magnified in the subsequent period: house price rises and increasing transactions volumes fuel residential investment and increasing repossessions depress residential investment. (The negative sign on the lagged dependent variable seems anomalous but can be explained by the fact that the impacts of this variable are also being captured by the Boom, Bubble and Crash variables.) These results confirm a Minskian view of financial fragility.

A Keynesian demand and finance model

In a Keynesian world, real factors such as disposable income and affordability, as reflected in the ratio of disposable income to house prices, are as important as financial factors as they will capture the demand side of residential investment. To capture these demand factors, the following model was estimated:

$$RI_t = \alpha + \lambda RI_{t-1} + \beta F_t + \delta y_t + \xi p_{ht} + \gamma_1 \text{Boom}_t + \gamma_2 \text{Bubble}_t + \gamma_3 \text{Crash}_t + \phi t + \varepsilon_t$$

where y is real personal disposable income and p_h is real house prices. The results from the estimation of these models are outlined in Table 15.4. The diagnostic tests were again insignificant at relatively high significance levels. The regressors in this model accounted for about 69 per cent of the variability in residential investment. The estimated elasticity of residential investment in

Table 15.4 Demand augmented bubble-crash models

Dependent variable: Residential investment, logged
Estimation period: 1980Q2 to 1999Q4

	Model 1		*Model 2*		*Model 3*	
	Parameter Estimate	*t ratio [p value]*	*Parameter Estimate*	*t ratio [p value]*	*Parameter Estimate*	*t ratio [p value]*
Constant	−1.59	−1.4 [0.150]	4.47	5.9 [0.000]	−1.06	−1.4 [0.177]
RI_{t-1}	−0.278	−2.3 [0.027]	0.236	2.0 [0.054]	−0.269	−2.2 [0.031]
F_t	0.124	3.3 [0.001]	0.134	2.9 [0.005]	0.121	3.3 [0.002]
y_t	0.745	5.7 [0.000]	...	...	0.694	7.7 [0.000]
p_{ht}	−0.011	−0.39 [0.696]	...	...	...	...
A_t	...	...	−0.087	−3.1 [0.003]	...	...
Bubble	0.0589	5.6 [0.000]	0.023	2.0 [0.049]	0.056	5.4 [0.000]
Crash	−0.005	−1.196 [0.236]	−0.008	−1.6 [0.110]	−0.006	−1.5 [0.144]
R^2 (adjusted)	0.68889		0.51317		0.69469	
Diagnostic tests – probability values						
Serial correlation	0.487		0.435		0.324	
Functional form	0.521		0.371		0.809	
Heteroscedasticity	0.387		0.305		0.405	

response to changes in the availability of finance was 0.12. The elasticity on real personal disposable income was 0.74 and a test of a null hypothesis of a unitary elasticity of residential investment with respect to real personal disposable income gave a estimated t ratio of 1.96 suggesting that the elasticity was insignificantly different from one at a 1 per cent significance level, but not at a 5 per cent significance level. The parameter on the real house price variable was insignificantly different from zero at high significance levels (of close to 70 per cent). This could reflect the fact that the impacts of house price rises are being captured via the bubble term.

A restricted form of this model was also estimated to capture the effects of affordability where affordability (A) is calculated as the ratio of real personal disposable income and real house prices.[2] The affordability parameter was insignificant, which is consistent with the results from the unrestricted form of the model. (These results suggest that real personal disposable income on its own, rather than as a component of affordability, is the important variable.)

In the initial estimation of the model, the boom term proved to be insignificant and this may reflect the fact that the disposable income variable is picking up some of the effects of rises in transaction volumes. Otherwise, the signs and significance of the Boom and Crash terms confirm the results from the Minskian model. Both these two models suggest that financial and demand factors are important and that effects of booms and crashes are magnified over time.

Neo-classical model

For the neo-classical model, relative price and output effects on residential investment are captured by incorporating various combinations of the user cost of housing and by using the volume of housing transactions as a proxy for the output variable:[3]

$$RI_t = \alpha + \lambda RI_{t-1} + \varphi Tr_t + \chi c_{ht} + \phi t + \varepsilon_t$$

where c_h is the user cost of housing and Tr is the volume of housing transactions.

The results from an estimation of these models, in levels and changes specifications, are outlined in Table 15.5. The R^2 (adjusted) for these models are lower than the adjusted R^2 in the previous models, ranging from 46 per cent to 57 per cent. In addition, the diagnostic tests from these models do reveal possible violations of key Gauss-Markov assumptions; the Breusch-Godfrey and Ramsey's RESET tests are significant at 10 per cent for almost all the regressions, perhaps suggesting the omission of important explanatory variables. Model 4, which incorporates a composite neo-classical variable Tr/c_h, performs the best in terms of statistical explanatory power so, while the models are poorly specified, relative cost factors do appear to play some role in capturing residential investment.

Table 15.5 Neo-classical models incorporating the user cost of housing investment

	Model 1		*Model 2*	
	Parameter Estimate	*t ratio [p value]*	*Parameter Estimate*	*t ratio [p value]*
Constant	3.5795	4.3183 [0.000]	0.24098	2.0767 [0.041]
RI_{t-1}	0.56907	5.6999 [0.000]	...	...
Δc_t	0.00662	0.14409 [0.886]	...	...
ΔTr_t	0.38478	3.0876 [0.003]	...	...
c_t	...	...	−0.0144	−0.30750 [0.759]
c_{t-1}	...	...	−0.0186	−0.37657 [0.708]
Tr_t	...	...	0.49707	3.8429 [0.000]
Tr_{t-1}	...	...	−0.0685	−0.51946 [0.605]
Trend	0.00154	2.1626 [0.034]	0.00418	3.5550 [0.001]
R^2 (adjusted)	0.46394		0.57324	
Diagnostic tests – probability values				
Serial correlation	0.001		0.034	
Functional form	0.688		0.069	
Heteroscedasticity	0.304		0.979	

	Model 3		*Model 4*	
	Parameter Estimate	*t ratio [p value]*	*Parameter Estimate*	*t ratio [p value]*
Constant	5.6121	6.5014 [0.000]	5.1385	6.5166 [0.000]
RI_{t-1}	0.31216	2.9619 [0.004]	0.37125	3.8744 [0.000]
Tr_t/c_t	0.00189	2.6844 [0.009]	0.00241	4.111 [0.000]
Tr_t/c_{t-1}	0.00102	1.3162 [0.192]	insignificant	
Trend	0.00199	2.9387 [0.004]	0.00186	2.7669 [0.007]
R^2 (adjusted)	0.54281		0.51299	
Diagnostic tests – probability values				
Serial correlation	0.078		0.065	
Functional form	0.041		0.087	
Heteroscedasticity	0.278		0.294	

Model comparison

The results outlined above do suggest that the models incorporating demand factors, financial factors and boom and crash terms out-perform the neo-classical models. To confirm these findings, the models were tested against one another using a range of model selection tests. (The non-nested testing methodology is explained in the Statistical Appendix.)

The non-nested test results are recorded in Table 15.6. As for Chapters 11 and 12, the probability values (*p* values) from the non-nested tests of alternative models against each other refer to tests of the null hypothesis that Model 1 contributes no significant additional explanatory power when imposed on top of Model 2. As explained in the Statistical Appendix, a low

Table 15.6 Non-nested test results, p values

	Model 1: Keynesian *Model 2: Minskian*	*Model 1: Minskian* *Model 2: Keynesian*
Cox test	0.000	0.378
Adjusted Cox test	0.000	0.526
Wald test	0.000	0.536
J test	0.000	0.247
JA Test	0.002	0.739
Encompassing F test	0.001	0.189
Akaike's Information Criterion = −5.8209 and favours the Keynesian model		
	Model 1: Neo-classical *Model 2: Keynesian*	*Model 1: Keynesian* *Model 2: Neo-classical*
Cox test	0.895	0.000
Adjusted Cox test	0.840	0.000
Wald test	0.839	0.000
J test	0.918	0.000
JA Test	0.880	0.000
Encompassing F test	0.036	0.000
Akaike's Information Criterion = 15.1371 and favours the Keynesian model		

p value implies that H_0 should be rejected. In this case, this will imply that Model 1 does contribute significant additional explanatory power independently of Model 2. (The terms 'Minskian', Keynesian and 'neo-classical' refer to the preferred models outlined in Tables 15.3, 15.4 and 15.5 respectively.)

The non-nested tests suggest that the Keynesian demand boom-bust model out-performs the Minskian boom-bust model. These tests also reveal that, overall, the Keynesian demand boom-bust model outperforms the neo-classical specification although the Encompassing F test does suggest that the neo-classical model contributes its own independent explanatory power at significance levels less that 4 per cent.

Overall, these results indicate that the UK residential investment market was affected by a complex range of factors during the 1980s and 1990s. The herd behaviours and instability emphasized by Post Keynesian economists had a profound influence but there is also some evidence that more objective, rationally-based variables, namely the user cost of housing, also had an influence. This finding parallels the findings about the influence of the user cost of capital on computing investment, as outlined in Chapter 13. The findings suggest that theoretical concepts have more power when applied to investment activity at a more disaggregated level.

Conclusion

UK residential investment has been affected by a large degree of political and financial change since the 1980s. The empirical evidence presented above indicates that whilst volumes of transactions and the user cost of capital have had an influence, financial and speculative factors have had substantial impacts on the path of residential investment too. This suggests that moves by New Labour, to moderate speculative forces via higher property taxes; to increase the housing stock by developing brown-field sites; and to smooth the legal process by removing contractual rigidities, will be important if the UK housing market is to experience more stability in the next 30 years than it has in the last 30 years.

Chapter summary

1. Residential investment is distinctly different from business fixed investment because housing combines the characteristics of production goods and consumption goods. However, residential investment is a crucial form of investment because housing is a main source of household wealth and household debt.
2. Like any other form of investment, residential investment can be explained using some of the theoretical concepts presented in earlier chapters. In this analysis, residential investment is analyzed using a variant of Jorgenson's user cost of capital as a measure of the relative cost of housing. The relative cost of housing will be determined by relative house prices, house price inflation, net imputed rent and mortgage interest costs.
3. Residential investment is also analyzed using Minskian-Keynesian approaches in which the availability of finance is captured using mortgage lending data and aggregate demand is captured using income/affordability variables. Feedback effects are captured using bubble, boom and crash variables, constructed to assess whether or not upward and downward movements in residential investment are magnified. If they are, then this suggests that the housing market is susceptible to the destabilizing forces of herd behaviour and crowd psychology.
4. The empirical evidence presented in this chapter indicates that the explanatory power of the neo-classical model is relatively low. In addition, all variants of the neo-classical model are characterized by serial correlation, possibly indicating missing variables, and/or incorrect functional form. In contrast, the explanatory power of the Keynesian models is relatively high and there were no significant econometric problems with these models.
5. The empirical results suggest that a Keynesian approach to the modelling of residential investment is more illuminating than the application of Keynesian principles to the models in Chapters 11 and 12, perhaps because house buyers are more susceptible to the influences of herd behaviour and crowd psychology than business investors. It also indicates that neoclassical concepts, namely the user cost of housing, have some influence on residential investment decisions.

Data appendix

Variables in the models

Monetary boom-bust model: Lagged residential investment (logged), mortgage lending (logged), boom variable and crash variable.

Demand boom-bust model: Lagged residential investment (logged), mortgage lending (logged), real personal disposable income (logged), boom variable and crash variable.

Neo-classical model: Lagged residential investment (logged), composite neo-classical user cost/transactions variable, deterministic trend.

Data sources

Residential investment (RI)	*Economic Trends Annual Supplement* (ETAS), Office of National Statistics (ONS)
Mortgage lending	Council of Mortgage Lenders
Real disposable income	ETAS, ONS
Housing transactions	*Economic Trends*, ONS
Repossessions	Council of Mortgage Lenders (CML)
User cost of housing	Calculated from CML and ETAS data

Explanation of the bubble, boom and crash terms

Bubble = RI_{t-1} × house price inflation
Boom = RI_{t-1} × number of housing transactions
Crash = RI_{t-1} × number of repossessions

Data limitations

Note that there may be data problems, for example, house price indicies may not control for quality improvement completely. Also, the house price data is collected from building societies but the shift in mortgage market lending means that the building societies are no longer the only major lenders. If different types of lenders are dealing with different types of properties, then the building society data may be subject to sample bias.

Part V Conclusion

16 Concluding remarks 211

16 Concluding remarks

The competing theories 212
The empirical evidence 214
Unresolved questions 215

This book traces the evolution of investment theory from Fisher and Keynes through to modern real options theories about investment under uncertainty. As explained in Chapter 3, Irving Fisher's mathematical analysis of the rate of return over cost forms the basis of modern orthodox theories that describe the rational, optimizing behaviour of investors. Fisher's theory is built to describe a world in which the determinants of investment are quantifiable and investment behaviour can be described mathematically. In contrast, Keynes did not believe that reality is always quantifiable, an issue that he analyzes in detail in *A Treatise on Probability* (1921). His ideas about limits to quantification resonate in *The General Theory of Employment, Interest and Money* (1936). Whilst Keynes's concept of the marginal efficiency of capital is analytically similar to Fisher's rate of return, for Keynes, limits to quantification limit the capacity for rational behaviour under conditions of uncertainty. Within Keynes's analysis, mathematical tools are of limited use. As a result, real-world investment is often propelled by psychological motivations, such as animal spirits, conventions and herd instincts. *The General Theory* is an inspired work but it is full of contradictions and it raises as many questions as it answers. But it is path-breaking in terms of the insights it presents about the effects of financial instability and uncertainty on the process of expectations formation that is central to fixed investment behaviour.

The competing theories

After Keynes and Fisher, the development of investment theories diverged into two quite separate paths. In the orthodox neo-classical literature, Fisherian concepts of net present value and the rate of return were refined and extended. As explained in Chapters 5–7, in Jorgenson's neo-classical theory, Fisher's basic ideas about rational calculating investors were modified to describe rational profit-maximizing investors balancing the marginal benefits and marginal costs of their investment decisions. In Jorgenson's theory, the marginal cost is captured by the relative factor cost of capital, or the 'user cost of capital'. In turn, Jorgenson's theory led the way for *q* theorists to deal with expectations in a logically consistent way. As described in Chapter 8, the *q* theorists (such as Brainard, Tobin and Abel) adopt the rational expectations hypothesis in assuming that agents do not make systematic errors and that the distribution of their subjective forecasts of future events correspond to the objective distribution of actual outcomes; thus expectations of a given variable are, on average, equal to subsequent realizations. The *q* theorists incorporate expectations explicitly into investors' optimization problems and, by incorporating internal adjustment costs, they solve one of the key theoretical problems with Jorgenson's model, i.e. that the rate of investment over time is undefined. This combination of the rational expectations hypothesis with that of the optimizing investor leads to coherent, though some would say unrealistic, models of investor behaviour.

Overall within the orthodox literature, given assumptions of quantifiable expectations and quantifiable uncertainty, investment is described within mathematical models of investor behaviour. Chirinko (1993) argues that this sort of rigorous theoretical approach is defensible because:

> Without some guidance from theory, noisy, non-experimental data are generally insufficient to discriminate among competing hypotheses . . . Whilst explicit models may not produce high R^2s and may fail specification tests . . . [they] are the preferred vehicle for furthering our knowledge of economic behaviour. (Chirinko, 1993, p. 1901)

However, empirical difficulties remain because econometric evidence tends to suggest that Jorgensonian and *q* theories do not capture real-world aggregate investment behaviour adequately. It is difficult to assess whether the poor empirical performance of these models reflects the data limitations or theoretical problems. Summers (1991) argues that the econometric evidence from mathematical models is relatively uninspiring:

> Successful empirical research has been characterized by attempts to gauge the strength of associations rather than to estimate structural parameters, verbal characteristics of how causal relations might operate rather than explicit mathematical models, and the skilful use of carefully chosen natural experiments rather than sophisticated statistical technique to achieve identification. (Summers, 1991, p. 2)

So, just as the *q* theorists introduced expectations into Jorgenson's theory, the real options theorist introduced uncertainty into *q* theories. The real options theories (such as those of Dixit and Pindyck) are explained in Chapter 9. The development of these models reflects a gradual recognition in orthodox literature of the importance of expectations, uncertainty and psychological forces in determining aggregate investment. The empirical evidence from real options analysis suggests that uncertainty is negatively correlated with investment and this result has been replicated in a large number of empirical models incorporating a wide range of measures of uncertainty. But this empirical finding does not resolve fundamental theoretical debates about rational investor behaviour because most economists would agree that uncertainty has a depressing effect. In addition, in a number of real options models, uncertainty is introduced on an *ad hoc* basis, which does seem to be inconsistent with other building blocks of the theory, for example, *q* models, in which Stock Market valuations are meant to capture all factors affecting expectations.

Following Keynes, the Post Keynesian theorists adopt a quite distinctive approach to that seen in orthodox analyses by emphasizing that uncertainty limits human capacity for rational calculation. They react against the orthodox belief in rational maximizing investor behaviour in a quantifiable world. Instead Post Keynesian analysis focuses on non-rational and irrational investor behaviour in a 'non-ergodic' world, i.e. a world that is always changing.

Interactions between different actors within an economy will mean that aggregating atomistic, individual behaviours is not a valid approach. The Post Keynesians argued that uncertainty exerts a depressing effect well before this insight was adopted within orthodox models: in Post Keynesian theories, uncertainty has always been central. Given non-measurable uncertainty, investor behaviour is non-rational or irrational. Investors will be propelled by animal spirits, herd instincts and conventions and they will be forced to concentrate focus on the short-term, with depressing effects in terms of fixed investment and destabilizing effects in terms of speculation.

Money is an important element in Post Keynesian analyses of investment because it acts as a barometer of uncertainty. In addition, money is endogenous within Post Keynesian models: banks and lending institutions will respond to faltering business confidence by limiting their lending decisions. For this reason, investment, finance and uncertainty are inextricably inter-linked. This insight contrasts with the orthodox Modigliani–Miller assumption that financing decisions do not determine real investment activity: in Post Keynesian analysis, different financial instruments will affect investment activity in distinctive ways. For example, Minsky argues that the structure of financing and debt will introduce instability into the macroeconomy and he develops this idea in his financial fragility model of the business cycle. Post Keynesian aproaches are outlined in more detail in Chapter 10.

The empirical evidence

In the empirical section, basic ideas about investment outlined in the theoretical chapters are applied to the analysis of investment in a series of real-world situations. In Chapter 11, accelerator and neo-classical specifications of investment functions are compared, in the context of UK investment activity from 1970–2001. Each of these models seems to possess some independent explanatory power, so a hybrid model of investment, incorporating user cost, output and capacity utilization terms is estimated. This model confirms findings from previous analyses that capacity utilization and output have the strongest effects on aggregate investment activity. In Chapter 12, Kaleckian-Keynesian models based around quantity factors and profits are estimated, using US data from 1970–98. The results from these models are compared with an orthodox form of *q* model. Again, both these models seem to have merits but the key finding from this analysis is that uncertainty did appear to have a depressing effect on US aggregate investment over this time period. This confirmed results from a wide range of other empirical analyses.

In the next section of the book, investment principles are applied to a range of topical problems. In Chapter 13, the behaviour of computing investment in the New Economy is assessed. The growth of high-tech IT products has meant that investment patterns have changed since widespread computerization began in the early 1970s: inventory investment has declined and replacement investment has increased. In addition, the empirical evidence in Chapter 15 suggests that the availability of funding, for example in the form of venture capital disbursements, will be particularly important if technological progress in IT is to be sustained. Patterns in computing investment will also be affected by developments in the macroeconomy in general; the evidence presented suggests that Stock Market exuberance will encourage computing investment but Stock Market volatility will discourage computing investment.

In Chapter 14, the investment theories are applied to international data on a cross-section of countries. The first part of this empirical analysis focuses on assessing the extent of convergence in investment rates across countries, following a Post Keynesian approach in which investment is a leading variable. Neo-classical theory suggests that equilibrating processes will ensure the convergence of savings and therefore investment. These basic insights are tested in Chapter 14. Overall, the results indicate that processes of persistence are stronger in developed countries than in less-developed countries. In addition, the estimation of the conditional convergence models indicated that output growth is a key determinant of comparative investment rates across countries but that proxies for the user cost of capital are not, thus providing some more empirical support for accelerator theories.

In Chapter 15, investment theories are applied to analysis of UK housing investment in the 1980s and 1990s. The models estimated included variables to capture the demand for housing, including the user cost of housing. The estimations indicated that a range of variables appear to be central to the determination of residential investment in the UK. In particular, the introduction of variables to capture cyclical forces, as propelled by the volume of transactions, house price rises and repossessions, were significant. These results suggest that processes of cumulative causation and path dependency characterized UK residential investment in the 1980s and 1990s, although there is also some evidence that the user cost of housing is important.

Unresolved questions

In order fully to understand fixed asset investment, we need more information about the nature of and limits to the rationality of real-world investors. We also need more information about the way in which economic reality is formed. Can reality be described by objective probability distributions? Are investors rational on average and/or over longer time horizons? If so, then orthodox analysis will be useful. But is economic reality path-dependent and malleable? Does unquantifiable uncertainty limit our capacity for rational calculation? If so, then a Post Keynesian approach will be more appropriate. Macroeconometric evidence often cannot resolve these questions because fundamental theoretical differences do not necessarily lead to fundamentally different predictions. As seen above, a key example relevant to investment comes in the analysis of uncertainty. Although the assertion of negative relationship between investment and uncertainty is now widely confirmed in orthodox literature, it is consistent with both orthodox and Post Keynesian theories. In this sense the empirical finding is a-theoretical and it leaves many of the fundamental questions unanswered: i.e. can we rely on free markets to secure adequate levels of investment? Or do uncertainty and other limits to rational maximizing behaviour mean that markets will never encourage sufficient investment unless governments intervene? Some other objective means of comparing competing theoretical models is needed in addition to standard econometric techniques. Perhaps future resolution to these theoretical and methodological questions will be found in survey evidence and experimental psychology.

The ideas presented in this book each contribute something to our understanding of investment activity and it does seem that there has been a growing convergence in empirical approach, with expectations and uncertainty now forming the basis of a wide range of modern investment models. However, differences in the methodological and philosophical bones of the competing theories can never be removed because, in comparing the relative merits of different theories, judgements of the extent to which a given theory increases our understanding of economic processes almost always contain subjective elements. It is important to assess the relative merits of the competing explanations if economic policy is to be implemented properly. Policies to suit a world of rational investors will be profoundly different from policy designed to suit a world of inherent instability and crisis.

Notes

Chapter 3

1. Harcourt and Sardoni (1995) warn, however, that to place too much emphasis on individual psychology may be a mistake because, in general, Keynes addresses issues of social psychology and conventional behaviour rather than individual psychological responses.
2. More detailed analyses of these issues are presented in Araujo (1994) and Asimakopulos (1991).
3. See also Davidson (1978) on the role of spot and forward markets in determining investment expenditure and Harcourt and Spajic (1999) and Araujo and Harcourt (1993) on the demand price/supply price approach to the analysis of investment.
4. For a fuller analysis of some of these issues, see Keynes's *A Treatise on Probability* (1921).
5. Shackle (1967) argues that Keynes's message about the limits to rational investor conduct under uncertainty is stated more effectively in his 1937 *Quarterly Journal of Economics* article, 'The general theory of employment'.
6. Rational expectations versions of q models are analyzed in Chapter 8. It should also be noted that a q approach is also consistent with a Post Keynesian view of investment.
7. In addition, Harcourt (1994) argues that the influence of speculation will mean cumulative processes rather than equilibrating tendencies will characterize the path of investment.

Chapter 4

1. The 'top down' modelling approach was pioneered by Hendry (for example, see Hendry and Wallis, 1984) but is vulnerable to accusations of 'data-mining'. Critics of this approach would argue that *a priori* theoretical arguments should underpin econometric specifications, if the dangers of spurious findings are to be avoided.
2. See Nickell (1978) and Junankar (1972) for surveys of the empirical evidence.

Chapter 5

1. Keynes (1936) also introduced a concept that he called the user cost of capital. Whilst there are some parallels between the two concepts (for example, depreciation is a component in both concepts), they are theoretically quite distinct.

Chapter 6

1. Gordon (1992, 1994) provides an extensive analysis of the financial aspects of investment decisions and their implications for neo-classical and Post Keynesian theories of finance and investment.

2. Ideas about financing constraints are explored throughout the Post Keynesian literature, for example by Minsky (1978, 1986), Gordon (1994) and Davidson (1965, 1978).

Chapter 7

1. In some versions of neo-classical investment theory, expected output is assumed to be a function of relative factor prices and thus the investment rate can be expressed solely in terms of the user cost of capital (Chirinko, 1993).
2. See also Nickell (1978) and Baddeley (1996) for a summary of econometric findings.

Chapter 8

1. 'q theory' is used to refer to a general approach to investment, based around the convention that defines q as the shadow price of capital, i.e. the discounted value of all future marginal products from production and investment activities. However, the term q theory is also used more specifically to refer to Brainard and Tobin's q model, in which financial market valuations are used to capture rational expectations. Both approaches are analyzed in this chapter. To prevent confusion, the latter will be referred to as 'Tobin's q' in this book. Post Keynesians such as Minsky have also formulated q models based around financial variables. Davidson (1965, 1967, 1978) provides an alternative, Post Keynesian interpretation of the role of stock markets, drawing more closely on Keynes's insights about the relationship between financial markets and fixed investment, as outlined in Keynes (1936, 1937). Davidson claims that his model of q precedes Brainard and Tobin's 1968 elaboration of q theory. Araujo (1994) presents a more detailed comparison of the essential elements of Davidson's and Tobin's q theories. For an interesting discussion of some of these issues, see Palley (2001).

Chapter 9

1. See *A Treatise on Probability* (Keynes, 1921) for an exploration of these issues.
2. The lemons principle describes a situation of asymmetric information in which purchasers of second-hand machinery have no information about the quality of a given piece of second-hand equipment. They will therefore be unwilling to pay a fair price to sellers of good quality machinery because they don't know whether or not they are purchasing a 'lemon' (Akerlof, 1970).
3. See also Summers (1987), who found that hurdle rates of return varied between 8 per cent and 30 per cent while nominal interest rates were only 4 per cent and the real interest rate was approximately 0%. He argues that these findings suggest that fixed asset investors are implicitly taking account of the opportunity cost of exercising options to invest.
4. However, it should be noted that Pindyck and Solimano did not include an output uncertainty variable in their analysis although they did include a real interest rate uncertainty variable.
5. The relative price of factors of production used in Driver and Moreton's (1992*b*) model is very similar to the user cost of capital except that their cost of capital is measured relative to wages rather than output prices. So it is not directly related to Jorgenson's model. Driver and Moreton (1992*b*) also estimate a logged levels investment equation with a lagged dependent variable. A problem with this model is that, while the model estimates a unitary elasticity of investment with respect to required new capacity, the current and lagged capacity variables are insignificant and much of the explanatory power is contributed by the lagged dependent variable. This approach is also adopted in Driver and Temple (1999) and Temple, Driver and Urga (2001).

Chapter 10

1. Fuller surveys of Post Keynesian ideas can be found in Hamouda and Harcourt (1988), Harcourt and Spajic (1999) and Sawyer (1991).
2. See Blanchard and Watson (1982) and Topol (1991) for orthodox explanations of mimickery as a rational device. See Baddeley and McCombie (2001) for a discussion of alternative models of speculative behaviour.
3. The overlap between individual and aggregate behaviour and the problems with precise quantification are some of the reasons why the investment demand schedule is seen as an inappropriate construction which is in many senses unnecessary for, and contradictory with, the rest of Keynes's theory. See also Davis (1996) on the interdependence of individual economic agents in Keynes's *General Theory*.
4. There is also a distinction between individual and institutional rationality. Hodgson (1985) argues that Keynes's emphasis on the behaviour of the entrepreneur as a determinant of investment decisions is misplaced because the agency forming expectations within the firm is rarely a single commanding individual (p. 17). Firms' decisions reflect expectations and objectives of a large number of people.
5. Skildelsky (1992, pp. 86–9) presents a survey of the different interpretations of Keynes's analysis of economic behaviour, which centres around the extent to which these interpretations focus on rational, irrational or non-rational forces.
6. See Gordon (1992, 1994) and Davidson (1978) for more comprehensive criticisms of the neo-classical theory of finance and the associated Modigliani–Miller theorem.
7. Another departure from neo-classical analysis; early neo-classical analysis is based around the loanable funds theory of interest rates, i.e. that interest rates are determined by the interaction of investment demand and savings (loanable funds).
8. Fuller analyses of Kalecki's ideas are provided in Courvisanos (1996), Laramie, Mair and Miller (2001), Laski (1998) and Sawyer (1985, 1991, 2000).

Chapter 11

1. The key variables were tested for non-stationarity using Augmented Dickey-Fuller tests. These revealed that investment, manufacturing output, the user cost of capital and the capital stock were all I(1), i.e. first-order integrated and stationary in their differences. A fuller explanation of these tests and concepts is outlined in the Statistical Appendix.
2. See Chapter 13.

Chapter 12

1. See also Baddeley (1996) and Chirinko (1993).
2. The rational expectations theorists do not have sole claim on *q* theory: variants of *q* models are consistent with Keynes and Post Keynesian theory, as was explained in Chapter 10.
3. Topol (1991) attempts to reconcile some of these issues in his analysis of speculative behaviour.

Chapter 14

1. See Barro and Sala-I-Martin (1995) for a comprehensive survey and analysis of economic growth models.

Chapter 15

1. A mortgage arrears version of these models was also estimated but the arrears variables were insignificant and so the results from the arrears models are not

included in the regressions reported here. Dummy variables to capture the introduction of MIRAS were also included in an initial specification but were found to be insignificantly different from zero.

2. In essence, the restricted model is incorporating the restriction $\delta + \xi = 0$. An F test of H_0: $\delta + \xi = 0$ leads to a rejection of this restriction with a p value of 0.000.
3. For a fuller explanation of Jorgenson's neo-classical model of investment more generally applied, see Chapter 5.

Glossary

Absolute convergence is a cross-sectional concept and occurs when all countries in a cross section are moving towards a common equilibrium. *See also* conditional convergence, β convergence and σ convergence.

Accelerator theory is the theory of investment in which expected output growth determines firms' decisions to augment their capital stock.

Adjustment costs are the costs involved with implementing investment projects and bolting down capital equipment. Internal adjustment costs arise out of disruptions to an individual firm's production process; external adjustment costs will reflect forces outside the individual firm, for example the rising capital goods prices that accompany increasing demand for capital goods from many firms.

Aggregate uncertainty is uncertainty in the macroeconomy.

Asset specificity occurs when capital assets are specialized for a particular production process and cannot easily be used for other purposes.

Autocorrelation is an econometric problem that occurs when the errors in a regression are correlated with each other.

Bad news principle describes irreversible investments as being more sensitive to bad news than good news.

Bandwagon effects occur when economic agents follow the crowd in making decisions.

Best is a statistical term used to denote an estimator with the minimum variance or spread.

Beta (β) convergence occurs in cross-sectional analysis when the growth or change in a cross-sectional variable over a period is negatively correlated with its starting value. It implies that countries or regions lagging behind will catch up with leading countries or regions.

BLUE is a statistical term meaning Best Linear Unbiased Estimator. OLS estimators are BLUE given certain assumptions.

Borrower's risk the risk that borrowers face of defaulting on their loans.

Call option is the right to buy a financial asset.

Cambridge Capital Controversies are the controversies that arose out of criticisms of neo-classical production functions and neo-classical approaches to defining and measuring capital. It is generally associated with the economists of the Cambridge (UK) school, who were following in the tradition of Keynes and Kalecki.

Capacity utilization rates measure the proportion of productive capacity currently in use and are an indicator of the stage of the business cycle.

Capital accumulation is another word for investment i.e. the flow into the capital stock.

Capital Asset Pricing Model (CAPM) is a model that assumes asset prices adjust to reflect systematic risk.

Clay models are models of the production process in which ratios of capital and labour inputs are not responsive to changes in the relative costs of these factors.

Conditional convergence occurs when different cross-sectional groups (for example, of countries) are moving towards different equilibria depending upon the structural characteristics of their economies.

Convexity is a mathematical term used to describe the shape of functions: if a line is drawn between two points of a curve, then the function is convex if that line lies above the curve. In adjustment costs theories of investment, adjustment costs are convex in investment and this implies that they are increasing in investment at an increasing rate.

Demand price of capital refers to the present value of expected future returns from a fixed capital asset.

Depreciation is the reduction in the value of capital assets, for example, because of wear and tear.

Diagnostic tests are econometric tests used to assess whether or not econometric procedures are working well. (See the Statistical Appendix for further details.)

Diffusion lag hypothesis is the hypothesis that technological innovations take a while to affect economies because of lags in the technological diffusion process.

Direct forecasting models are rational expectations models of investment in which investors judge the future returns from investments by using past values as a proxy for expectations of future values.

Discount rates are used to capture the fact that present income will always be preferred to an equivalent amount of future income. The discount rate is the rate at which a given amount of future income is judged to be equivalent to current income.

Dummy variables are categorical variables that take discrete values, usually zero or one, and thereby allow econometricians to separate different categories of observations within one sample.

Efficient markets hypothesis is the hypothesis that financial markets respond instantaneously to news and so asset prices fully reflect all available information about the fundamental value of an asset.

Elasticity of factor substitution is the responsiveness of the capital–labour ratio to changes in relative factor costs.

Endogenous money is associated with the creation of money by banks and other financial institutions in response to changes within the economic system. It is associated with Post Keynesian economics and contrasts with the assumptions of exogenous money and financing neutrality seen in orthodox analyses of investment.

Ergodicity is an assumption that economic processes are regular, measurable and determinate and that the determinants of economic behaviour are immutable.

Ex ante decisions are planned decisions, taken 'before the event'.

Ex post decisions are realised decisions, taking place 'after the event'.

Financial fragility hypothesis is the hypothesis, associated with Minsky, that the financial instability associated with depressions and recessions is created by over-optimism during expansionary phases.

Gazumping occurs in housing markets when the seller reneges on an informal agreement with a buyer in order to take advantage of house price rises.

Gearing ratio is the extent to which investment decisions are financed via borrowings. A high gearing ratio means that capital gains and losses will be magnified.

Granger causality means that one variable leads another variable. This phenomenon is captured by Granger causality tests.

Gauss Markov theorem is the theorem that states OLS is BLUE given certain assumptions many of which relate to the random behaviour of disturbance/error terms.

Hedge finance is a safe form of investment financing for which current cash flows are expected to exceed short-term cash flows and long-term capital repayments.

Hedonic price indexes are price indexes that reflect improvements in the quality of products over time.

Heteroscedasticity occurs when the spread of errors in a statistical model is not constant.

Homogeneity, linear, is a mathematical term used to describe the relationship between variables and is often used to describe the relationship between capital, labour and output as captured by production functions. In this context, the production is linearly homogeneous, it exhibits constant returns to scale: i.e. a given increase in inputs leads to an equi-proportionate increase in output.

Hurdle rate of return is the expected rate of return from an investment that must be exceeded before the investment takes place.

Idiosyncratic uncertainty is the uncertainty that just affects an individual firm.

Impatience principle is associated with Fisher's theory of the determinants of interest rates and describes the impatience of people to spend money today, rather than wait to spend it tomorrow. This means that money today has more value than money tomorrow.

Imputed rent is the rent that householders would pay if they did not own their own home.

Increasing risk, principle of, is associated with Kalecki and describes the increasing risk that develops as the stock of debt increases.

Installation costs *See* adjustment costs.

Intangible investment is investment not associated with tangible physical assets. Examples include investments in training, parts of R&D and new business processes.

Internal rate of return is the rate of discount that, when used to discount the value of expected future returns from an asset, equalizes those returns with the current costs of purchasing that asset. The concept was devised by Fisher as his rate of return over costs.

Irreversibility occurs because investment involves sunk costs and so investment purchases cannot be resold.

Isoquant is a relationship describing the different combinations of capital and labour inputs that can be used to produce a constant amount of output.

Just-in-time inventory control is a computing innovation that allows firms to track their stock of inventories very efficiently, allowing firms to respond their production patterns quickly in the face of changes in demand for their products.

Knightian risk is quantifiable risk or uncertainty.

Knightian uncertainty is unquantifiable uncertainty.

Koyck transformations incorporate a lagged dependent variable to represent all past values of explanatory variables.

Lender's risk is the risk financial institutions face when they lend money to borrowers who may later default on their loans.

Liquidity traps occur, in depressed economies, when increases in the supply of money do not lead to falls in the interest rate because people want to hold as much cash as possible, rather than taking the risk of buying assets. They occur when the elasticity of demand for money is infinite.

Long-run elasticity is the long-term responsiveness of a variable to changes in another. For example, when the long-run elasticity of investment with respect to output is equal to one, this implies that, in the long-run, a 1 per cent increase in output will be associated with a 1 per cent increase in investment.

Lumpy investment occurs when investment goods are not easily divisible into smaller units and so large investment expenditures take place at one time. This means that investment expenditure will not be smoothly distributed over time.

Marginal efficiency of capital is described by Keynes and is equivalent to Fisher's rate of return over costs internal rate of return. *See* internal rate of return.

Model comparison tests *See* non-nested tests.

Modigliani–Miller assumption is the assumption that, with perfect capital markets, the costs of all types of financing will be equal and so the way in which fixed investments are financed does not affect investment decisions.

Money illusion occurs when people confuse changes in the nominal value of variables with changes in the real value. For example, when workers see a fall in their nominal wage they may mistakenly believe that this affects their purchasing power, i.e. their real wage.

Multicollinearity occurs when two or more explanatory variables within an econometric model are correlated with each other.

Multiplier effects occur when changes in aggregate demand are magnified by the fact that money will flow through the economy and be respent by other people.

New Economy is the changed economic environment that has emerged as a consequence of innovations in high-tech, knowledge-based products and services.

Net domestic product (NDP) is GDP minus depreciation.

Net present value (NPV) is the difference between the discounted value of expected future returns and current costs, when the prevailing real, risk-adjusted interest rate is used to discount expected future returns. When the internal rate of return is equal to the prevailing interest rate, NPV will be equal to zero.

Network effects are the positive and negative externalities that emerge within networked industries e.g. in telecommunications and computing.

Non-ergodicity is an assumption that the determinants of economic processes are not immutable and determinate, and that economic processes will be changed by past events.

Non-nested tests are econometric tests used to assess whether or not an econometric model adds significant extra explanatory power when tested against alternative models. *See the* Statistical Appendix.

Non-stochastic means non-random, deterministic.

Non-stationarity occurs when a variable does not exhibit stable statistical properties.

Obsolescence occurs when structural and technological changes reduce the value of capital assets.

Opportunity cost is involved in all economic decisions. It is the cost associated with giving up the next best alternative.

Opportunity principle is the principle outlined by Fisher in his analysis of the determination of interest rates, and describes the demand for funds from investors facing various investment opportunities.

Options theory *See* real options theory.

Ordinary least squares (OLS) is an estimation procedure used to estimate parameters in models based around minimizing the sum of squared residuals.

Panel data is a data set that includes observations over time and across space. In other words, panel data sets consist of time series and cross-sectional observations together.

Paradox of thrift, in contrast to neo-classical theory, describes the possibility that increases in savings rates will mean that money will leak out of the circular flow of income, dampening the multiplier and reducing aggregate demand.

Pay-off period is the period of time that it takes for an investment expenditure to pay for itself.

Ponzi finance is a risky form of investment financing that is based on expectations of future profit bonanzas rather than a current cash flows.

Probability value (p value) is, essentially, the probability that a null hypothesis (H_0) will not be rejected. In practice it can be used as an exact significance level. A low probability value implies that the H_0 is unlikely and therefore could be abandoned.

Procedural rationality is a rationality assumption described by Simon (1979) that economic decisions are a process of 'appropriate deliberation' rather than a mathematical assessment of benefits and costs.

Prospective yield is a concept outlined by Keynes, describing the discounted value of expected future returns from an asset. *See also* demand price of capital.

Putty-clay models are models of production in which capital–labour ratios are flexible (like putty) before investment decisions are made but inflexible (like clay) once investments have been installed.

q_A **(average q)** is the ratio of market capitalization and current replacement cost of the capital stock and is often called Tobin's q. It can be shown, given various assumptions, that average q is equal to marginal q and if this is the case, average q gives a measure of the incentive to invest. The theory is applied to both microeconomic and macroeconomic analyses of investment.

q_M **(marginal q)** is sometimes described as the shadow price of capital and is the expected value of future returns from increments to the capital stock, relative to the cost of those increments.

Rate of return over costs *See* internal rate of return.

Rational expectations hypothesis assumes that economic agents make full use of all available information and do not make systematic mistakes.

Real interest rate is the nominal interest rate minus expected inflation. It is a concept originally associated with Fisher and captures the fact that real debt burdens are reduced by inflation and this reduces the real cost of borrowing.

Real options theory is a corollary of financial options theories. Real options theories of fixed investment analyze the costs of exercising an option to invest in fixed assets relative to the costs of doing nothing.

Rental cost of capital *See* user cost of capital.

Representative agents hypothesis is the hypothesis that by describing the microeconomic behaviour of one representative firm or household, macroeconomic theories can be constructed.

Reverse multiplier effects occur when *falls* in aggregate demand are magnified. *See also* multiplier effect.

Risk *See* lender's risk, borrower's risk, Knightian risk and inflationary risk.

Second mover advantage occurs when an economic agent does well out of waiting for other economic agents to act first.

Shadow price of capital *See* marginal q.

Sigma (σ) convergence occurs when the dispersion of variables across a cross-sectional sample is decreasing over time.

Solow's computer paradox applies to the phenomenon of decreasing productivity between the 1970s and 1990s despite widespread technological change, including computerization. *See also* diffusion lag hypothesis.

Speculative finance is a sustainable form of investment financing when current cash flows will meet current interest obligations and future cash flows will meet capital repayment costs.

State of confidence is the general state of optimism or pessimism in an economy and is a concept discussed by Keynes.

State of credit refers to the confidence of lending institutions and is interdependent with the state of confidence. It is also a concept associated with Keynes.

Stochastic means random, non-deterministic.

Structural breaks occur when the relationships between variables changes, reflecting structural change. They can be modelled econometrically, for example, by using dummy variables. *For more details, see the* Statistical Appendix.

Sunk costs are costs that cannot be recouped. *See also* irreversibility.

Surrogate production functions are associated with Samuelson who showed that, even in a world in which capital and labour are not substitutes, substitutability of techniques can replace factor substitutability.

Tobin's q *See* q_A.

Top-down modelling strategy is an econometric approach associated with Hendry in which an econometrician includes a large number of plausible variables within a model and just excludes the insignificant variables. *More details are outlined in the* Statistical Appendix.

Total factor productivity (TFP) is the contribution to changes in output that cannot be accounted for by changes in factor inputs of capital and labour.

Transformation models are rational expectations models of investment in which current values of variables are substituted for expected future values, based around an assumption that current values represent all currently available information.

Type I error refers to the mistake of incorrectly rejecting a true null hypothesis.

Type II error refers to incorrectly retaining a false null hypothesis.

Uncertainty *See* aggregate uncertainty, idiosyncratic uncertainty, Knightian uncertainty.

User cost of capital (Jorgenson's definition) is the marginal cost of consuming a unit of capital, including interest costs, depreciation and losses/gains in the value of capital assets.

User cost (Keynes's concept) Keynes does not define his user cost concept very clearly but it is generally assumed to describe the costs for investors associated with wear and tear, depreciation and fluctuations in value of capital assets.

Venture capital refers to the funds used to finance innovative investment projects.

Vintage effects emerge from the fact that capital stocks are made up of different pieces of machinery and equipment acquired at different times and embedding different capital–labour ratios.

Statistical appendix: some basic econometric techniques

This Statistical Appendix is not intended as a comprehensive guide to econometric technique. Instead, it is a quick introduction to some of the estimation techniques used in the analyses of investment discussed in this book. Recognizing that statistical analysis can sometimes be unnecessarily confusing, the statistical techniques used have been kept simple for those without much experience of econometrics. There are a number of more sophisticated techniques, tests and solutions than those outlined briefly here and good introductory texts that cover these in more detail include:

P. Kennedy (1998) *A Guide to Econometrics* (4th Edition). Oxford: Basil Blackwell.

R.L. Thomas (1997) *Modern Econometrics.* Harlow: Addison Wesley Longman.

D.N. Gujarati (2003) *Basic Econometrics* (4th Edition). New York: McGraw-Hill.

W.E. Griffiths, R. Carter Hill and George G. Judge (1993) *Learning and Practicing Econometrics.* New York: Wiley.

The regressions in this book were estimated using Microfit 4.0 so an additional guide to the tests and procedures used in with this package is:

M.H. Pesaran and B. Pesaran (1997) *Microfit 4.0.* Oxford: Oxford University Press.

OLS estimation techniques

Ordinary least squares (OLS) estimation techniques are based around the classical linear regression model (CLRM) and are a way of estimating the parameters within a model. As a linear technique, OLS can only be applied to linear, or additive, statistical models. For example, for a model of investment with output as the explanatory variable, the natural log of investment (i) can be described as a linear function of the natural log of output (o):

$$i_t = \alpha + \beta o_t + u_t$$

where u_t is the disturbance term or non-deterministic component and the deterministic relationship between i_t and o_t is described by $\alpha + \beta o_t$; α and β are the 'parameters' of the model.

OLS is based around minimizing the sum of squared residuals within a regression to get estimates of the parameters, where the residuals are the deviations of the observed values of a dependent variable from its estimated value, for each observation. The two main advantages of OLS estimation techniques are that they are simple and they are accurate, given certain assumptions. The accuracy emerges because, on average, OLS techniques will give the right answer and the likelihood of getting the right answer will be maximized (and the variance of answers minimized). The reason that OLS techniques are so widely used is this combination of simplicity and accuracy: there is a wide range of accurate estimation techniques but they are based on more restrictive assumptions, do not have the same desirable properties as OLS estimators, or are computationally complicated.

A word on causality: an econometrician can never really know whether, for example, investment causes output or output causes investment and so they can only make assertions about *correlations* between variables, keeping in mind that variables could be determined by each other (a phenomenon known as simultaneity) or by some other factor.

Probability values (*p* values) and significance levels

In this book, estimates of parameters are tested against various hypotheses using t and F versions of hypothesis tests. F tests are also reported with the diagnostic test results (discussed below). The interpretation of these tests can be speeded up by using 'probability values'; these are reported with the regression results in this book. The probability value is a measure of the probability of retaining a null hypothesis. As it is a probability it will range in value between zero and one. The closer is the probability value to one, the more likely is the null hypothesis. The closer is the *p* value to zero, the less likely is the null.

Following from this, *p* values can be used in two ways:

1. They can be used to define simple decision rules for interpreting hypothesis tests. For example if you are using a 5 per cent significance level:
   If $p > 0.05$ then do not reject H_0
   If $p < 0.05$ then do reject H_0
   However, before a decision rule can be formulated, some decision must be made about the significance level to be used in the decision rule. Essentially, this decision is somewhat arbitrary and implicitly reflects a judgement about the relative desirability of Type I error (falsely rejecting a true null) and Type II error (retaining a false null). By convention, relatively low significance levels are used (for example 1 per cent, 5 per cent and 10 per cent are common). This is based on an assumption that the null hypothesis reflects prior knowledge that an econometrician does not want to abandon too easily on the basis of results from one sample. This approach may be suitable for simple t tests of the null hypothesis that a given parameter is equal to zero. However, for some hypotheses, you may be more worried about Type II error. For example, with diagnostic tests you may want to be reassured that there are no problems. The consequences of retaining a false null on diagnostic tests are more worrying as they will have implications for the accuracy of OLS.
2. There is a way of using *p* values that is not dependent on arbitrary decisions about the significance level and that is to use the *p* value as an 'exact significance level', for example, if the *p* value is 0.37, then the test is significant at a 37 per cent significance level. This means that interpretation of results will not be completely dependent upon one researcher's selection of significance levels.

Obviously, in interpreting *p* values it is important to state your null hypothesis clearly. For simple t tests on the explanatory variable parameters (such as that a parameter is equal to zero), you will probably be looking to *reject* a null that a particular parameter is equal to zero because this will suggest that the variable is statistically important. However, for the p values reported with the diagnostic tests, you will probably want to *not reject* the null hypothesis, because the null is usually one of the Gauss-Markov assumptions, i.e. that there is no econometric problem.

The Gauss-Markov theorem

As explained above, OLS works if certain restrictive assumptions are met. These assumptions form part of the 'Gauss-Markov Theorem'. The Gauss-Markov theorem states that OLS estimators will be the 'BLUE' (best linear unbiased estimators) only if the 'Gaussian' or 'Gauss Markov' assumptions are satisfied. These assumptions generally focus on the form of the population disturbance term in an econometric model, where this disturbance term is the random component (u_t) in the econometric model.

So for OLS to work properly, the following assumptions must be true:

1. $E(u_i) = 0$ — on average, the disturbance terms equal zero.
2. $E(u_i u_j) = 0 \; i \neq j$ — there is no autocorrelation between the disturbance terms.
3. $E(u_i^2) = \sigma^2$, a constant — homoscedasticity: the pattern of spread of disturbances does not change over time (in time-series analysis) or over space (in cross-sectional analysis). Heteroscedasticity occurs when the spread does change.
4. $E(u_i X_i) = 0$ — there is no correlation between explanatory variables and disturbances.
5. The model is 'correctly specified', i.e. is an accurate description of reality, and is 'linear in the parameters', i.e. the dependent variable is an additive function of the explanatory variable(s).

Inferences about the behaviour of population disturbance terms can be made by looking at the residuals from the estimation of a sample of data. Looking at patterns of residuals forms the basis of a large number of diagnostic tests.

Other problems may affect the use of OLS. For example, if there is multicollinearity, i.e. a linear correlation between one or more explanatory variables, then your results may not be as accurate as you would like. But, in its simplest form, multicollinearity does not involve a violation of the Gauss-Markov assumptions and so OLS may still be the best technique in the presence of multicollinearity. The exceptional case is when there is 'perfect multicollinearity' which occurs when there is a perfect linear association (i.e. a correlation coefficient of one) between one or more explanatory variables. In this case, the OLS estimates will be undefined.

The diagnostic tests for the violation of Gauss-Markov conditions used in the analyses discussed in this book include:

1. Breusch-Godfrey LM test for serial correlation
2. Ramsey's RESET test for incorrect functional form
3. LM test for dependent variable heteroscedasticity
4. Chow's 'second' test for predictive failure
5. Chow's test for structural break

Many of these tests focus on describing patterns of residuals (the sample equivalent of the disturbance term) and estimated values of the relevant dependent variable. These diagnostic tests are explained in the following section.

Diagnostic tests

Breusch-Godfrey test

This test assesses the correlation between residuals in one period and residuals in previous periods. It involves regressing residuals on past residuals and the explanatory variables to test the past residuals for their relationship with the current residual. It is superior to other tests for autocorrelation because it will capture relatively complex forms of autocorrelation and can be used when a lagged dependent variable is being used as an explanatory variable. However, the Breusch-Godfrey test does suffer from the limitation that it is an asymptotic test, in other words it will only work well if there are lots of observations in the sample of data.

Ramsey's RESET test

Ramsey's RESET test involves incorporating some function of the estimated or 'fitted' value of the dependent variable into an 'auxilliary' regression. If this additional variable is significant, then this suggests that something has been left out of the original model. Consequently, Ramsey's RESET test will capture some problems reflecting incorrect functional form, for example, if levels of variables are used when logged values would have been better.

LM test for heteroscedasticity

This test involves regressing the squared residuals (the residual variance, given that the mean of residuals will be zero) on the square of the fitted values on the dependent variable. The assumption of homoscedasticity suggests that there should be no systematic pattern in the variance of the disturbance terms and therefore no systematic pattern in the variance of the residuals. The LM test for heteroscedasticity will pick up any systematic pattern; if there is a systematic pattern, then the OLS estimators will be inefficient. This test suffers from the same limitation that faces the Breusch-Godfrey test: it is an asymptotic or large sample test.

Structural break and predictive failure tests

These tests involve looking at econometric predictions versus real-world observations. For structural break tests, regressions are run on sub-samples of data and compared with results from the full sample to test whether or not the parameters are stable over time. For predictive failure tests, regressions are run leaving a few observations spare at the end. The regression results are extrapolated forward and these extrapolations are compared with observed values, to give a measure of forecast errors.

Interpreting diagnostic tests

When diagnostic tests reveal significant econometric problems, a range of explanations exist and some of these explanations will overlap. Some possibilities include:

True autocorrelation

It may be that the Gauss-Markov condition of non-autocorrelation in the disturbances is violated and that there is no more complex reason for this. If this is the case, then the model can be estimated using generalized least squares (GLS) techniques (see below).

Structural breaks and/or predictive failure

If there is a structural break in a model, for example, in time-series analysis, this may reflect some historical event or political change. This may be reflected in systematic patterns in residuals as well, so the tests for autocorrelation may also be significant. If there is a structural break or predictive failure, then dummy variables can be incorporated into models to capture breaks. (Dummy variables are simple categorical variables that take the value zero or one, depending upon whether a particular characteristic is present or not.)

Model misspecification

Systematic patterns in residuals may reflect omitted influences which are being picked up by the error term. These omitted influences may reflect an incorrect functional form or the exclusion of an important explanatory variable in which case incorrect functional form tests may also be significant. The solution is to try different specifications of the model but this solution may be constrained by theoretical considerations, if an econometrician is to avoid being accused of data mining!

Non-stationarity in the variables

Signs of econometric problems, e.g. autocorrelation or structural breaks, may reflect a problem with 'non-stationarity' in the variables. Common forms of non-stationarity include random walks and random walks with drift. These patterns occur when a variable has a unit root, as described below. OLS estimation procedures will only work if all the variables (dependent and explanatory) are stationary. (An exception to this occurs when non-stationary variables are co-integrated: that is, when a linear combination of the variables is stationary.) When non-stationary variables are regressed on non-stationary variables, this can result in spurious regressions: i.e. models that appear to possess a high degree of explanatory power. A spurious regression can be picked up in the residuals. So a combination of a high R^2 and significant autocorrelation is often an indication of non-stationarity in the variables.

The Dickey-Fuller (DF) and Augmented Dickey-Fuller (ADF) tests test whether or not a given variable is non-stationary. This is done by testing the H_0 that the variable has a 'unit root'. A unit root can be described by looking at the relationship between a variable and its lagged value, for example:

$$i_t = \rho i_{t-1} + \varepsilon_t$$

ε_t is a non-serially correlated error term.
If $\rho = 1$, then the system is characterized by a unit root. Another way to describe a unit root process is as a random walk: if ρ is equal to one, then Δi_t will be completely random, i.e. it will equal to ε_t.

A random walk with drift is much the same except a constant term is included to capture drift upwards in the variable:

$$i_t = \alpha + \rho i_{t-1} + \varepsilon_t$$

if $\rho = 1$ then this process is a random walk with drift.

In constructing DF tests, for statistical reasons, this specification is reformulated by subtracting y_{t-1} from both sides to give:

$$\Delta i_t = \delta i_{t-1} + \varepsilon_t \quad \text{where } \delta = \rho - 1$$

H_0: $\rho = 1$ or $\delta = 0$ versus H_1: $\rho < 1$ or $\delta < 0$ tested using a τ test, where the critical values on τ are presented by Dickey and Fuller (1981).

If the DF and ADF tests are insignificant then this means that the H_0 of a unit root cannot be rejected. In this case, variables should be 'differenced' to eliminate the non-stationarity.

When the DF test is characterized by serial correlation in the residuals the results are unreliable and so ADF tests must be used instead. The ADF test is much the same as the DF test in that the τ test of $\rho = 1$ or $\delta = 0$ is still used but lagged Δys are included as well, to 'mop-up' any autocorrelation in ε_t,:

$$\Delta i_t = \delta i_{t-1} + \phi_1 \Delta i_{t-1} + \phi_2 \Delta i_{t-2} + \phi_3 \Delta i_{t-3} + \phi_4 \Delta i_{t-4} + \varpi_t$$

where ϖ_t is the non-serially correlated stochastic error term.

Other econometric issues

Other estimation techniques

A couple of variants of OLS are used in this book, i.e. generalized least squares (GLS) and instrumental variable estimation (IV). GLS involves modifying OLS to eliminate econometric problems such as autocorrelation and/or heteroscedasticity. This is done by 'restricting' or modifying the models, thus eliminating econometric problems such as autocorrelation and heteroscedasticity.

Simultaneity

Instrumental variable (IV) estimation is used when there is simultaneity between variables, in other words when the variables are mutually dependent, for instance, in the above example if i_t determines o_t and o_t determines i_t. If this is the case then Gauss-Markov assumption 4 will be violated because u_t is a component of i_t and i_t is a component of o_t. The simplest form of IV estimation involves lagging explanatory variables because, in the above example, o_{t-1} will not be a component of u_t.

Cointegration

As mentioned above, non-stationarity will not cause problems if the dependent and explanatory variables are cointegrated, i.e. if a linear combination of non-stationary variables is itself stationary. If variables are co-integrated, then the error terms from a regression of the variables will be stationary and errors will not be correlated with past values. This insight is incorporated into autoregressive distributed lag (ARDL) co-integrating models, for example, see Banerjee *et al.* (1993). An example of an ARDL model is:

$$i_t = \alpha + \lambda i_t + \beta_1 o_t + \beta_2 o_{t-1} + u_t$$

i.e. there is a lagged dependent variable and a distributed lag on the explanatory variable on the right-hand side.

How to find a good econometric model

Top-down modelling strategy

Econometricians face many trade-offs in estimating good econometric models. If a 'data-mining' approach is adopted it is almost inevitable that some sort of relationship will be discovered. So economic theory should be the first guide in the construction of econometric models. On the other hand, it is best to include all relevant variables at the beginning rather than adding in new explanatory variables one at a time. This is because, if an important explanatory variable is omitted, then the parameter estimates on the remaining explanatory variables may be biased if they reflect the influence of the neglected variables. The tests on these parameters will not be reliable because of this bias and tests for autocorrelation may also be significant if the error terms are picking up omitted influences. For this reason, Hendry and Wallis (1984) recommend a 'top-down' modelling strategy – starting off with a large model and gradually excluding insignificant variables, but keeping an eye all the time on the diagnostic tests to make sure that excluding insignificant variables is not creating econometric problems that might suggest model misspecification.

The merits of alternative econometric models can be assessed by examining their explanatory power, for example, by assessing the proportion of variability in the dependent variable that is captured by the explanatory variables. This can be captured by looking at the adjusted R^2, adjusted for the number of explanatory variables within a model. However, as noted above, a high R^2 is not always a good sign if it reflects a spurious relationship, such as in the case of non-stationary variables.

So more rigorous approaches to model comparison are needed. Other statistics that are used to judge a model include Akaike's Information Criterion and Schwartz's Bayesian Information Criterion. These are tests constructed by looking at the trade-off between minimizing the sum of square residuals and limiting the number of regressors (Griffiths, Hill and Judge, 1993; Kennedy, 1992).

Model comparison tests

Another way to judge an econometric model is to look at how it performs against other econometric models. Non-nested tests are a way of doing this. They involve comparing two models that are not nested within each other, i.e. each retain some distinctive components relative to the other model. So if two different models pick up variability in a dependent variable then the independent explanatory power of each model can be captured in the non-nested testing stage.

The non-nested tests used in the analyses outlined in this book include the Cox, Cox (adjusted), Wald, J, JA and F (encompassing) tests. The simplest forms of these tests involve using an alternative model to derive predicted values for investment. These predicted values are then used as an additional explanatory variable. If the coefficient on this additional variable is insignificant when added to alternative model, then the alternative model contributes no significant additional explanatory power. Non-nested tests can also be interpreted as model specification tests because if a model is not able to explain the results of alternative models then this indicates that the maintained model may be misspecified (Bean, 1981, p. 116; Davidson and MacKinnon, 1981).

The rationale underlying different non-nested testing procedures used in this book is explained in more detail in the MICROFIT manual and in Davidson and MacKinnon (1981), Griffiths, Hill and Judge (1993), Gujarati (2003), Mizon (1984), Pesaran and Deaton (1978).

Ultimately, it should be remembered that if econometric results are bad, it may be because the economic theory underlying the econometric model is flawed!

Bibliography

Abel, A.B. (1980) Empirical Investment Equations: An Integrative Framework. In K. Brunner and A.H. Meltzer *On the state of macroeconomics*, in Carnegie-Rochester Conference Series on Public Policy. Supplementary series in *Journal of Monetary Economics*: 39–91.

Abel, A.B. (1983) Optimal Investment under Uncertainty. *American Economic Review*, **73**(1): 228–33.

Abel, A.B. (1990) Consumption and Investment. In B.M. Friedman and F.H. Hahn *Handbook of Monetary Economics*. New York: North-Holland: 726–78.

Abel, A.B. and Blanchard, O.J. (1986) The Present Value of Profits and Cyclical Movements in Investment. *Econometrica*, **54**(2): 249–83.

Abel, A.B. and Eberly, J.C. (1996) Optimal Investment with Costly Reversibility. *Review of Economic Studies*, **63**(4): 581–93.

Abel, A.B. and Eberly, J.C. (1999) The Effects of Irreversibility and Uncertainty on Capital Accumulation. *Journal of Monetary Economics*, **44**(3): 339–77.

Acemoglu, D. (1993) Learning About Others' Actions and the Investment Accelerator. *Economic Journal*, **103**: 318–28.

Aiginger, K. (1987) *Production and Decision Theory Under Uncertainty*. Oxford: Basil Blackwell.

Akerlof, G.A. (1970) The Market for Lemons: Quantity, Uncertainty and the Market Mechanism. *Quarterly Journal of Economics*, **84**: 488–500.

Alvarez, L.H.R. and Koskela, E. (2002) *Irreversible Investment under Interest Rate Variability: New Results*. CESifo Working Paper Series No. 640. Munich: Centre for Economic Studies and Ifo Institute.

Anderson, G.J. (1981) A New Approach to the Empirical Investigation of Investment Expenditures. *Economic Journal*, **91**: 88–103.

Anderson, W.H.L. (1964) Business Fixed Investment: A Marriage of Fact and Fancy. In R. Ferber (ed.) *Determinants of Investment Behaviour*. Universities National Bureau Conference Series, **18**. New York: Columbia University Press for the National Bureau of Economic Research.

Araujo, J.A. (1994) On the Keynesian Investment Demand Schedule. Essay III of PhD thesis, University of Cambridge.

Araujo, J.A. and Harcourt, G.C. (1993) Maurice Dobb, Joan Robinson and Gerald Shove on Accumulation and the Rate of Profits. *Journal of the History of Economic Thought*, **15**: 1–30.

Arrow, K.J. (1968) Optimal Capital Policy with Irreversible Investment. In J.N. Wolfe *Value, Capital and Growth*. Edinburgh: Edinburgh University Press: 1–19.

Asimakopulos, A. (1971) The Determination of Investment in Keynes's Model. *Canadian Journal of Economics*, **4**: 382–8.

Asimakopulos, A. (1991) *Keynes's General Theory and Accumulation.* Cambridge: Cambridge University Press, Modern Cambridge Economics Series.

Auerbach, A.J. and Hassett, K. (1992) Recent US Investment Behaviour and the Tax Reform Act of 1986: A Disaggregate View. *Carnegie-Rochester Conference Series on Public Policy*, **35**: 185–215.

Baddeley, M.C. (1996) Rationality, Expectations and Investment. PhD thesis, University of Cambridge.

Baddeley, M.C. (2000), *Is e-money Real Money? An Economic Analysis of Virtual Currencies.* Paper presented to the Institute of Electrical Engineers Seminar, University of Cambridge, December 2000.

Baddeley, M.C. (2002 forthcoming) Accelerator Theory. In H. Vane and B. Snowdon (eds) *Encyclopaedia of Macroeconomics.* Aldershot: Edward Elgar.

Baddeley, M., Martin, R. and Tyler, P. (1998) European Regional Unemployment Disparities: Convergence or Persistence? *European Urban and Regional Studies* **5**(3): 195–215.

Baddeley, M. and McCombie, J. (2001) An Historical Perspective on Speculative Bubbles and Financial Crises: Tulipmania and the South Sea Bubble. In P. Arestis, M. Baddeley and J. McCombie (eds) *What Global Economic Crisis?* London: Macmillan.

Banerjee, A., Dolad, J.J., Galbraith, J.W. and Hendry, D.F. (1993) *Cointegration, Error Correction and the Econometric Analysis of Non-Stationary Data.* Oxford: Oxford University Press.

Barna, T. (1962) *Investment and Growth Policies in British Industrial Firms.* Cambridge: Cambridge University Press.

Barro, R.J. (1990) The Stock Market and Investment. *Review of Financial Studies*, **3**(1): 115–31.

Barro, R.J. and Sala-I-Martin, X. (1995) *Economic Growth.* New York: McGraw-Hill.

Bateman, B.W. (1990) The Elusive Logical Relation: An Essay on Change and Continuity in Keynes's Thought. In D.E. Moggridge (ed.) *Perspectives on the History of Economic Thought*, **IV**. Aldershot: Edward Elgar.

Bean, C.A. (1989) Capital Shortage. *Economic Policy*, April 1989: 11–54.

Bean, C.R. (1981) An Econometric Model of Manufacturing Investment in the UK. *Economic Journal*, **91**: 106–21.

Belassa, B. and Nelson, R. (eds) (1977) *Economic Progress, Private Values and Public Policy: Essays in Honour of William Fellner.* New York: North-Holland.

Bernanke, B.S. (1983) Irreversibility, Uncertainty and Cyclical Investment. *Quarterly Journal of Economics*, **98**(1): 85–106.

Berstein, J.I. and Nadiri, M.I. (1989) Rates of Return on Physical and R&D Capital and the Structure of the Production Process: Cross Section and Time Series Evidence. In B. Raj *Advances in Econometrics and Modelling.* Hingham: Kluwer Academic: 169–87.

Bertola, G. (1989) Irreversible Investment. Cited in R.S. Pindyck (1991) Irreversibility, Uncertainty and Investment. *Journal of Economic Literature*, **XXIX**: 1110–48.

Biais, B., Hilton, D., Mazurier, K. and Pouget, S. (2002) *Psychological Traits and Trading Strategies.* CEPR Discussion Paper **3195**, February.

Bischoff, C.W. (1969) Hypothesis Testing and the Demand for Capital Goods. *Review of Economic Statistics*, **51**(3): 354–68.

Blanchard, O.J. and Fischer, S. (1993) *NBER Macroeconomics Annual.* National Bureau of Economic Research. Cambridge, MA: MIT Press.

Blanchard, O.J. and Watson, M.W. (1982) Bubbles, Rational Expectations and Financial Markets. In P. Wachtel (ed.) *Crises in Economic and Financial Structure.* Lexington: M.A. Heath.

Blanchard, O.J. and Wyplosz, C. (1981) An Empirical Structural Model of Aggregate Demand. *Journal of Monetary Economics*, 7(1): 1–28.

Blinder, A.S. (1986) Can the Production Smoothing Model of Inventory Behaviour be Saved. *Quarterly Journal of Economics*, **101**: 431–53.

Bradford, W. and Harcourt, G.C. (1996) Units and Definitions. In G.C. Harcourt and P. Riach (eds) *A Second Edition of* The General Theory. London: Routledge.

Brainard, W.C. and Tobin, J. (1968) Pitfalls in Financial Model Building. *American Economic Review*, **58**(2): 99–122.

Brainard, W.C. and Tobin, J. (1977) Asset Markets and the Cost of Capital. In B. Belassa and R. Nelson (eds) *Economic Progress, Private Values and Public Policy: Essays in Honour of William Fellner*. New York: North-Holland.

Braithwaite, R.B. (1972) Editorial Foreword. In J.M. Keynes (1921) *A Treatise on Probability*. London: Macmillan: xv–xxii.

Brunner, K. and Meltzer, A.H. (1980) *On the State of Macroeconomics*, **12**. Carnegie-Rochester Conference Series on Public Policy. Supplementary series in *Journal of Monetary Economics*.

Bulmer, M.G. (1989) *Principles of Statistics*. New York: Dover Publications.

Caballero, R.J. (1991) On the Sign of the Investment-Uncertainty Relationship. *American Economic Review*, **81**(1): 279–88.

Caballero, R.J. and Pindyck, R.S. (1992) Uncertainty, Investment and Industrial Revolution. National Bureau of Economic Research. Working Paper **4160**. Cambridge, MA: National Bureau of Economic Research.

Carabelli, A. (1988) *On Keynes's Method*. London: Macmillan.

Carrado, C. and Slifman, L. (1999) The Reliability of Aggregate Statistics: Decomposition of Productivity and Unit Costs. *American Economic Review*, **89**(2): 328–32.

Cecchetti, S.G. (2002) The New Economy and Challenges for Macroeconomic Policy. National Bureau of Economic Research. Working Paper **8935**. Cambridge, MA: National Bureau of Economic Research.

Chatterji, M. and Dewhurst, J.H. (1996) Convergence Clubs and Relative Economic Performance in Great Britain, 1977–91. *Regional Studies*, **30**(1): 31–40.

Chenery, H.B. (1952) Overcapacity and the Acceleration Principle. *Econometrica*, **20**(1): 1–28.

Chirinko, R.S. (1987) Tobin's Q and Financial Policy. *Journal of Monetary Economics*, **19**(1): 69–87.

Chirinko, R.S. (1993) Business Fixed Investment Spending: Modelling Strategies, Empirical Results and Policy Implications. *Journal of Economic Literature*, **XXXI**: 1875–911.

Chirinko, R.S. and Fazzari, S.M. (1988) Tobin's Q, Nonconstant Returns to Scale and Imperfectly Competitive Product Markets. Cited in R.S. Chirinko Business Fixed Investment Spending: Modelling Strategies, Empirical Results and Policy Implications. *Journal of Economic Literature*, **XXXI**: 1875–911.

Clark, J.M. (1917) Business Acceleration and the Law of Demand: A Technical Factor in Economic Cycles. *Journal of Political Economy*, **25**(1): 217–35.

Clark, P.K. (1979) Investment in the 1970s: Theory, Performance, and Prediction. *Brookings Papers on Economic Activity*, **1**: 73–124.

Coates, J. (1990) Ordinary Language Economics – Keynes and Cambridge Philosophers, PhD thesis, University of Cambridge.

Coates, J. (1996) Keynes, Vague Concepts and Fuzzy Logic. In G.C. Harcourt and P. Riach (eds) *A Second Edition of* The General Theory. London: Routledge.

Coen, R.M. (1968) Tax Policy and Investment Behaviour. *American Economic Review*, **58**(2): 200–11.

Coen, R.M. (1969) Tax Policy and Investment Behaviour: Comment. *American Economic Review*, **59**(3): 370–7.

Colander, D.C. and Guthrie, R.S. (1980) Great Expectations: What the Dickens Do 'Rational Expectations' Mean. *Journal of Post Keynesian Economics*, **3**(2): 219–34.

Confederation of British Industry (1994) *Industrial Trends Survey*. CBI.

Courvisanos, J. (1996) *Investment Cycles in Capitalist Economies: A Kaleckian Behavioural Contribution*. Cheltenham: Edward Elgar.

Craine, R. (1975) Investment, Adjustment Costs and Uncertainty. *International Economic Review*, **16**(3): 648–61.

Crotty, J.R. (1992) Neo-classical and Keynesian Approaches to the Theory of Investment. *Journal of Post Keynesian Economics*, **14**(4): 483–96.

Cukierman, A. (1980) The Effects of Uncertainty on Investment Under Risk Neutrality with Endogenous Information. *Journal of Political Economy*, **88**(3): 462–75.

Cyert, R.M. and March, J.G. (1963) *A Behavioural Theory of the Firm*. Englewood-Cliffs, NJ: Prentice-Hall.

Darby, M.R. and Zucker, L.G. (2002) Going Public When You Can in Biotechnology. National Bureau of Economic Research, Working Paper **8954**. Cambridge, MA: National Bureau of Economic Research.

Davidson, P. (1965) Keynes's Finance Motive. *Oxford Economic Papers*, **17**: 47–65.

Davidson, P. (1967) The Importance of the Demand for Finance. *Oxford Economic Papers*, **19**: 245–53.

Davidson, P. (1970) Discussion Paper: Money in Britain, 1959–69. Reprinted in P. Davidson (ed.) (1990) *Money and Employment: The Collected Works of Paul Davidson*, **1**. London: Macmillan.

Davidson, P. (1978) *Money and the Real World* (2nd Edition). London: Macmillan.

Davidson, P. (1980) The Dual-Faceted Nature of the Keynesian Revolution. *Journal of Post Keynesian Economics*, **2**: 291–307.

Davidson, P. (1987) User Cost. In P. Davidson (1991b) *Inflation, Open Economies and Resources*. London: Macmillan: 139–42.

Davidson, P. (1991a) Comment. In R.M. O'Donnell 1991a: 61–72.

Davidson, P. (1991b) *Inflation, Open Economies and Resources*. London: Macmillan.

Davidson, P. (1995) Uncertainty in Economics. In S. Dow and J. Hillard (eds) *Keynes, Knowledge and Uncertainty*. Aldershot: Edward Elgar: 107–16.

Davidson, R. and MacKinnon, J.G. (1981) Several Tests for Model Specification in the Presence of Alternative Hypotheses. *Econometrica*, **49**(3): 781–93.

Davis, J.B. (1996) J.M. Keynes on History and Convention. In G.C. Harcourt and P. Riach (eds) *A Second Edition of* The General Theory. London: Routledge.

DeLong, J.B. and Summers, L.H. (1986) The Changing Cyclical Variability of Economic Activity in the United States. In R.J. Gordon (ed.) *The American Business Cycle: Continuity and Change*. National Bureau of Economic Research, Studies in Business Cycles, **25**: 679–719.

DeLong, J.B. and Summers, L.H. (2001) The 'New Economy': Background, Historical Perspective, Questions and Speculations. In *Economic Policy of the Information Economy*. Proceedings of the symposium sponsored by the Federal Reserve Bank of Kansas City: 11–46.

Diamond, J.J. (1962) Further Development of a Distributed Lag Investment Function. *Econometrica*, **30**(4): 788–800.

Dickey, D.A. and Fuller, W. (1981) Likelihood Ratio Statistics for Autoregressive Time Series with a Unit Root. *Econometrica*, **49**: 1057–72.

Dittrich, D, Gueth, W. and Maciejovsky, B. (2001) *Overconfidence in Investment Decisions: An Experimental Approach*, CESifo Working Paper Series No. 626. Munich: Centre for Economic Studies and Ifo Institute.

Dixit, A.K. and Pindyck, R.S. (1994) *Investment Under Uncertainty*. Princeton, NJ: Princeton University Press.

Domar, E. (1946) *Toward a Dynamic Economics.* London: Macmillan.
Dougherty, C. (1992) *Introduction to Econometrics.* New York: Oxford University Press.
Dow, A. and Dow, S. (1985) Animal Spirits and Rationality. In T. Lawson and M.H. Pesaran *Keynes' Economics – Methodological Issues.* Beckenham: Croom Helm.
Dow, S. and Hillard, J. (eds) (1995) *Keynes, Knowledge and Uncertainty.* Aldershot: Edward Elgar.
Driver, C. and Moreton, D. (1992a) *Investment, Expectations and Uncertainty.* Oxford: Blackwell.
Driver, C. and Moreton, D. (1992b) The Influence of Uncertainty on UK Manufacturing Investment. *Economic Journal,* **101**: 1452–9.
Driver, C. and Temple, P. (1999) A Survey of Recent Issues in Investment. In C. Driver and P. Temple (eds) *Investment, Growth and Employment.* London: Routledge.
Driver, C., Temple, P. and Urga, G. (2001) Profitability, Capacity and Uncertainty: A Model of UK Manufacturing Investment. Unpublished paper.
Duesenberry, J.S., Fromm, G., Klein, L.R. and Kuh, E. (eds) (1965) *The Brookings Quarterly Model of the United States.* Amsterdam: North-Holland.
Dunne, T. (1991) *Technology Usage in US Manufacturing Industries.* Washington, DC: US Census Economic Studies.
Dwyer, G.P., Williams, A.W., Battalio, R.C. and Mason, T.L. (1993) Test of Rational Expectations in a Stark Setting. *Economic Journal,* **103**: 586–601.
Earl, P.E. (1983) *The Economic Imagination: Towards a Behavioural Analysis of Choice.* New York: Sharpe.
Earley, J.S. (1956) Marginal Policies of Excellently Managed Companies. *American Economic Review* **46**(1): 44–70
Eisner, R. (1965) Realisation of Investment Anticipations. In J.S. Duesenberry, G. Fromm, L.R. Klein and E. Kuh (eds) *The Brookings Quarterly Model of the United States.* Amsterdam: North-Holland.
Eisner, R. (1970) Tax Policy and Investment Behaviour: Further Comment. *American Economic Review,* **60**(4): 746–52.
Eisner, R. (1974) Econometric Study of Investment Behaviour: A Comment. *Economic Inquiry,* **12**(1): 91–104.
Eisner, R. (1996) The Marginal Efficiency of Capital and Investment. In G.C. Harcourt and P. Riach (eds) *A Second Edition of* The General Theory. London: Routledge.
Eisner, R. and Nadiri, M.I. (1968) Investment Behaviour and the Neo-classical Theory. *Review of Economic Statistics,* **50**(3): 369–82.
Eisner, R. and Strotz, R.H. (1963) Determinants of Business Investment. In M.J.C. Surrey (ed.) *Macroeconomic Themes – Editing Reading in Macroeconomics.* Oxford: Oxford University Press: 127–136.
Elliott, J. (1973) Theories of Corporate Investment Behaviour Revisited. *American Economic Review,* **63**: 195–207.
Engle, R.F. and Foley, P.K. (1975) An Asset Price Model of Aggregate Investment. *International Economic Review,* **16**(3): 625–47.
Evans, M.K. (1967) A Study of Industry Investment Decisions. *Review of Economic Statistics,* **53**(1): 151–64.
Fazzari, S.M., Hubbard, R.G. and Peterson, B.C. (1988) Financing Constraints and Corporate Investment. *Brookings Papers on Economic Activity,* **1**: 141–95.
Federer, J.P. (1993) Does Uncertainty Affect Investment Spending. *Journal of Post Keynesian Economics,* **16**(1): 19–35.
Feldstein, M. and Flemming, J. (1971) Tax Policy, Corporate Saving and Investment Behaviour in Britain. *Review of Economic Studies,* **38**: 314–34.
Feldstein, M.S. (1987) *The Effects of Taxation on Capital Accumulation.* National Bureau of Economic Research. Chicago: University of Chicago Press.

Ferber, R. (ed.) (1964) *Determinants of Investment Behaviour*. Universities National Bureau Conference Series, **18**. New York: Columbia University Press for the National Bureau of Economic Research.

Fisher, I. (1906) *The Nature of Capital and Income*. New York: Macmillan.

Fisher, I. (1907) *The Rate of Interest*. New York: Macmillan.

Fisher, I. (1930) *The Theory of Interest*. New York: Macmillan.

Fisher, I. (1932) *Booms and Depressions*. New York: Adelphi.

Friedman, B.M. and Hahn, F.H. (1990) *Handbook of Monetary Economics*. New York: North-Holland.

Friedman, M. (1953) The Methodology of Positive Economics. In F.H. Hahn and M. Hollis (eds) (1979) *Philosophy and Economic Theory*. Oxford: Oxford University Press: 18–35.

Garber, P.M. and King, M.A. (1983) Deep Structural Excavation? A Critique of Euler Equation Methods. National Bureau of Economic Research, Working Paper **31**.

Gerrard, B. (1994) Beyond Rational Expectations: A Constructive Interpretation of Keynes's Analysis of Behaviour Under Uncertainty. *Economic Journal*, **104**: 327–37.

Gomes, J.F. (2001) Financing Investment. *American Economic Review*, **91**(5): 1263–85.

Glazer, A., Kanniainen, V. and Mustonen, M. (2002) *Innovation of Network Goods: A Non-innovating Firm Will Gain*. CESifo Working Paper Series Number 692, Munich: Centre for Economic Studies and Ifo Institute for Economic Research.

Goodwin, R.M. (1948) Secular and Cyclical Aspects of the Multiplier and Accelerator. In A. Metzler (ed.) *Income, Employment and Public Policy (Essays in Honor of Alvin H. Hansen)*. New York: W.W. Norton & Co.

Gordon, M.J. (1992) The Neoclassical and Post Keynesian Theory of Investment. *Journal of Post Keynesian Economics*, **14**(4): 425–43.

Gordon, M.J. (1994) *Finance, Investment and Macroeconomics*. Aldershot: Edward Elgar.

Gordon, R.A. (1948) Short-period Price Determination in Theory and Practice. *American Economic Review* **38**(3): 265–88.

Gordon, R.J. (2000) Does the 'New Economy' Measure up to the Great Inventions of the Past? *Journal of Economic Perspectives*, **14**: 49–74.

Gould, J.P. (1968) Adjustment Costs in the Theory of Investment of the Firm. *Review of Economic Studies*, **35**(1): 47–55.

Gowrisankaran, G. and Stavins J. (2002) Network Externalities and Technology Adoption: Lessons from Electronic Payments. National Bureau of Economic Research, Working Paper **8943**. Cambridge, MA: National Bureau of Economic Research.

Griffiths, W.E., Hill, R.C. and Judge, G.G. (1993) *Learning and Practising Econometrics*. New York: Wiley.

Griliches, Z. (1967) Distributed lags: a Survey. *Econometrica*, **35**: 16–49.

Griliches, Z. (1979) Issues in Assessing the Contribution of R&D to Productivity Growth. *Bell Journal of Economics*, **10**(1): 92–116.

Griliches, Z. (1994) Productivity, R&D and the Data Constraint. *American Economic Review*, **84**(1): 1–23.

Grunfeld, Y. (1960) The Determination of Corporate Investment. In A.C. Harberger *The Demand for Durable Goods*. Chicago: Chicago University Press: 211–66.

Gujarati, D.N. (2003) *Basic Econometrics* (4th Edition). New York: McGraw-Hill.

Gullickson, W. and Harper, M.J. (1999) Possible Bias in Aggregate Productivity Growth. *Monthly Labor Review* **125**(3): 32–40.

Haavelmo, T. (1960) *A Study in the Theory of Investment*. Chicago: University of Chicago Press.

Hahn, F.H. (1973a) The Winter of Our Discontent. *Economica*, **40**: 322–3.

Hahn, F.H. (1973b) *On the Notion of Equilibrium in Economics: Inaugural Lecture*. Cambridge: Cambridge University Press.

Hahn, F.H. (1985) *In Praise of Economic Theory: 1984 Jevons Memorial Lecture.* London: University College.

Hahn, F.H. and Hollis, M. (eds) (1979) *Philosophy and Economic Theory.* Oxford: Oxford University Press.

Hahn, F. (1990) Expectations. In J.D. Hey and D. Winch (eds) *A Century of Economics: 100 years of the Royal Economic Society.* Oxford: Basil Blackwell.

Hahn, F. and Matthews, R.C.O. (1964) The Theory of Economic Growth – A Survey. *Economic Journal*, **74**: 779–902.

Hall, R.E. and Jorgenson, D.W. (1967) Tax Policy and Investment Behaviour. *American Economic Review*, **57**(3): 391–414.

Hall, R.L. and Hitch, C.J. (1939) Price Theory and Business Behaviour. *Oxford Economic Papers* **1939**(2): 12–45.

Hamouda, O.F. and Harcourt, G.C. (1988) Post Keynesianism: From Criticism to Coherence. *Bulletin of Economic Research*, **40**(1): 1–33.

Harberger, A.C. (1960) *The Demand for Durable Goods.* Chicago: Chicago University Press.

Harcourt, G.C. (1965) The Accountant in the Golden Age. *Oxford Economic Papers*, **17**: 66–80. Reprinted in G.C. Harcourt (1992) *On Political Economists and Modern Political Economy* (ed. C. Sardoni). London: Routledge: 14–27.

Harcourt, G.C. (1966) Biases in Empirical Estimates of the Elasticities of Substitution of CES Production Functions. *Review of Economic Studies*, **33**: 227–33.

Harcourt, G.C. (1968) Investment Decision Criteria, Investment Incentives and the Choice of Technique. *Economic Journal*, **78**: 77–95.

Harcourt, G.C. (1969) Some Cambridge Controversies in the Theory of Capital. *Journal of Economic Literature*, 7: 369–405.

Harcourt, G.C. (1972) *Some Cambridge Controversies in the Theory of Capital.* Cambridge: Cambridge University Press.

Harcourt, G.C. (1976) The Cambridge Controversies: Old Ways and New Horizons – or Dead End? *Oxford Economic Papers*, **28**(1): 25–65.

Harcourt, G.C. (1986) The Legacy of Keynes: Theoretical Methods and Unfinished Business. Reprinted in G.C. Harcourt (1992) *On Political Economists and Modern Political Economy* (ed. C. Sardoni). London: Routledge: 235–50.

Harcourt, G.C. (1992) *On Political Economists and Modern Political Economy* (ed. C. Sardoni). London: Routledge.

Harcourt, G.C. (1994) Taming Speculators and Putting the World on Course to Prosperity: A 'Modest Proposal'. *Economic and Political Weekly*, **XXIX**: 2490–2.

Harcourt, G.C. and Kenyon, P. (1976) Pricing and the Investment Decision. *Kyklos*, **29**: 449–77.

Harcourt, G.C. and Laing, N.F. (1962) *Capital and Growth.* Harmondsworth: Penguin.

Harcourt, G.C. and Riach, P. (eds) (1996) *A Second Edition of* The General Theory. London: Routledge.

Harcourt, G.C. and Sardoni, C. (1995) The General Theory of Employment, Interest and Money: Three Views. In Philip Arestis (ed.) *Keynes, Money and the Open Economy: Essays in Honour of Paul Davidson*, **1**. Cheltenham: Edward Elgar: 1–13.

Harcourt, G.C. and Spajic, L. (1999) Post Keynesianism. In Shri Bhagwan Dahuya (ed.) *The Current State of Economic Science* **2**. Tohtak: Spellbound: 909–34.

Harrod, R.F. (1936) *The Trade Cycle.* Oxford: Oxford University Press.

Harrod, R.F. (1939) An Essay in Dynamic Theory. *Economic Journal*, **49**: 14–33.

Hartman, R. (1972) The Effects of Price and Cost Uncertainty on Investment. *Journal of Economic Theory*, **5**: 258–66.

Hartman, R. (1976) Factor Demand with Output Price Uncertainty. *American Economic Review*, **66**(4): 675–81.

Harvey, A.C. (1990) *The Econometric Analysis of Time Series Data* (2nd Edition). New York: Philip Allan.

Hay, D.A. and Morris, D.J. (1991) *Industrial Economics and Organisation: Theory and Evidence*. Oxford: Oxford University Press.

Hayashi, F. (1982) Tobin's Marginal q and Average q: A Neoclassical Interpretation. *Econometrica*, **50**: 213–24.

Hayashi, F. (1985) Corporate Finance Side of the Q Theory of Investment. *Journal of Public Economics*, **27**(3): 261–80.

Hendry, D.F. and Wallis, K.F. (1984) *Econometrics*. Oxford: Basil Blackwell.

Hendry, D.F. and Mizon, G.E. (1978) Serial Correlation as a Convenient Simplification, Not a Nuisance. *Economic Journal*, **88**: 549–63.

Hey, J.D. and Winch, D. (eds) (1990) *A Century of Economics: 100 Years of the Royal Economic Society*. Oxford: Basil Blackwell.

Hilton, K. and Heathfield, D. (1979) *The Econometric Study of the UK*. London: Macmillan.

Hines, A.G. and Catephores, G. (1979) Investment in the UK Manufacturing Industry. In K. Hilton and D. Heathfield *The Econometric Study of the UK*. London: Macmillan: 203–24.

Hobijn, B. and Jovanovic, B. (2001) The Information Technology Revolution and the Stock Market: Evidence. *American Economic Review*, **91**(5): 1203–20.

Hodgson, G.M. (1985) Persuasion, Expectations and the Limits to Keynes. In T. Lawson and M.H. Pesaran *Keynes' Economics – Methodological Issues*. Beckenham: Croom Helm.

Howitt, P. (1996) Expectations and Uncertainty in Contempary Keynesian Models. In G.C. Harcourt and P. Riach (eds) *A Second Edition of* The General Theory. London: Routledge.

Hutton, W. (1996) *The State We're In*. London: Vintage.

Hylleberg, S. and Paldam, M. (1991) *New Approaches to Empirical Macroeconomics*. Oxford: Basil Blackwell.

Ingersoll, J. and Ross, S.A. (1992) Waiting to Invest: Investment and Uncertainty. *Journal of Business*, **65**: 1–29.

Jenkinson, N.H. (1981) *Investment, Profitability and the Valuation Ratio*. Bank of England Discussion Paper **17**.

Jorgenson, D.W. (1963) Capital Theory and Investment Behaviour. *American Economic Review*, **53**: 247–59.

Jorgenson, D.W. (1964) Anticipations and Investment Behaviour. In D.W. Jorgenson (1996) *Investment – Volume I: Capital Theory and Investment Behaviour*. Cambridge, MA: MIT Press.

Jorgenson, D.W. (1967) The Theory of Firm Behaviour. In R. Ferber (ed.) *Determinants of Investment Behaviour*. Universities National Bureau Conference Series, **18**. New York: Columbia University Press for National Bureau of Economic Research.

Jorgenson, D.W. (1971) Econometric Studies of Investment Behaviour: A Survey. *Journal of Economic Literature*, **9**(4): 1111–47.

Jorgenson, D.W. (1996) *Investment*. Cambridge, MA: MIT Press.

Jorgenson, D.W. and Siebert, C.D. (1968) A Comparison of Alternative Theories of Corporate Investment Behaviour. *American Economic Review*, **58**(4): 681–712.

Jorgenson, D.W. and Stephenson, J.A. (1967) Investment Behaviour in US Manufacturing 1947–60. *Econometrica*, **35**: 169–220.

Jorgenson, D.W. and Stiroh, K.J. (2000) Raising the Speed Limit: U.S. Economic Growth in the Information Age. Harvard University and Federal Reserve Bank of New York, mimeo.

Junankar, P.N. (1972) *Investment: Theories and Evidence.* London: Macmillan.

Kalecki, M. (1933) Essays on Business Cycle Theory. Translated in M. Kalecki (1966) *Studies in the Theory of Business Cycles 1933–39* Oxford: Basil Blackwell.

Kalecki, M. (1937a) Some Remarks on Keynes' Theory. In F. Targetti and B. Kinda-Hass (1982) Kalecki's Review of Keynes' General Theory. *Australian Economic Papers*, **21**(39): 245–53.

Kalecki, M. (1937b) The Principle of Increasing Risk. *Economica*, **4**: 440–7.

Kalecki, M. (1943) The Determinants of Investment. In *Studies in Economic Dynamics.* London: Allen & Unwin.

Kalecki, M. (1954) *Theory of Economic Dynamics on Cyclical and Long-run Changes in Capitalist Economy.* London: Allen & Unwin.

Katz, M. and Shapiro, C. (1986) Technology Adoption in the Presence of Network Externalities. *Journal of Political Economy*, **94**: 822–41.

Kennedy, P. (1992) *A Guide to Econometrics* (3rd Edition). Oxford: Blackwell.

Keynes, J.M. (1921) *A Treatise on Probability.* London: Macmillan.

Keynes, J.M. (1923) *A Tract on Monetary Reform.* London: Macmillan.

Keynes, J.M. (1936) *The General Theory of Employment, Interest and Money.* London: Macmillan.

Keynes, J.M. (1937) The General Theory of Employment. *Quarterly Journal of Economics*, **51**: 209–23.

Keynes, J.M. (1979a) *My Early Beliefs*, **X**. *Collected Writings of John Maynard Keynes* (ed. D.E. Moggridge). London: Macmillan and Royal Economic School.

Keynes, J.M. (1979b) *The General Theory and After: A Supplement*, **XXIX**. *Collected Writings of John Maynard Keynes* (ed. D. Moggridge). London: Macmillan and Royal Economic Society.

King, M.A. (1972) Taxation and Investment Incentives in a Vintage Investment Model. *Journal of Public Economics*, **1**: 121–47.

Klein, L.R. (1958) The Estimation of Distributed Lags. *Econometrica*, **26**: 553–65.

Koutsoyiannis, A. (1979) *Modern Microeconomics* (2nd Edition). Houndmills: Macmillan Education.

Koyck, L.M. (1954) *Distributed Lags and Investment Analysis.* Amsterdam: North-Holland.

Kregel, J.A. (1972) *The Theory of Economic Growth.* London: Macmillan.

Kregel, J.A. (1976) Economic Methodology in the Face of Uncertainty: The Modeling Methods of the Keynesians and Post Keynesians. *Economic Journal*, **86**: 209–25.

Kregel, J.A. (1996) The Theory of Value, Expectations and Chapter 17 of The General Theory of Employment, Interest and Money. In G.C. Harcourt and P. Riach (eds) *A Second Edition of The General Theory.* London: Routledge.

Kuh, E. (1971) *Capital Stock Growth: A Microeconometric Approach.* Amsterdam: North-Holland.

Kuznets, S. (1935) Relation Between Capital Goods and Finished Products. In *Essays in Honor of Wesley Clair Mitchell.* New York: Columbia University Press.

Kuznets, S. (1961) *Capital in the American Economy.* Princeton, NJ: Princeton University Press.

Landefeld, J.S. and Fraumeni, B.M. (2000) Measuring the New Economy. Bureau of Economic Analysis Advisory Committee Meeting.

Laramie, A.J., Mair, D. and Miller, A.G. (2001) *A Kaleckian Investment Model: UK Evidence.* Paper presented at the Annual Meeting of the Eastern Economic Association, February 2001.

Laski, K. (1998) Michal Kalecki. In J. Eatwell, M. Milgate and P. Newman (eds) *The New Palgrave: A Dictionary of Economics.* London: Macmillan: 10–14.

Lawson, T. (1981) Keynesian Model Building and the Rational Expectations Critique. *Cambridge Journal of Economics*, **5**: 311–26.

Lawson, T. (1985) Uncertainty and Economic Analysis. *Economic Journal*, **95**: 902–27.

Lawson, T. (1995) Economics and Expectations. In S. Dow and J. Hillard (eds) *Keynes, Knowledge and Uncertainty.* Aldershot: Edward Elgar: 77–106.

Lawson, T. and Pesaran, M.H. (1985) *Keynes' Economics – Methodological Issues.* Beckenham: Croom Helm.

Leahy, J.V. and Whited, T.M. (1995) The Effect of Uncertainty on Investment: Some Stylized Facts. National Bureau of Economic Research, Working Paper **4986**.

Lerner, A.P. (1944) *The Economics of Control.* London: Macmillan.

Levacic, R. and Rebmann, A. (1982) *Macro-economics – An Introduction to Keynesian-Neoclassical Controversies.* London: Macmillan.

Littleboy. B. (1990) *On Interpreting Keynes: A Study in Reconciliation.* London: Routledge.

Lucas, R.E. (1976) *Studies in Business Cycle Theory.* Cambridge: MIT Press.

Lucas, R.E. and Prescott, E.C. (1971) Investment under Uncertainty. *Econometrica*, **39**(5): 659–81.

Machlup, F. (1946) Marginal Analysis and Empirical Research. *American Economic Review* **36**(4): 519–54.

Mahdavi, S., Sohrabian, A. and Kholdy, S. (1994) Cointegration and Error Correction Models: the Temporal Causality Between Investment and Corporate Cash Flow. *Journal of Post Keynesian Economics*, **16**(3): 478–98.

Malkiel, B., von Furstenberg, G. and Watson, H (1979) Expectations, Tobin's q and Industry Investment. *Journal of Finance*, **34**: 549–61.

Mankiw, N.G. (1989) Real Business Cycles – A New Keynesian Perspective. *Journal of Economic Perspectives*, **3**(3): 79–90.

Manne, A.S. (1961) Capacity Expansion and Probabilistic Growth. *Econometrica*, **29**: 632–49.

Matthews, R.C.O. (1959) *The Trade Cycle.* Cambridge: Nisbet & Co and Cambridge University Press.

Mayer, T. (1960) Plant and Equipment Lead Times. *Journal of Business*, **33**: 127–32.

McConnell, M.M. and Quiros, G.B. (2000) Output Fluctuations in the United States: What has changed since the early 1980s? *American Economic Review*, **90**: 1464–76.

McDonald, R. and Siegel, D.R. (1986) Investment and the Valuation of Firms When There is an Option to Shut Down. *International Economic Review*, **26**(2): 331–49.

Meeks, J.G. (1991) Keynes on the Rationality of Decision Procedures Under Uncertainty: the Investment Decision. In J.G. Meeks *Thoughtful Economic Man.* Cambridge: Cambridge University Press.

Melliss, C.L. and Richardson, P.W. (1976) Value of Investment Incentives for Manufacturing Industry 1946 to 1974. In A. Whiting (ed.) *The Economics of Industrial Subsidies.* London: HMSO: 23–31.

Mensch, G.O. (1979) *Stalemate in Technology: Innovations Overcome the Depressions.* Cambridge, MA: Ballinger Publishing.

Messe, R. (1980) Dynamic Factor Demand Schedules for Labor and Capital Under Rational Expectations. *Journal of Econometrics*, **14**(1): 141–58.

Meyers, S.C. and Majluf, N.S. (1984) Corporate Financing and Investment Decisions When Firms have Information that Investors do not have. *Journal of Financial Economics*, **13**(2): 187–221.

Mini, P. (1990) *Keynes, Bloomsbury and The General Theory.* London: Macmillan.

Minsky, H. (1975) *John Maynard Keynes.* New York: Columbia University Press.

Minsky, H.P. (1978) The Financial Instability Hypothesis. Thames Polytechnic Working Paper.

Minsky, H.P. (1986) *Stabilizing an Unstable Economy.* New Haven: Yale University Press.

Mizon, G.E. (1984) The Encompassing Approach in Econometrics. In D. Hendry and K.F. Wallis *Econometrics.* Oxford: Basil Blackwell.

Modigliani, F. and Miller, M.H. (1958) The Cost of Capital, Corporation Finance, and the Theory of Investment. *American Economic Review*, **48**: 261–97.

Modigliani, F. and Weingartner, H.M. (1958) Forecasting Uses of Anticipatory Data on Investment and Sales. *Quarterly Journal of Economics*, **LXXII**(1): 23–54.

Moggridge, D.E. (ed.) (1990) *Perspectives on the History of Economic Thought*, **IV**. Aldershot: Edward Elgar.

Morris. D.J. (1974) *The Structure of Investment Decisions*. D.Phil, Oxford.

Morrison, C.J. (1986) Structural Models of Dynamic Factor Demands with Nonstatic Expectations: An Empirical Assessment of the Alternative Expectations Specifications. *International Economic Review*, **27**(2): 365–86.

Muellbauer, J. and Murphy, A. (1997) Booms and Busts in the UK Housing Market. *Economic Journal*, **107**(445): 1701–27.

Mussa, M.L. (1977) External and Internal Adjustment Costs and the Theory of Aggregate and Firm Investment. *Economica*, **44**: 163–78.

Muth, J. (1961) Rational Expectations and the Theory of Price Movements. *Econometrica*, **29**: 315–35.

Neild, R.R. (1964) Replacement Policy. *National Institute Economic Review*. London: National Institute of Economics.

Nerlove, M. (1972) Lags in Economic Behaviour. *Econometrica*, **40**: 221–51.

Nickell, S.J. (1978) *The Investment Decision of Firms*. Cambridge: Cambridge University Press.

Nobay, A.R. (1970) Forecasing Manufacturing Investment 1959–67: Some Preliminary Results. National Institute Economic Review. Reported in R. Levacic and A. Rebmann (1982) *Macro-economics – An Introduction to Keynesian-Neoclassical Controversies*. London: Macmillan.

O'Donnell, R.M. (1989) *Keynes: Philosophy, Economics and Politics*. London: Macmillan.

O'Donnell, R.M. (ed.) (1991a) *Keynes as Philosopher-Economist*. Proceedings of the Ninth Keynes Seminar, University of Kent at Canterbury. London: Macmillan.

O'Donnell, R.M. (1991b) Keynes on Probability, Expectations and Uncertainty. In O'Donnell, R.M. (ed.) *Keynes as Philosopher-Economist*. London: Macmillan: 3–60.

Oi, W.Y. (1961) The Desirability of Price Stability. *Econometrica*, **29**: 58–64.

Oswald, A.J. (1997) The Missing Piece of the Unemployment Puzzle. Inaugural Lecture, University of Warwick.

Oulton, N. (1981) Aggregate Investment and Tobin's q: the evidence from Britain. *Oxford Economic Papers*, **33**(2): 177–202.

Palley, T. (2001) The Stock Market and Investment: Another Look at the Microfoundations of q Theory. *Cambridge Journal of Economics*, **25**(5): 657–67.

Pasinetti, L.L. (1974) *Growth and Income Distribution – Essays in Economic Theory*. Cambridge: Cambridge University Press.

Pasinetti, L.L. (1996) The Marginal Efficiency of Investment. In G.C. Harcourt and P. Riach (eds) *A Second Edition of* The General Theory. London: Routledge.

Pesaran, M.H. (1990) Expectations in Economics. Department of Applied Economics, Working Paper **9016**. University of Cambridge.

Pesaran, M.H. and Deaton, A.S. (1978) Testing Non-Nested Non-linear Regression Models. *Econometrica*, **46**: 677–94.

Pindyck, R.S. (1982) Adjustment Costs, Uncertainty and the Behaviour of the Firm. *American Economic Review*, **72**(3): 415–27.

Pindyck, R.S. (1988) Irreversible Investment, Capacity Choice and the Value of the Firm. *American Economic Review*, **78**(5): 969–85.

Pindyck, R.S. (1991) Irreversibility, Uncertainty and Investment. *Journal of Economic Literature*, **XXIX**: 1110–48.

Pindyck, R.S. (1993) A Note on Competitive Investment under Uncertainty. *American Economic Review*, **83**(1): 273–8.

Pindyck, R.S. and Rotemberg, J.J. (1983a) Dynamic Factor Demands under Rational Expectations. *Scandinavian Journal of Economics*, **85**(2): 223–38.

Pindyck, R.S. and Rotemberg, J.J. (1983b) Dynamic Factor Demands and the Effects of Energy Price Shocks. *American Economic Review*, **73**(5): 1066–79.

Pindyck, R.S. and Solimano, A. (1993) Economic Instability and Aggregate Investment. In D.J. Blanchard and S. Fischer *NBER Macroeconomics Annual*. National Bureau of Economic Research. Cambridge, MA: MIT Press: 259–300.

Pressman, S. (1999) *Fifty Major Economists*. London: Routledge.

Price, S. (1995) *Aggregate Uncertainty, Investment and Asymmetric Adjustment in the UK Manufacturing Sector*. University of Essex, Discussion Paper Series **441**.

Rae, J. (1834) *Statement of Some Principles on the Subject of Political Economy*. Boston: Hilliard Gray & Co.

Raj, B. (1989) *Advances in Econometrics and Modelling*. Hingham: Kluwer Academic.

Ramsey, F. (1931a) *The Foundations of Mathematics and Other Logical Essays* (ed. R.B. Braithwaite). London: Kegan Paul, Trency, Trabner and Co.

Ramsey, F. (1931b) Truth and Probability. In F. Ramsey *The Foundations of Mathematics and Other Logical Essays* (ed. R.B. Braithwaite). London: Kegan Paul, Trency, Trabner and Co.: 156–98.

Richardson, G.B. (1959) Equilibrium, Expectations and Information. *Economic Journal*, **69**: 223–37.

Roach, S.S. (1998) *The Boom for Whom: Revisiting America's Technology Paradox*. New York: Morgan Stanley Dean Witter.

Roberts, K. and Weitzman, M.L. (1987) Fundamental Criteria for Research Development and Exploration Projects. *Econometrica*, **49**(5): 1261–88.

Robinson, J.V. (1953/4) The Production Function and the Theory of Capital. *Review of Economic Studies*, **21**: 81–106.

Robinson, J.V. (1960a) Introduction. In *Collected Economic Papers*, **3** (2nd Edition). Oxford: Blackwell.

Robinson, J.V. (1960b) Some Problems of Definition and Measurement of Capital. *Collected Economic Papers*, **7**: 369–405. Oxford: Basil Blackwell.

Robinson, J.V. (1962) *Essays in the Theory of Economic Growth*. London: Macmillan.

Robinson, J.V. (1964a) Pre-Keynesian Theory After Keynes. *Australian Economic Papers*, **3**(1): 25–35.

Robinson, J.V. (1964b) Kalecki and Keynes. In *Collected Economic Papers*, **3**. Oxford: Basil Blackwell.

Robinson, J.V. (1965) The General Theory after Twenty-Five Years. *Collected Economic Papers*, **3**. Oxford: Basil Blackwell.

Robinson, J.V. (1973a) Capital Theory Up to Date. *Collected Economic Papers*, **4**. Oxford: Basil Blackwell.

Robinson, J.V. (1973b) The Measurement of Capital: the End of the Controversy. *Collected Economic Papers*, **4**. Oxford: Basil Blackwell.

Robinson, J.V. (1975) *Collected Economic Papers* (2nd edition). Oxford: Basil Blackwell.

Robinson, J.V. (1979) What has become of the Keynesian Revolution. *Collected Economic Papers*, **5**. Oxford: Basil Blackwell.

Rockley, L.E. (1973) *Investment for Profitability*. London: Business Books.

Rothschild, K.W. (1947) Price Theory and Oligopoly. *Economic Journal*, **57**: 299–30.

Runde, J.H. (1991) 'Keynesian Uncertainty and the Instability of Beliefs'. *Review of Political Economy*, **3**(2): 125–45.

Runde, J. (1996) Keynesian Methodology. In G.C. Harcourt and P. Riach (eds) *A Second Edition of* The General Theory. London: Routledge.

Sakellaris, P. (1994) A Note on Competitive Investment Under Uncertainty: Comment. *American Economic Review*, **84**(4): 1107–12.

Salter, W.E.G. (1966) *Productivity and Technical Change* (2nd edition). Cambridge: Cambridge University Press.

Samuelson, P. (1962) Parable and Realism in Capital Theory: the Surrogate Production Function. In G.C. Harcourt and N.F. Laing *Capital and Growth*. Harmondsworth: Penguin.

Sawyer, M.C. (1985) *Economics of Michal Kalecki*. London: Macmillan.

Sawyer, M. (1991) Post-Keynesian Macroeconomics. In D. Greenaway, M. Bleaney and I. Stewart (eds) *Companion to Contemporary Economic Thought*. London: Routledge: 184–206.

Sawyer, M. (2000) Kalecki. In P. Arestis and M. Sawyer (eds) *A Biographical Dictionary of Dissenting Economists* (2nd edition) Aldershot: Edward Elgar: 302–10.

Scarth, W.M. (1988) *Macroeconomics – An Introduction to Advanced Methods*. Toronto: Harcourt Brace Jovanovich.

Schumpeter, J.A. (1911) *Theory of Economic Development*. Cambridge Massachusetts: Harvard University Press.

Schumpeter, J.A. (1939) *Business Cycles: A Theoretical, Historical and Statistical Analysis of the Capitalist Process*. New York: McGraw-Hill.

Sen, A. (ed.) (1970) *Growth Economics – Selected Readings*. Harmondsworth: Penguin.

Shackle, G.L.S. (1955) *Uncertainty in Economics and Other Reflections*. Cambridge: Cambridge University Press.

Shackle, G.L.S. (1967) *The Years of High Theory*. Cambridge: Cambridge University Press.

Shackle, G.L.S. (1972) *Epistemics and Economics*. Cambridge: Cambridge University Press.

Simon, H.A. (1979) From Substantive to Procedural Rationality. In F.H. Hahn and M. Hollis, (eds) *Philosophy and Economic Theory*. Oxford: Oxford University Press: 65–86.

Skidelsky, R. (1992) *John Maynard Keynes – The Economist As Saviour 1920–1937*. London: Macmillan.

Small Business Research Centre (1992) *The State of British Enterprise*. University of Cambridge.

Solow, R.M. (1970) A Contribution to the Theory of Economic Growth. In A. Sen *Growth Economics – Selected Readings*. Harmondsworth: Penguin: 161–92.

Solow, R.M. (1987) *We'd Better Watch Out*. New York Times Book Review, 12 July: 36.

Solow, R.M. (1988) Growth Theory and After. *American Economic Review*, **78**(3): 307–17.

Stegman , T. (1982) The Estimation of an Accelerator-Type Investment Function with a Profitability Constraint by the Technique of Switching Regressions. *Australian Economic Papers*, **21**: 379–91.

Stegman, T. (1983) The Effects of Changes in the Functional Distribution of Income on Aggregate Demand in Australia in the 1970s. PhD dissertation, University of New South Wales.

Summers, L.H. (1981) Taxation and Corporate Investment: A q-Theory Approach. *Brookings Papers on Economic Activity*, **1**: 67–127.

Summers, L.H. (1987) Investment Incentives and the Discounting of Depreciation Allowances. In M.S. Feldstein *The Effects of Taxation on Capital Accumulation*. National Bureau of Economic Research. Chicago: University of Chicago Press: 295–304.

Summers, L. (1991) The Scientific Illusion in Empirical Macroeconomics. In S. Hylleburg and M. Paldam *New Approaches to Empirical Macroeconomics*. Oxford: Basil Blackwell: 1–20.

Surrey, M.J.C. (ed.) (1976) *Macroeconomic Themes – Edited Reading in Macroeconomics.* Oxford: Oxford University Press.

Targetti, F. and Kinda-Hass, B. (1982) Kalecki's Review of Keynes' General Theory. *Australian Economic Papers*, **21**(39): 244–60.

Tinbergen, J. (1938) Statistical Evidence on the Acceleration Principle. *Economica*, **5**: 164–76.

Tobin, J. (1969) A General Equilibrium Approach to Monetary Theory. *Journal of Money, Credit and Banking*, **1**(1): 15–29.

Tobin, J. (1998) Fisher. In J. Eatwell, M. Milgate and P. Newman (eds) *The New Palgrave Dictionary of Economics*, **2**: 369–76.

Topol, R. (1991) Bubble and Volatility of Stock Prices: Effects of Mimetic Contagion. *The Economic Journal*, **101**: 786–800.

Torr, C. (1996) User Cost. In G.C. Harcourt and P. Riach (eds) *A Second Edition of* The General Theory. London: Routledge.

US Department of Commerce (1999) *The Emerging Digital Economy II.*

Viner, J. (1931) Cost Curves and Supply Curves. *Zeitschrift für National ökonomie*, **3**: 23–46.

von Furstenberg, G. (1977) Does Market Value Matter in the Aggregate. *Brookings Papers on Economic Activity*, **1977**(2): 347–408.

Wan M.Y. (1971) *Economic Growth.* New York: Harcourt Brace Jovanich.

West, D. (1986) A Variance Bounds Test of the Linear Quadratic Inventory Model. *Journal of Political Economy*, **94**: 374–401.

Whelan, K. (2000) Computers. Obsolescence and Productivity. *Finance and Economics Discussion Series Paper 2000–06.* New York: Board of Governors of Federal Reserve System.

Whiting, A. (ed.) (1976) *The Economics of Industrial Subsidies.* London: HMSO.

Wildasin, D.E. (1984) The q Theory of Investment with Many Capital Goods. *American Economic Review*, **74**(1): 203–10.

Winslow, E.G. (1986) Keynes and Freud: Psychoanalysis and Keynes's Account of the 'Animal Spirits' of Capitalism. *Social Research*, **53**(4): 549–78.

Wolfe, J.N. (1968) *Value, Capital and Growth.* Edinburgh: Edinburgh University Press.

Yang, S. and Brynjolfsson, E. (2001) Intangible Assets and Growth Accounting: Evidence from Computer Investments. Massachusetts Institute of Technology, mimeo.

Index

Abel, A.B. 14, 63, 69, 88, 89, 96, 97, 101, 103, 105, 106, 111, 151, 212
absolute convergence 183–4, 185–8, 221
abstraction 74, 76
accelerator theory xii, 12–13, 18, 48–56, 58, 61, 72, 82–3, 85, 90, 93, 140, 142–3, 147–8, 221
  causality in 55
  empirical evidence 53–5, 56, 68, 86–8, 101
  flexible 48, 51–3, 56
  simple 48, 49–51, 56
Acemoglu, D. 119
adaptive expectations 55, 70, 71, 72
adjustment costs 14, 15, 25, 63, 70, 72–3, 77, 96–108, 221
aggregate uncertainty 113–14, 118, 221
aggregation 15, 16, 61, 65, 67, 74–5, 76, 77, 90
Aiginger, K. 107, 121
Akaike Information Criterion 233
Akerlof, G.A. 113, 218
Alvarez, L.H.R. 121
Anderson, W.H.L. 54, 69, 70, 72, 87, 88, 105
animal spirits 15, 37–8, 41, 44, 45
Araujo, J.A. 217, 218
Arrow-Debreu model 28
Asimakopulos, A. 33, 217
asset specificity 14, 111, 221
Augmented Dickey-Fuller (ADF) test 154, 231–2
autocorrelation 221, 229, 230–1
Automated Clearing House (ACH) system 164
Auto Regressive Distributed Lag (ARDL) models 232
availability of finance 15, 77, 127–8, 133–4, 152–3
average cost pricing 67
average productivity of capital 103
average *q* 99–100, 103, 104, 151

bad news principle 113, 114, 122, 221
Baddeley, M. 38, 67, 88, 101, 179, 184, 218, 219
balanced growth, Marris on 67
bandwagon effects, and innovation 174, 221
banking system, role of 130–1, 133, 134
Barro, R.J. 120, 184, 219
Bateman, B.W. 127
Baumol's theory of sales maximization 67
Bean, C.R. 54, 69, 86, 87, 143, 147, 233
beauty contest analogy 40
behavioural theory of firm 67
Bernanke, B.S. 112
Bertola, G. 115
Best Linear Unbiased Estimator (BLUE) 221, 229
beta (β) convergence 183–4, 185–90, 191
Biais, B. 107
bi-modal lags 54
biotechnology sector, investment in 173
Bischoff, C.W. 85, 86, 142, 147, 175, 219
Blanchard, O.J. 101, 106
Bloomsbury set 32
borrower's risk 35, 129, 153, 221
Brainard, W.C. 14, 93, 99, 100, 212, 218
Breusch-Godfrey test 154, 228, 229
Brynjolfsson, E. 102, 165, 167, 172, 173
bubbles 41
  in housing market 196, 201–4, 207
building societies 200–1
business motive 127–8
  see also finance motive

Caballero, R.J. 113, 118
call options 14, 114, 221
Cambridge capital controversies 73–6, 221
capacity scrapping 84
capacity utilisation 84, 104, 111, 151, 155, 156, 221
capital
  and aggregation problems 74
  heterogeneity of 74–5, 77
  measurement and definition of 67, 74, 77
  accumulation xii, 75, 221
  consumption 25
  controversies 73–6

re-switching 75–6
reversal 75–6
scarcity 44, 75 (*see also* full investment)
stock, nature of 9, 18, 80
stock adjustment 49, 56, 59–61, 62, 64, 65, 67, 69, 77, 96
Capital Asset Pricing Model (CAPM) 118, 221
capitalism 34, 44, 133
capital–labour ratio 13, 48, 49, 51, 58, 62, 74, 75, 75–6, 81, 84, 90
Carabelli, A. 127
Carrado, C. 167
Carter-Hill, R. 227, 233, 234
Catephores, G. 88
causality 55, 120
CBI Industrial Trends survey 38
Cecchetti, S.G. 165, 169, 170
Chenery, H.B. 51, 53
Chirinko, R.S. 62, 68, 69, 72, 89, 93, 95, 99, 100, 101, 102, 103, 104, 105, 106, 218, 219
Chow tests 229
Clark, J.M. 12, 48
Clark, P.K. 101, 120
Classical Linear Regression Model (CLRM) 227
clay-clay models 80, 82–3, 90, 91, 221
see also accelerator theory
Cobb Douglas Production function 60, 64
Coen, R.M. 85, 143
cointegration 232
Colander, D.C. 127
complementarity of factors 49, 80, 82–3
computing investment 164–80, 214–15
definition 170
depreciation 169–70, 178–9
empirical evidence 175–80
externalities in 168–9, 179
and hedonic pricing 171
and intangible investment 165–6, 172–3, 179
measurement difficulties 170–3, 179
network effects 168–9, 179
and New Economy 165–6, 175–80, 214–15
by new firms 173–4, 180
replacement investment 169–70, 178–9, 215
and venture capital funds 173–4, 176, 177, 179, 180, 215
see also New Economy
conditional convergence 184, 187, 188–90, 191, 222
continuity, in Keynes's ideas 127
conventions 15, 16, 37, 39–42, 45, 126–7, 133, 134, 179, 217
convergence, absolute 183–4, 185–8
beta (β) 183–4, 185–90, 191
conditional 184, 187, 188–90, 191
gap 185–90, 191
sigma (σ) 184, 185–90, 191
in investment 183–91
empirical evidence 184–90, 191
theoretical 15, 121, 123, 212–16
convexity 95–6, 222
cost of capital 73
see also user cost of capital
costs of financing 73
Cox test 233
credibility, of monetary policy 42
credit, state of 127–8
Crotty, J.R. 127
crowd psychology 41, 45, 207
see also mass psychology
Cukierman, A. 112, 114
current replacement cost, of capital 99–100, 102
Cyert, R.M. 67

Deaton, A.S. 234
Darby, M.R. 173
data mining 233
Davis, J.B. 219
Davidson, P. 87, 127, 128, 153, 217, 218, 219
Davidson, R. 87, 145, 234
debt–equity ratios 129
De Long, J.B. 167
demand price of capital 34, 129–30, 153, 217, 222
depreciation 9, 18, 58, 59, 64, 88, 97, 102, 222
in the New Economy 169–70, 178–9
straight-line methods 102
deregulation, financial 196–7, 198–9, 200–1
developed countries, investment in 182–91
developing countries, investment in 182–91
diagnostic tests 222
Diamond 53
Dickey-Fuller (DF) test 154, 219, 231–2
diffusion, technological 167
diffusion lag hypothesis 167, 222
diminishing returns to scale 72
direct forecasting approaches 14, 93, 105, 106, 108, 222
discontinuities, in the production function 75–6
discount rate 11, 16–17, 24, 35, 59, 222
distributed lags 68–9, 70, 72, 93
Dittrich, D. 107
Dixit, A.K. 14, 63, 110, 112, 114, 116, 117, 122
double-sided relationship, between profits and investment 129, 134
Dow, A. and S. 127
Driver, C. 117, 121, 218
Dwyer, G.P. 107

Earley, J.S. 68
Eberly, J.C. 63
Economic Consequences of the Peace, The 32
economic obsolescence 10, 18
efficient markets hypothesis 100, 130, 151, 222
Eisner, R. 33, 53, 72, 85, 86, 87, 94, 95, 143
elasticity of capital stock 61–2
elasticity of demand for money 42, 76
elasticity of factor substitution 13, 49, 54–5, 58, 75, 80, 81, 81–3, 84, 85–6, 89, 90, 91, 222
  of money demand 42, 76
Electronic Funds Transfer at Point of Sale (EFTPOS) 164
electronic payment systems 169, 179
eligible options 27
Elliott, J. 87
Encompassing test 233
endogeneity of money 127–33, 134, 222
Engle, R.F. 101
Enterprise Resource Planning (ERP) systems 172
entrepreneurship 40–1
equation of exchange 28
ergodicity 222
Evans, M.K. 54
ex ante investment 33, 58, 80, 81, 83, 84, 91
ex post investment 58, 80, 81, 83, 84, 91
expansionary monetary policy 76
expectations 11, 13, 15, 22, 24, 34, 36, 39, 40, 42, 52–3, 55, 56, 63, 67, 70–2, 77, 88, 90, 93–4, 110, 152, 212–13
  and reversibility 65
  direct forecasting approaches to 14, 93, 108, 105, 106
  explicit treatment in adjustment cost models 98
  in Jorgenson's model 59–60
  in Tobin's *q* theory 14, 99–104, 108
  inflationary 28
  in Post Keynesian theory 126–7
  transformation approaches to 14, 93, 105–6, 108
  undershooting and overshooting 38
expenditure policies 43–4
experimental psychology 107
external adjustment costs 94–5, 107
external consistency 138
external economies 119–20
external economies, in computing investment 168–9, 178–9
extrapolative expectations 55, 70, 71, 72

factor
  prices 81
  substitutability 49, 75, 80, 81–4
  substitution, elasticity of
    see elasticity of factor substitution
factors of production, as complements 49, 80, 84
factors of production, as substitutes 58, 80
Fazzari, S.M. 104
Federer, J.P. 120
feedback effects 16, 76, 77, 201–4, 207
Feldstein, M. 86, 143
finance motive, for investment 127–8, 133, 134, 152, 217–18
finance units 131–2
finance, availability of 127–8, 152, 196
financial, deregulation 196–7, 198–9, 200–1
financial fragility hypothesis, Minsky's 29, 130–3, 134, 201
financial markets 9, 14, 18, 39–42, 45, 93, 99–104, 128
financial posture 131–3, 134
financing, and risk 73
  costs 73
  neutrality 73, 77
  neutrality, in Fisher 25
firm specific risk 73
Fisher, I. xii, 10, 13, 18, 22, 24–30, 33, 34, 44, 45, 58, 59, 63, 64, 212
  biographical details 28, 29
  on circulating capital 25
  contributions to economics 25, 28
  and discount rates 26–7
  equation of exchange 28
  impatience principle 25, 26
  and index numbers 28
  influence of 25, 28
  and internal rate of return 10, 12
  investment opportunity principle 25, 26–7
  rate of return over costs 26–7
  streams and pools analogy 25
  on stocks and flows 24–5
  and *The Nature of Capital and Income* 24
  and *The Theory of Interest* 10, 18
  theory of interest determination 25–8
Fisher's separation theorem 25
Fisher's ideal index 28
Flemming, J. 86, 143
flexible accelerator 12–13, 18, 48, 56, 51–3, 87
  see also accelerator theory
flow theories of investment 96
flows, versus stocks 24
Foley, P.K. 101
forecaster discord, as measure of uncertainty 120
Fraumeni 167, 170
frenzy effects 196, 197
Friedman, M 67, 125
full investment 34, 35, 44
fundamental value 41, 100, 101

gap convergence models 184, 185–90, 191
Garber, P.M. 105
gazumping 195, 222
Gauss-Markov theorem 141, 222, 229
gearing ratios 196, 200, 222
General Theory of Employment, Interest and Money, The 18, 30–44, 36, 45, 71, 126, 127, 217, 219
Generalized Least Squares (GLS) 232
Gerrard, B. 127
Gomes, J.F. 73
Goodwin, R.M. 51
Gordon, M.J. 217, 218, 219
Gordon, R.J. 167
Gould, J.P. 70
government, role of 11, 42–4, 179, 180, 182
Gowrisankaran, G. 169
Granger causality 120, 222
Grant, Duncan 32
Griffiths, W.E. 227, 234
Griliches, Z. 55, 69, 72, 176
gross investment 9, 18
growth accounting, and computing investment 172
Grunfeld, Y. 101
Gueth, W. 107
Gujarati, D.N. 142, 227, 234
Guthrie, R.S. 127

Haavelmo, T. 62, 72, 94
Hahn, F.H. 125
Hall, R.L. 53, 67
Hall, R.E. 85
Hamouda, O.F. 219
Harcourt, G.C. 74, 75, 88, 128, 217, 219
Harrod, R.F. 48, 51
Hartman, R. 111
Hay, D.A. 86, 88, 89, 95
Hayashi, F. 99, 101, 103, 104
Hazard, Margaret (wife of Fisher) 29
hedge finance 131–2, 134, 222
hedonic pricing, of computing 171, 222
Hendry, D.F. 142, 217, 233
herd behaviour 15, 16, 37, 41, 76, 119–20, 133, 134, 179, 201–4, 207
heterogeneity of capital 88, 90, 74–5, 77, 119–20, 126–7
heteroscedasticity 154, 223, 228
Hines, A.G. 88
Hitch, C.J. 53, 67
Hobijn, B. 166, 173
Hodgson, G.M. 219
homogeneity, linear 223
homogeneity of capital 62, 74–5
homoscedasticity 229
housing investment
  see residential investment
housing stock, public 199, 200
Howitt, P. 127
hurdle rate of return 115, 117, 118, 218, 223
Hutton, W. 199
hybrid models 145–6, 147, 148
hypothesis testing 228

idiosyncratic uncertainty 113–14, 118, 223
impatience, principle of 26, 28, 223
imputed rent 195, 196, 223
incorrect functional form 154, 228, 231, 229
increasing risk, principle of 129, 153, 223
index number problem 74
individualism, in Keynes 42, 43
Industrial Trends Survey 38
industrialisation 182
ineligible options 27
inflationary expectations 28
inflationary risk 35
Information Technology (IT) Revolution 102, 164–80, 214–15
informational constraints 14, 112–13
Ingersoll, J. 117
innovation 29, 164–80
installation costs *see* adjustment costs
instrumental variables 89, 105, 232
intangible investment 9, 18, 102, 165, 172–3, 223
interest rates
  determinants of 25, 26–8
  and investment 17, 28, 34, 35, 38, 39, 42–3, 58, 75, 76, 97, 121, 128, 218
  nominal 17
  real 17
  and the user cost of capital 88
internal
  adjustment costs 95–8, 107
  consistency 138
  finance, and investment 73, 129
  rate of return 10, 12, 16, 17, 18, 24, 26, 33, 38, 44, 45, 115, 117, 118, 119, 223
  see also marginal efficiency of capital, rate of return over costs
inventory investment 9, 18, 117, 170, 178, 180, 214
investment
  accelerator theory of 12–13, 18, 48–56, 82–3
  adjustment cost models 14, 25, 93, 94, 95, 96–108
  axiomatic approaches to 74
  bad news principle of 113, 114, 122
  business motive for 127–8
  as circulating capital 25
  computing 165–6, 168–80
  conventions and 126–7
  convergence 183–91
  and cyclical factors 50, 104, 105
  definitions of 9, 18
  and development 182–91, 214

double-sided relationship with profits 129, 134
dynamic structure of 67, 69
empirical evidence 6, 68, 77, 84–9, 90, 100–1, 104–5, 117–22, 142–6, 147–8, 153–7, 158, 175–8, 180, 184–90, 191, 201–6, 207, 214–16
evolution of theories 90, 110
ex ante 58
and expectations 11, 13, 15, 22, 24, 34, 36, 39, 40, 42, 52–3, 55, 56, 59, 63, 67, 70–2, 77, 88, 90, 93–4, 110, 212–13
explicit models of 103
ex post 58
and external economies 119–20
and financial constraints 67, 73, 104, 127–33, 134, 217, 218
finance motive, and the 127–8
Fisher's theory of xii, 5, 10–11, 24–30
flow theories of 96–7
housing 9, 18, 194–208
importance of 4
intangible 102, 165, 172–3
interest rates, and 17, 28, 34, 35, 38, 39, 42–3, 58, 75, 76, 97, 121, 128, 218
internal finance and 73, 129
and irrationality 126–7
irreversibility of 70, 77, 111–15, 122
and IT revolution 102, 117, 164–80, 214–15
Jorgenson's theory xii, 5, 13, 14, 15, 22, 54–5, 58–65, 67–77, 84–90, 93, 96, 97, 107, 110, 140–1, 144–5, 147–8, 150, 212
Kalecki's theory of xii, 128–9
Keynes's theory of xii, 5, 10–11, 30–45, 125–8
lags in 56, 68–72, 77, 85–6, 91, 94, 142
and long-term expectations 44
lumpiness 170, 173
and marginal efficiency of capital 10, 18, 12, 31–4, 38, 43, 44, 45, 49
mathematical modelling of 11–12, 18, 22, 28, 44–5
microfoundations of aggregate models 61, 65, 76, 77, 100
neo-classical theory of xii, 5, 13, 58–65, 84, 212
and the New Economy 102, 117, 164–80, 214–15
objective determinants of 32–5
opportunity cost of 11, 18, 59
optimal path of 96, 97, 106, 108
and output growth 91 (*see also* accelerator theory)
physical versus financial 39–42
and political uncertainty 118
Post Keynesian theory of xii, 5, 15, 212, 213–14, 217, 218, 219
prospective yield of 31
psychological determinants 24, 38–41, 42, 55, 126–7, 217
and uncertainty 36–8
q theory of xii, 5, 14, 15, 39, 45, 77, 90, 94, 96–108, 150, 151–2, 153–5, 157–8, 213, 218, 219
real options theories xii, 5, 14, 15, 22, 45, 63, 77, 90, 114–17, 122–3
residential 9, 18, 194–208
and savings 28, 183, 219
sequencing of 117
and share prices 39–42
and sources of finance 73
and Stock Markets 39–42, 45, 99–104, 128, 173, 214–15, 218
subjective determinants 41–2, 44, 45, 55, 126–7
supply price of 31
timing of 76, 112–17, 123
and uncertainty 110–23, 152–6, 157–8, 175–8, 179, 180, 196–7, 212–16, 218
undefined rate of 62, 65, 72, 77, 94
appraisal techniques 11, 16–17, 18, 115–17
demand schedule 32, 33, 38, 39–42
opportunity principle 26
policy 42–4
investor psychology 38
involuntary unemployment 84
irrationality, in Post Keynesian models 126–7
irreversible investment 39, 70, 77, 90, 111–15, 122, 223
iso-cost line, described 81–2
isoquant, described 80–2, 223

jelly models 80, 84
J test 233
JA test 233
Jenkinson, N.H. 100
Jorgenson, D.W. xii, 13, 14, 15, 22, 25, 58–77, 80, 85, 86, 87, 89, 90, 93, 97, 107, 122, 140–1, 167, 172, 212
Jorgenson's model
assumptions in 58, 61–3, 65
empirical evidence 54–5, 68, 77, 85–9, 144–5, 147–8, 150–1
in continuous time 63–5
influence of 63, 77, 110
problems with 61–3, 67–77, 93, 94, 96
refinements of 77, 80–2, 83–91
roots in Fisher 25
undefined rate of investment in, 62, 65, 72, 77, 94
Jovanovic, B. 166, 173
Judge, G.G. 227, 233, 234
Junankar, P.N. 62, 72, 94, 217
just-in-time inventory control 170, 180, 223

Kalecki, M. xii, 33, 128–30, 134, 152
  and principle of increasing risk 129, 130, 153
  profits and investment 128–30
  theory of investment 128–30, 150, 152–3, 155–6, 157–8, 214
Katz, M. 169
Kennedy, P. 227, 233
Kenyon, P. 75
Keynes, J.M. xii, 10, 13, 15, 18, 22, 24, 28, 33, 34, 35–45, 48, 71, 110, 125, 126–8, 134, 150, 152, 153, 212, 217, 218, 219
  and beauty contest analogy and 40
  biographical details 31
  and bubbles and whirlpools analogy 41
  continuity in ideas 127
  and finance motive 127–8
  and *The General Theory* 18, 30–44, 36, 45, 71, 126, 127, 212
  on investment policy 42–4
  on mathematical modelling 44
  and objective determinants of investment 36
  and practical theory of the future 36, 40, 126–7
  on probability and weight 110
  and problems measuring/defining capital 74
  and *q* theory 99, 102
  and the role of speculation 40–1
  and the subjective determinants of investment 36
  and *The Tract on Monetary Reform* 28
  and *A Treatise on Probability* 71, 126, 127, 212
  and user cost of capital definition 217
  Florence Ada 31
  Geoffrey 31
  John Neville 31
  Margaret 31
Kholdy, S. 129
Kinda-Hass, B. 33
King, M.A. 105, 121
Knightian risk 15, 18, 24, 71, 94, 223
Knightian uncertainty 15, 18, 24, 71, 223
  see also uncertainty
Koskela, E. 121
Koyck, L.M. 51, 52–3, 54
Koyck transformation 52–3, 54, 69, 142, 223
Kregel, J.A. 75
Kuh, E. 53
Kuznets, S. 51

labour-intensive production 76
lags 25, 51–3, 56, 68–72, 77, 85–6, 91, 94, 97
  bi-modal 54
  empirical evidence 53–4, 72, 85–6, 88, 91, 142
  in expectations formation 52–3
  in putty-clay models 84, 85–6
  in putty-putty models 81–2
  in *q* models 103–4, 105, 106
  problems separating the sources 51, 53–4, 56, 69, 72
  problems with estimation 53–4, 89
Landefeld, J.S. 167, 170
Laramie, A.J. 219
Laski, K. 219
Laspeyres index 28
Lawson boom 200
Leahy, J.V. 111, 118
Lemons Principle 113, 218
lender's risk 35, 129, 223
Lerner, A.P. 33, 72, 94
life cycle theory of consumption smoothing 28
liquidity 39, 41, 42
  in Post Keynesian models 127–8
  in *q* models 104
  preference 35, 127–8, 152
  premia 35
  traps 76, 223
Littleboy, B. 127
LM test for heteroscedasticity 154, 228, 229
loanable funds theory 219
long-run elasticity, defined 223
long-run elasticity of factor substitution 80, 84
long-term expectations, state of 36–8, 44
Lopokova, Lydia 32
Lucas, R.E. 95, 96, 110, 113
lumpy investment 95, 170, 174, 223

Machlup, F. 68
Maciejovsky, B. 107
MacKinnon, D.G. 87, 145, 234
Mahdavi, S. 129
Mair, D. 219
Majluf, N.S. 73
Malkiel, B. 101
management objectives, influence on investment 102
Mankiw, N.G. 138
Manne, A.S. 111
March, J.G. 67
marginal efficiency of capital 10, 12, 18, 31–4, 38, 43, 44, 45, 49, 152, 223
  and marginal productivity of capital 33
  see also internal rate of return, rate of return over costs
marginal productivity of capital 33, 59, 60, 63–4, 103
marginal productivity of labour 60, 63–4
marginal *q* 96, 99–100, 103, 151
marginal rate of return over cost 27
marginalism 59, 67–8

market capitalisation 14, 41, 99, 100, 101–2, 173
Marris, R. 67
Martin, R. 184
Marx, K. xii
mass psychology 40
mathematics, role of 22, 28, 37, 44–5
Matthews, R.C.O. 49, 50
Mayer, T. 54, 69
McCombie, J. 219
McConnell, M.M. 170
McDonald, R. 115
Meeks, J.G. 127
Mensch, G.O. 174
Messe, R. 106
methodological holism 16
methodological individualism 16
Meyers, S.C. 73
microfoundations in macroeconomic theories 15, 16, 65, 67, 74, 76, 77, 100
microprocessors 164–5
Miller, A.G. 219
Miller, M.H. 73, 99, 127
Mini, P. 127
Minsky, H.P. 33, 34, 127, 130–3, 134, 153, 196, 218
  and banking system 130–1, 133, 134
  and financial fragility hypothesis 29, 130–3, 134, 201
Mizon, G.E. 142, 234
model misspecification 231
model selection tests 86–7
Modigliani, F. 53, 73, 99, 127
Modigliani–Miller theorem 73, 99, 127, 129, 152, 219, 224
monetary policy 42, 53, 67, 76, 86, 88, 89
money, endogeneity of 127–33, 134
money illusion 29, 224
money supply 35
Moore's Law 165
Moreton, D. 121, 218
Morris, D.J. 86, 88, 89, 95
mortgage arrears 219
Mortgage Interest Relief at Source (MIRAS) 199–200, 220
mortgage lending 197, 200–1
Muellbauer, J. 197, 200
Murphy, A. 197, 200
multicollinearity 88, 224, 229
multiplier 43, 51, 55, 224
Muth, J. 93

Nadiri, M.I. 85, 86, 87, 143
Nature of Capital and Income, The 25
Neild, R.R. 53, 67
neo-classical
  parables 74
  theory xii, 13, 38, 45, 56, 58–65, 68, 74, 77, 80, 90, 183, 212
  empirical evidence 54–5, 68, 77, 85–9, 144–5, 147–8, 150–1, 204–6, 207
  theory, problems of axiomatic approach 74, 76
Nerlove, M. 55, 69, 70
Net Domestic Product (NDP) 170, 224
net investment 10, 18
Net Present Value (NPV) 16–17, 18, 27, 45, 63–4, 115, 116–17, 123, 224
network effects 168–9, 178–9, 224
New Economy 102, 117, 224
  computing investment, and 165–6, 175–80, 214–15
  definition 170
  depreciation in 169–70, 178–9
  empirical evidence 175–80
  externalities in 168–9, 179
  intangible investment and 165–6, 172–3, 179
  inventory investment in 170, 178, 180
  investment 144, 164–80, 214–15
  measurement difficulties 170–3, 179
  microprocessors and 164–5
  network effects in 168–9, 179
  new firms in 173–4, 180
  replacement investment in 169–70, 178–9, 215
  transistors and 164–5
  venture capital funds in 173–4, 176, 177, 179, 180, 215
Nickell, S.J. 72, 73, 94, 110, 217, 218
Nobay, A.R. 54
non constant returns to scale 103
non-ergodicity 15, 224
non-nested tests 86–7, 145, 148, 156–7, 158, 205–6, 224, 233–4
non-stationarity 224, 231–2, 233

obsolescence, economic 10, 18, 224
O'Donnell, R.M. 127
Oi, W.Y. 111
oligopoly 67
opportunity
  cost of investment 59, 97
  cost, of exercising options to invest 14, 114–17, 123
  cost, of waiting to invest 14
  Fisher's principle of 28, 224
optimal capital stock, definition of 60
  adjustment 59–61, 67, 70–1
optimal path of investment 96, 97, 106, 108
optimal waiting period 112
options 27
options theories of investment 27, 114–17, 122–3, 213
ordinary least squares (OLS) 141, 224, 227–8, 229

Oswald, A.J. 194
Oulton, N. 101
output effect, of changes in
factor prices 81–2
output elasticities 61–2
output growth 80, 91
owner occupation rates 197, 198

p value *see* probability value
Paasche index 28
Palley, T. 130, 155, 218
panel data 224
parables of neo-classical theory 74
paradox of thrift 25, 183, 224
partial adjustment models 51
Pasinetti, L.L. 33, 34
payback method 17, 224
perfect factor substitutability 81
Pesaran, B. 227
Pesaran, M.H. 227, 234
Pesaran-Deaton tests 87, 234
Pigou, A.C. 29
and the real balance effect 29
Pindyck, R.S. 14, 63, 105, 110, 112, 113, 114, 115, 116, 117, 118, 122, 218
political uncertainty 118
Ponzi finance 131–3, 134, 224
portfolio shift 133, 134
positivist approach, defences of 68
Post Keynesian economics 15, 16, 18, 24, 29, 45, 63, 71, 76, 121, 122, 125–34, 150, 152–3, 155–6, 157–8, 179, 183, 196, 201–4, 205–6, 207, 208, 212, 213–14, 217, 218, 219
predictive failure 230, 231
Prescott, E.C. 110
present value 11, 12, 13, 16, 26
Price, S. 119
principle of impatience 28
principle of increasing risk 129, 153
principle of opportunity 28
probability 71, 110, 126–7, 212
probability value 224, 228
procedural rationality 126, 134, 224
production functions, discontinuities in 75–6
profits 52, 75, 128–30
double-sided relationwith investment 129, 134
projection 36
prospective yield 31, 33, 35, 224
psychological factors 24, 38, 42, 43, 45, 126–7, 217
psychological testing, of rational expectations 107
public housing stock 199, 200
public investment 16
pure rate of time preference 26
putty-clay models 13, 75, 80, 91
putty-putty models 58, 80, 81–2, 90

q, average 99–100, 103, 104, 151, 225
q, marginal 96–100, 99, 103, 151, 225
q theory xii, 14, 15, 39, 45, 73, 77, 90, 93, 94, 96–108, 213, 214, 218, 219
roots in Fisher 25
Tobin's 99–104, 150, 151–2, 153–5, 157–8
see also Tobin's *q*
quantity adjustment 58
quantity theory of money 28
Quiros, G.B. 170

R&D expenditure 102
Rae, J. 26
Ramsey's RESET test 154, 228, 229
rate of return over costs 24, 26, 45, 115, 117, 118, 119
see also internal rate of return; marginal efficiency of capital
rational expectations
in adjustment cost models 99–107
in Tobin's *q* models 99–104, 151, 218, 219
hypothesis 55, 69, 70, 71, 72, 93, 94, 107, 108, 110, 122, 212, 217, 225
rationality 36, 45, 63, 67, 110, 122, 212, 217, 218, 219
limits on 36–42, 196
in Post Keynesian models 126–7, 133, 134, 212, 213–14
substantive versus procedural 126, 134
experimental psychology tests 107
reaction lags 51
real balance effect 29
real interest rate 17, 225
real options theory 14, 15, 22, 45, 63, 77, 90, 114–17, 122–3, 213, 225
real world investment appraisal techniques 11, 16–17, 18, 116–17
regressive expectations 55
relative cost of financing 73
relative factor cost effects
in clay-clay models 82–3
in putty-clay models 83–4
in putty-putty models 81–2
relative factor costs 90, 141
rental cost of capital *see* user cost of capital
replacement investment 9, 18, 169–70, 178
repossessions 201
representative agents hypothesis 16, 61, 76, 100, 134, 151, 225
research and development (R&D) 172
residential investment 9, 18, 194–208, 215
affordability of 196, 204
empirical evidence 201–6, 207
and frenzy effects 196, 197
and gearing 196, 200
and legal constraints 195, 198
and mortgage lending 194, 197, 200–1

and policy changes 197–201
public 199
rate of return on 195
and supply lags 195
and transactions costs 195
and user cost of capital 195
re-switching, capital 75–6
retained profits 73, 129
reversal, of capital 75–6
reverse multiplier effects 153, 225
risk 17, 34
borrower's 129, 134, 153
financing 73
Knightian 71
lender's 129, 134
Roach, S.S. 169
Roberts, K. 111
Robinson, J.V. 33, 38, 74, 127, 129
Rockley, L.E. 53
Ross, S.A. 117
Rotemberg, J.J. 105
Runde, J.H. 127

Sakellaris, P. 111
Sala-I-Martin, X. 184, 219
sales maximization, Baumol's theory of 67
Salter, W.E.G. 75
Samuelson, P. and surrogate production functions 75, 83
Sardoni, C. 128, 217
savings, and investment 183, 219
savings, in Fisher's theory 25–6
Sawyer, M.C. 219
scale effects 81–2, 141
Scarth, W.M. 96
Schumpeter, and innovation 29, 174
Schumpeter, debt-deflation theory 29
Schwarz's Bayesian Information Criterion 233
second-mover advantage, and computing investment 169, 225
Sen, A. 75, 76
sequencing, of investment projects 117, 123
serial correlation 154
serial correlation, in *q* models 101, 105, 106
Shackle, G.L.S. 33, 38, 127, 217
shadow price of capital 14, 96, 108, 218
Shapiro, C. 169
share prices 39, 40
shareholder value 101
short-term expectations 36–8
Siebert, C.D. 69, 86, 87
Siegel, D.R. 115
sigma (σ) convergence 184, 185–90, 191, 225
Simon, H.A. 126, 134
simple accelerator theory 12–13, 18, 48, 49–51, 56
see also accelerator theory
simultaneity 89, 232
Skidelsky, R. 28, 127, 219
Slifman, L. 167
Sohrabian, A. 129
Solimano, A. 115, 118, 218
Solow, R.M. 76, 84, 172
and putty-clay models 75, 83–4
computer paradox 167, 225
vintage model 84
Spajic, L. 217, 219
specification error 69
speculation 39–42, 40–1, 44
speculative bubbles 41, 196, 201–4, 207
speculative finance 131–3, 134, 225
state of confidence 41, 43, 152, 225
state of credit 127–8, 225
state of long-term expectation 36, 38, 44
static expectations 58, 70, 77, 93
Stegman, T. 130
Stephenson, J.A. 61, 69, 85, 87
sticky prices 49
Stiroh, K.J. 167, 172
stocks versus flows 21, 96
stock markets 14, 39–42, 45, 93, 99–104, 128, 150, 173, 214–15, 218
Strachey, Lytton 32
Stavins, J. 169
Strotz, R.H. 94, 95
structural breaks 225, 228, 231
subjective versus objective factors 44, 45, 55, 126–7
substantive rationality 126, 134
substitutability of techniques 83
substitution effect 81, 81–2, 83, 84
Summers, L.H. 101, 167, 213, 218
sunk costs 14, 111–12, 113
supply price of investment 31, 34, 217
surrogate production function 75, 83, 225
survey evidence, about investment 68, 69
switching regressions 130

tangible investments 9, 18
Targetti, F. 33
technical progress 73–4
techniques, substitutability of 75, 83
technology 89, 90, 164–80
technological transfer 182
Temple, P. 117, 121, 218
Thatcher, M. 197
theoretical convergence 15, 121, 123, 212–16
theories of the firm, microeconomic 67
Theory of Interest, The 18, 25
time preference, rate of 26
timing of investment projects 76, 112–17, 123
Tinbergen, J. 51, 55
Tobin, J. xii, 5, 14, 28, 29, 93, 99, 100
Tobin's *q* 99–104, 105, 106, 107, 108, 150, 151–8, 212, 218

average versus marginal *q* 99–100, 103, 108
mismeasurement of capital stock in 102
theory, problems of 100, 101–7, 108
theory, role of additional variables in 103–4, 108
theory, role of lags 103–4, 105, 106
top-down modelling strategy 54, 142, 217, 225, 233
Topol, R. 219
Total Factor Productivity (TFP) 226
Tract on Monetary Reform 28
transformation approaches 14, 93, 105–6, 108, 226
transistors, in microprocessors 164–5
Treatise on Probability, A 71, 126, 127, 212
trickle down 182
trigger rates of return 115, 117, 118
see also hurdle rate of return
Tyler, P. 184
Type I error 226, 228
Type II error 226, 228

uncertainty 24, 26, 67, 70–2, 76, 90, 93, 152–3, 196–7, 212–16, 218
aggregate 113–14, 118
empirical evidence 117–22, 123, 153–6, 157–8
idiosyncratic 113–14, 118
and internal rate of return 115, 117
investment appraisal techniques, effects on 115–17
Knightian 71
in the New Economy 175–8, 179, 180
NPV calculations, and 115, 115–17
political 118
positive effects on investment 111
in Post Keynesian theory 125–33, 134
quantification of 117–22
in real options theories 114–17, 122, 123
see also Knightian uncertainty, Knightian risk
risk 11, 12, 15, 16, 17, 18, 34–42
unemployment 84, 201
Urga, G. 121, 218
user cost of capital 58, 65, 70, 75, 76, 85–6, 89, 90, 141, 144, 145, 147, 148, 218, 226
components of 59–60, 141
computing 175–6, 177–8
housing 195–6, 204, 207
Keynes's definition 217, 226
mathematical derivation 63–4
measurement of 88
utility maximization, Williamson's model of 67

value, problems of measurement and definition 74
value-weighted aggregation 74–5
venture capital, and computing investment 173–4, 176, 177, 180, 226
Viner, J. 112
vintages 62, 67, 70, 74–5, 84, 173, 226
von Furstenberg, G. 101

Wald test 233
Wallis, K.C. 217, 233
Wan, M.Y. 75
Watson, M.W. 101, 219
weight, of probability 110
Weingartner, H.M. 53
Weitzman, M.L. 111
Whelan, K. 167
Whited, T.M. 111, 118
Williamson's model 67
winner's curse 107
Winslow, E.G. 127
Woolf, Virginia 32
Wyplosz, C. 101

Yang, S. 102, 165, 167, 172, 173

Zucker, L.G. 173